ATTENTION, PLEASE!

ATTENTION, PLEASE!

A Comprehensive Guide for Successfully Parenting
Children with Attention Deficit Disorders and Hyperactivity

Edna D. Copeland, Ph.D.
Valerie L. Love, M.Ed.

Specialty Press, Inc.

Plantation, Florida
1995

Copeland, Edna D. and Love, Valerie L.
Attention, Please! A Comprehensive Guide for Successfully
Parenting Children with Attention Disorders and Hyperactivity
p. 352

ISBN 1-886941-02-5 (hardcover)

  1. Attention Deficit Disorder - Treatment
  2. Attention-deficit/Hyperactivity Disorder - Treatment

Library of Congress Card Number: 91-062565

First Printing: September 1991
Second Printing: August 1992
Third Printing: September 1995
Fourth Printing: October 1998

Specialty Press, Inc. • First edition 1995
300 Northwest 70th Avenue
Plantation, Florida 33317
(800) 233-9273 • (954) 792-8100

Manufactured in the United States of America

To Frank and Terry, Frank, III and Anne, Todd and Jennifer.

Acknowledgments

A book is often the culmination of the collective experiences of many individuals who share, in some way, a common purpose. *Attention, Please!* has been most directly influenced by the children, adolescents and adults with attention disorders whose lives have been shared with us and from whom we have learned so much. We are grateful to them and especially thank those who have permitted us to tell their stories.

We also wish to thank Terrence Love for endless hours of artistic preparation of the illustrations; Ron Walker for his commentary; Vivian Bozeman, Leigh Ann Butler and Kerri Ellis for their tireless proofreading and editing; Beverly Bailey of Graphic Works, Inc. for graphic assistance; and Lanie Shaw for the final preparation of the manuscript.

Table of Contents

Introduction

The satisfaction derived from successfully parenting a child with an attention disorder is tremendous. These children often possess creativity, a sense of individuality, and a genuine concern for others that is far greater than most children's. When they mature in an understanding and supportive environment, their capacity for becoming successful, fulfilled, productive individuals is enhanced. But, unlike the old adage, "Getting there is *not* always half the fun!"

Recent advances in modern science have greatly increased our understanding of the causes of and treatments for attention disorders. People formerly destined for lives filled with frustration, disappointment, heartache and failure now have an opportunity to live productive and fulfilled lives.

It is our hope that this book will provide all who parent or interact with those with attention disorders some tools and insights for understanding, motivating, and affirming these children and for guiding them toward meaningful, satisfying lives.

We understand that parenting is not easy—even under the most ideal of conditions. Parenting the ADHD or ADD child requires a courage, commitment and patience that can seem overwhelming even to the most dedicated. We hope this book will provide knowledge, skills and encouragement to the millions of parents who are trying every day to make a difference in their children's lives. We know from experience that you will survive; more importantly, we believe that your ADHD or ADD child will become a successful adult because of your efforts. Together, you and your child have embarked on an exciting journey of discovery. Slowly a young man or woman will begin to emerge from this child that you are now nurturing. All the hours, weeks, months and years you devote will seem well worth it when your child blossoms into a mature, competent and appreciative adult.

Use your tremendous power as a parent, combined with your love and knowledge, to make that journey exciting for both of you. In the process we anticipate that you may even discover that getting there *can* be half the fun.

UNDERSTANDING ATTENTION DEFICIT DISORDERS

If a man does not keep pace with his companions, perhaps he dances to the music of a different drummer.
—Thoreau

Benjy and Tracey – Different Drummers?

"Hello, Mrs. Adams. This is Mr. Phillips, Benjy's principal. Could you possibly come in to see me right away? We need to have another talk about Benjy."

Those who have received such a phone call know only too well the range of feelings which pour forth: embarrassment, frustration, anger, helplessness and despair. The majority of American families, fortunately, do not receive such a phone call often. It may occur once, twice, or even three times during their child's school years. In families of children and adolescents with attention disorders, however, it is a frequent event, often occurring once or twice a month, sometimes even once or twice a week.

It is conservatively estimated that out of every one hundred children in America five have moderate to severe attention deficit disorders. Some researchers feel that the number may be as high as ten percent. Thus, three to five million families may be affected by this disorder.

The phone call, itself, is not the problem. Parents become quite adept at dealing with frustrated teachers, perplexed principals, angry parents, and exasperated peers. The real issue is how to manage Benjy's attention disorder on a daily basis and how to help him mature into a competent, happy adult. The strife and turmoil created in the family as a result of the constant stress and strain caused by Benjy's behavior is also an important issue that must be addressed.

How did Benjy get to be this way? Is his inappropriate behavior intentional? Is he purposely frustrating his teacher? Does he enjoy tormenting his parents at home? What's wrong with him?

To gain some insight into Benjy's personality the following report given by his mother may be helpful:

"From the time Benjy was born I knew something was not right. Even before birth he was active and easily stimulated. I hated to laugh because afterwards he would kick for hours. I gave up many activities because he kicked so hard I could barely sit.

I had tried for months, unsuccessfully, to become pregnant. Finally, I took hormones and to our joy we conceived. Hormones were necessary for several months to maintain the pregnancy. We were thrilled when Benjy was finally born. You should have seen the nurses laughing

*at this tiny five-pound guy who was born after only eight
months. They laughed hysterically as he lay on his back,
kicking his little feet constantly when he was awake. We
thought it was cute, too, for a while. However, after we
brought Benjy home my uneasiness began to grow as his
cute, busy behavior never ceased.*

*John, Benjy's dad, was an easy-going man, who be-
lieved that everything works out if you are patient and
calm. He was surprised by my concerns but was certain
that I could handle the situation. "Aren't all new mothers
anxious?", he asked. As the days wore on and I became
both exhausted and frantic, he, too, had mild concerns.*

*I asked myself and the pediatrician constantly what
was wrong. "Aren't babies supposed to sleep?" "Do all
babies cry continually for six months?" "Do they all put
everything they can find in their mouths?" He assured
and reassured me until both he and I began to think I was
a truly neurotic mother. Finally, he reluctantly prescribed
medication to help Benjy sleep. To my surprise and his,
the medicine only made things worse. Benjy was in high
gear until dawn. My patient and gentle pediatrician finally
acknowledged that perhaps my son was overactive and
suggested that I take tranquilizers or see a therapist.*

*I suffered through those months trying to smile and not
appear to be the most bewildered mother around. We
stopped going out since I was tired and depressed most of
the time. Besides, sitters were impossible to find; they were*

surprised by this baby with so much energy. They left exhausted and rarely returned. I provided structure and routine. Wasn't that supposed to help? I read every book I could find on child behavior and tried every suggestion offered.

By this time, I suspected that I had a hyperactive child. At Christmas I saw a child psychologist who assured me the problem was Benjy and not me. She suggested that Benjy might have food intolerances, which he did. Things improved somewhat when milk was eliminated. Of course, I had never given Benjy sugar.

Even though active, Benjy did enjoy playing by himself. His playtime in his room, which the psychologist had suggested to give me a breather, became increasingly long. I eagerly anticipated the few activities I had managed to continue and left my husband to care for Benjy. John continued to feel, I sensed, though it was never stated, that the problem was more mine than Benjy's. Never having accepted defeat before, I was determined to prove I could raise this child. Inwardly, however, I resented John's lack of understanding. How I wished I could go off to work each day!

The terrible two's which descended upon us were just a continuation of the old behaviors. Benjy was active, aggressive, determined to have his own way, and an exhausting child with whom to live. I all but gave up *shopping since Benjy was uncontrollable in a supermarket. Food was far less important than my sanity. When I did take Benjy, I thought I would scream if one more person looked at me with that "Aren't you going to discipline that child?" look in their eyes. Not infrequently grandmothers forthrightly offered their advice: "A good spanking could really help your son." It was too frustrating to try to explain that I had used every discipline known to man and that none of them worked. The "Thinking Room" had, however, saved me from totally losing it. It wasn't that Benjy was a mean child; he obviously could not help his behavior. And there were times, when he was still enough, that he was the most sensitive, loving, responsive child any mother could want. He always seemed so angelic after he went to sleep. Many nights when finally I put my head on my pillow, I cried until the oblivion of exhaustion overtook me.*

Still determined to be a loving mother, I gave Benjy a fabulous second-birthday party. To everyone's surprise he was so overstimulated by the party that when the birthday cake arrived, he put his face down right in the middle of it. Needless to say, his aunts, uncles and grandparents were more than a little amazed. Their raised eyebrows only intensified my frustration.

I thought peer relations would help Benjy's development. That, too, was a disaster. After a few toddler play groups, when I was able to observe what I had suspected for so long, I was in tears. Benjy was different - very different. No matter how hard I tried to teach him not to shove or to take other children's toys, to settle down or to mind, it was to no avail. The other mothers were pleasant, but the look of relief was unmistakable when I offered to withdraw from the group: "We are so sorry, but we do understand. Benjy is a handful, isn't he?"

When Benjy was three I enrolled him in a small preschool program. When I arrived to pick him up and asked, hopefully, how the day had gone, his teacher was guarded but pleasant. Two days later she requested a conference. The pronouncement: "Benjy is a handsome, bright, alert, sweet and sensitive child, but more than I can handle in such a large group. It just isn't fair to the other children. He needs a smaller, more structured situation." I would hear these words often over the next few years.

Potty training was also a nightmare. At age three and a half when he still wasn't trained, I gave up. By age four, however, God smiled upon us and granted my fervent prayer....he could go to kindergarten without diapers.

Realizing that school was not going to be easy, I investigated every school available. I settled on the one that was considered the most structured and the most family-oriented. Despite my strategic efforts, problems occurred almost immediately. I had already accepted the fact that my child was hyperactive and I had tried every thing from Vitamin B to Primrose Oil to avoid medication. We changed Benjy's diet, trying everything from macrobiotics to an elimination and challenge diet for allergies. While these helped some, the problems were intense.

At this point I was willing to try medication. We saw a neurologist and Ritalin was prescribed. The help was immediate and immense. For a few weeks we felt relieved. Benjy then developed tics - blinking his eyes incessantly. However, he could not manage without medication, so Dexedrine, Cylert and Tofranil were investigated as well. After several months of trial-and-error, it seemed that

Benjy managed best on 10 mg. of Ritalin three times a day. Any more than that resulted in tics; any less and a teacher's call was inevitable.

We struggled through first and second grades. Benjy's fine-motor skills were never the best and writing was a hopeless disaster. Benjy was very verbal and impressed everyone with his intellect. However, his handwriting was the worst his teacher had ever seen. I tutored Benjy every afternoon and worked intensely on his handwriting. Nothing improved it. Finally in third grade we were advised to have him learn to type. Typing, word processing and the computer have truly saved this child's life—and mine!

By third grade the problems intensified even with medication. Benjy stood on the steps of his school one day and refused to enter. He stated he would never go through that school door again. We realized it was time for a change. Benjy had quite a reputation with both the teachers and his peers at this point, and school had become more than he could bear. If we did not do something soon, I feared that he might be a school dropout before the age of ten.

After much searching we found a school with a patient, structured, loving staff who tolerated Benjy even when he threw his shoes across the room, forgot his homework, or impulsively shoved another child. They saw Benjy's good qualities and were able to build on them. Still, however, there were many parent conferences. They knew how hard we were trying, or perhaps they would not have kept Benjy. His good intellect, his beloved computer and the grace of God kept us going."

Benjy is a fairly typical example of a child with Attention Deficit Hyperactivity Disorder (ADHD). The struggles his family have experienced are quite characteristic as well. Benjy was fortunate to have the support and determined efforts of his family, and his story has a happy ending as the following update from his mother indicates:

> *Benjy is seventeen now. He has managed with much assistance along the way, to maintain a B average, and even make an occasional A. He has lettered in a Varsity sport and is studying hard to prepare for college. I, too, can finally breathe more easily and be a real mother. Those years were very hard on me. I often felt more like an Army sergeant than a mother and I was certain Benjy would grow up to hate me. Amazingly, however, he expresses affection and appreciation. We can even laugh now at some of the disasters. Our relationship has the quality of strength gained only from overcoming many adversities together and never losing faith in each other or in the process.*
>
> *At this point I am very hopeful, for I see a mature young man emerging. All the qualities which matter most to us are there: honesty, integrity, responsibility and sensitivity to others. Benjy is deeply grateful to all those who worked with him along the way: physicians, psychologists, tutors, and the many teachers who gritted their way through a year of his antics. Benjy's goal is to be able to repay them by helping other children with similar problems."*

♦ UNDIFFERENTIATED ATTENTION ♦ DEFICIT DISORDER

While most research data, especially before 1990, would suggest that approximately 40% of the children with attention disorders are significantly overactive like Benjy, our experience and that of others is that a much smaller percentage truly fit that description.

Instead, the majority of the children and adolescents we see have undifferentiated attention deficit disorder (ADD). They are restless, inattentive, dreamy, off-task, impulsive, easily overstimulated or distractible, or they have some combination of these symptoms. While the problems are often not as intense as the difficulties associated with attention deficit hyperactivity disorder, children with ADD also experience problems both at home and at school. Tracey was such a child, as the following story told by her father illustrates:

> *Tracey was an exceptionally good baby - too good to be true. She slept through the night at two weeks of age and rarely cried except when hungry. She was in no hurry to move through the developmental stages, but managed to accomplish each one relatively on time. Her mother could not understand this talk about the "terrible two's." Tracey was as easy at two as she was as a baby.*
>
> *Ages three and four were uneventful and pleasant as well. Five-year kindergarten was an easy year, too. Her teacher endearingly named her, "my little dreamer." Tracey was often in another world at home, too. But, so was her mom, so we weren't concerned.*
>
> *First grade was a shock for Tracey, who found the demands too intense and the pace too fast. She had a hard time getting her work done and was teased by the other children. Her nickname changed from "dreamer" to "space cadet" as her disorganization and lack of awareness were noticed by her peers. Tracey withdrew at school and became quieter at home. We reassured her as best we could that she was okay and obligingly helped her finish her classwork at home in the evening.*
>
> *Second grade was harder and Tracey withdrew even more. While she was bright, she processed information*

slowly and took forever to respond. Tracey's teacher was concerned and an evaluation was suggested.

I must admit I was outraged with the teacher who suggested that my child had a problem. Tracey's mom shared the teacher's concerns, but I prevailed, insisting that our daughter was immature and over the summer she would catch up. I secretly believed my wife was not helping her enough with her homework. I guiltily acknowledged to myself that I avoided the struggle by working late, and I vowed to do better.

Third grade improved somewhat, for Tracey had a loving teacher who modified her demands to fit Tracey's needs. Written assignments were reduced, while other assignments were sent home so we could help her get a head start. Our pleasant "little dreamer", however, was increasingly unhappy and difficult at home. Getting her up and dressed for school became a daily battle. She often refused to go and missed the bus frequently. To avoid these disastrous morning struggles, I changed my schedule so I could drop her off at school and we planned wonderful treats if she would try her best.

Academics had not been a problem until multiplication was introduced. It was our first encounter with school failure. No amount of repetition locked in these facts. I now understand why math quizzes which require students to do a hundred problems in five minutes are called, "Mad Minutes." They are truly designed to drive both children and parents mad!

At this point I was too concerned to continue being proud, so we requested an evaluation. The school was cooperative, but the waiting list was unending. Third grade came to a close without any testing taking place.

During the summers Tracey usually returned to her good-natured self. This summer, however, was more difficult, because the struggle which had developed between Tracey and her mom during the school year continued. Four weeks at a fun, loving, esteem-building camp was both Tracey's reprieve and ours. She returned much happier and seemed once more to accept our love. By the end of the summer I was feeling hopeful again.

Fourth grade quickly dashed such optimism. School became an exhausting emotional and psychological struggle for us all. In mid-fourth grade an evaluation finally took place. Tracey was found to be above average in ability but was underachieving. However, she did not have a learning disability, which I later learned meant she was not underachieving enough, so no help was forthcoming.

Tracey's grades throughout elementary school and middle school continued to hover around C's with an occasional D or F and an occasional B. I remained concerned while my wife was frantic. She tried everything from teacher-signed homework assignment sheets to rewards for papers completed and returned to her teacher, to restrictions for poor performance. She continually asked for help from our daughter's teachers until both the school and Tracey considered my wife a pest. She, however, was unwilling to allow our daughter to fail.

High school proved to be the final straw. Ninth grade was disastrous. Tracey was excited about a new beginning and threw herself into the extracurricular activities with a zest not previously revealed. She was elected to the Student Council and was selected as a junior cheerleader. She proudly escorted visitors through her school and was excited for the first time since kindergarten. While her grades were no better, her social world suddenly blossomed.

At the end of the first semester Tracey received two failing grades. Then the bomb dropped! The "no pass, no play" ruling went into effect and she was dropped from cheerleading and the Student Council. She was no longer even able to host visitors to the school. Failures, I suppose, must be banished from sight.

Do I sound bitter? Perhaps I was...and still am. For eight years the school had failed my child and now they were making her pay the price for their failure to educate her. Her teachers were equally concerned and frustrated, but found the rules and regulations difficult to change.

"No pass, no play," was almost a death sentence for our daughter. She became so depressed she couldn't eat. Professional assistance was no longer a choice but a necessity. My pride and the cost of treatment were immaterial in the face of this new danger.

Tracey was evaluated by a private psychologist and found to have a significant attention deficit disorder. She was not hyperactive but rather spacey, inattentive and disorganized, and she had terrible memory problems. She still did not know her multiplication tables but had devised incredible strategies to compensate. Her I.Q. scores had declined dramatically, which I understand is what happens when ADD goes untreated for so long. We were assured, however, that her ability was still there. Her achievement was also considerably below grade level.

The psychologist referred us to an adolescent psychiatrist. Both Ritalin and counseling were begun. Individual remediation was recommended and obtained, and modifications were made at school.

Tracey is a sophomore now. She has made progress, but her recovery has not been miraculous. She did pass all seven of her courses and ran track for the first time this spring. Tracey makes A's and B's in small classes, but she still feels inadequate and disorganized in larger ones. She feels overwhelmed by the size of her high school with its 2,000 students and begs to attend a tutorial school. While it would be wonderful, we simply can't afford it.

Despite her friends' positive reports from college, Tracey vows she won't attend. She has decided instead to be a cosmetic consultant. She'll probably be excellent since she's always been visual and has a flare for design. Nevertheless, it troubles me greatly that school has been so negative for this child that she may never avail herself of its potential benefits. It saddens me, too, that her relationship with her mom is so strained. It seems unfair that parents must choose between policing their ADD children to help them succeed or letting them totally fail without their constant checking, reminders, teacher conferences and restrictions.

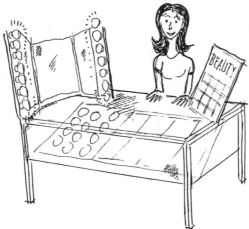

Therapy has begun the healing process as both Tracey and we understand her disorder and its devastating effects on her educational experiences and our family life. As she achieves new success she softens a little and is more open and responsive. We hope some day all the bad experiences will fade and those ten long and awful years will seem only like a bad dream. Both my wife and I are committed to educational reform, especially for ADHD/ADD students, and are determined to do everything possible to prevent other students from suffering this way.

While harder to recognize, children with undifferentiated attention deficit disorder and their families suffer immensely. Once recognized and understood, however, both types of attention disorders can be effectively treated and managed.

ADHD and ADD have progressed light years since the beginning of Benjy and Tracey's stories. Families no longer have to endure their experiences. Instead there is now both recognition of these disorders and assistance for them. Today many professionals understand and treat attention disorders, and schools can now, with the new education guidelines, address these childrens' needs.

In concluding Chapter 1, we would like to leave you with one last thought. We know that daily living with a child or adolescent with an attention disorder can be a challenge. However, we believe it will be a little easier if you can see your child not as one with problems, but rather as one who hears a different drummer as Thoreau suggested. Your child's drum may beat a little faster or slower than most and his notes may not always be in sync with the group, but in the end these differences may have the unexpected benefit of increasing his sensitivity, creativity, and concern for others. He may ultimately be the one who creates the most beautiful music of all. Taking great license with the writings of Thoreau, we might even say that ADD stands for <u>A</u> <u>D</u>ifferent <u>D</u>rummer.

If you treat an individual as he is, he will stay as he is, but if you treat him as if he were what he ought to be and could be, he will become what he ought to be and could be.

—Johann Wolfgang von Goethe

What are ADHD and ADD? What Is Living with Each Like?

Each of us enters parenthood with the hope and expectation that we will have healthy, happy children who will become confident, successful and contributing adolescents and adults. For many families that dream becomes a reality. For others, it does not.

Instead, life with an ADHD or ADD child or adolescent can be a struggle—an endless series of difficult behaviors, tormented siblings, poor grades, exasperated teachers, annoyed coaches, angry neighbors, family conflict, feelings of frustration, and sometimes even desperation.

Attention disorders are problems which usually begin in early childhood or in the elementary school years. They often continue into adolescence and adulthood, and can persist throughout life. Both ADHD and ADD can be difficult to recognize, for the symptoms masquerade as learning disabilities, emotional problems, bad behavior, poor parenting, stressed out environments, and overly demanding schools, among others.

Perhaps the most significant disorders of the twentieth century, ADHD and ADD affect millions of children, adolescents and adults in every country in the world. They do not discriminate. Rather, they occur in people of every ability level and in every socioeconomic group. They have traditionally been reported as occurring two to four times more frequently in boys than girls. However, it is becoming widely acknowledged that girls are significantly underidentified. Studies of American youth have reported statistics suggesting from three to twenty percent have ADHD or ADD. Other countries report the incidence of ADHD/ADD from eight to sixteen percent: New Zealand - 13%; West Germany - 8%; Italy - 12%; Spain - 16%; Great Britain - 10%; and China - 11% (Shaywitz and Shaywitz, 1988).

Attention disorders are not new problems; rather, they have existed for hundreds of years. Only in the last decade, however, have we begun to understand them and to know how to deal effectively with them. While still relatively unknown to the lay community, much scientific research has been devoted to unraveling the mysteries of attention deficit disorders and to treating them successfully.

◆ HISTORY OF ATTENTION DISORDERS ◆

The first mention of the constellation of symptoms we now call ADHD or ADD came in 1848, when Fidgety Phil appeared as a character in a story written by a German family doctor for his children. ADHD was next addressed in 1902 by Dr. George F. Still in *Lancet*, the premier medical magazine of its time. Dr. Still described ADHD symptoms as "a defect in moral control" which occurred despite the fact that the children came from good environments and had received adequate parenting. By *defect in moral control* he meant that these children knew the rules; they simply did not obey them. He noted that ADHD appears to be an inherited predisposition and that more boys suffer from the disorder than girls. "Problems in attention, responsiveness to discussion, emotional maturity, and social conduct" were described by Dr. Still, as well as persistence and "a headstrong disposition." While we no longer accept his explanation of their cause, his descriptions of the symptoms are still very accurate today, almost ninety years later.

Despite these astute observations, this disorder was not given much attention until 1940 when an outbreak of encephalitis left many children brain-damaged. The affected children had many of the symptoms characteristic of hyperactive children. It was deduced that hyperactive children must, therefore, be brain-damaged. ADHD children were regarded as brain-damaged from 1940 to 1960 and even today to some extent. We now know, of course, that most children with attention disorders do not have brain damage *per se* although some do.[1] However, it was not until 1960 that a task force studying *Minimal Brain Damage*, the new term given to this disorder, reached this conclusion. This task force came up with so many symptoms that no one paid any attention to the disorder. Because no evidence of true brain damage could be determined for most of the children diagnosed with Minimal Brain Damage, the name was changed to *Minimal Brain Dysfunction.* "MBD" was the term used for the next twenty years to describe children with ADHD and ADD symptoms.

In the mid-1960's the American Psychiatric Association (APA) was seriously addressing the problem. It determined that attention disorders, especially those with hyperactivity, were caused by environmental problems, especially in the home, and named this constellation of difficulties *Hyperkinetic Reaction of Childhood.* ADHD and ADD were at that point considered to be the results of poor child-rearing and disorganized environments. From 1965 to 1980, inadequate parenting was blamed consistently for these children's problems. Teachers, pediatricians and professionals unwittingly faulted parents, especially mothers, as the cause of their difficult children's behavior. Parents, in turn, blamed each other. Family life often became quite tense with many divorces being the inevitable result.

Hyperactivity, MBD, conduct disorder, inattention and learning disabilities—all continued to be investigated as increasing numbers of children experienced school failure not explained by

---

[1] It is crucial that people not think of attention deficit disorder as brain damage. As will be addressed in Chapter 3, ADHD/ADD are usually the result of neurotransmitter problems, rather than being injury to specific cortical areas. Children who suffer brain damage are often less responsive to the usual treatments for ADHD/ADD, even when hyperactive, than those who are not and frequently require more intensive interventions.

ability levels, teaching methods or parenting styles. The American Psychiatric Association became the leader in efforts both to understand these diverse problems and to establish the validity of a diagnosis of hyperactivity. Dr. Dennis Cantwell, a leading investigator of ADHD/ADD, notes that the term *attention deficit disorder* was chosen for the third edition of the *APA Diagnostic and Statistical Manual (DSM III)* because most investigators believed that attentional problems, rather than hyperactivity, were the cardinal symptom of this group of difficulties (Cantwell, 1985). While some children have poor attention and impulse control *and* are overactive (ADD with hyperactivity: ADDH), it was recognized that other children exhibit attentional deficits and impulsivity, but are *not* overactive. This second group was described as having ADD without hyperactivity (ADDnoH).

It was also apparent that many individuals continue to exhibit inattention and impulsivity without the hyperactivity into adulthood. This set of symptoms was categorized as *ADD Residual Type (ADD-RT)*. Thus DSM III criteria for ADD recognized three types of difficulties, each with an attentional deficit at its core:

ADDnoH:	Inattention, impulsivity
ADDH:	Inattention, impulsivity, hyperactivity
ADD-RT:	Inattention, impulsivity persist; hyperactivity does not persist

The problems exhibited in each of the categories of symptoms were detailed in the 1980 *Diagnostic and Statistical Manual of the American Psychiatric Association (DSM-III)* as follows:[2]

Inattention (at least three of the following):

- Often fails to finish things he or she starts.

---

[2]Reprinted with permission from the <u>Diagnostic and Statistical Manual of Mental Disorders</u>, Third Edition. Copyright © 1980, American Psychiatric Association.

- Often doesn't seem to listen.
- Easily distracted.
- Has difficulty concentrating on schoolwork or other tasks requiring sustained attention.
- Has difficulty sticking to a play activity.

Impulsivity (at least three of the following):

- Often acts before thinking.
- Shifts excessively from one activity to another.
- Has difficulty organizing work (this not being due to cognitive impairment).
- Needs a lot of supervision.
- Frequently calls out in class.
- Has difficulty awaiting turn in games or group situations.

Hyperactivity (at least two of the following):

- Runs about or climbs on things excessively.
- Has difficulty sitting still or fidgets excessively.
- Has difficulty staying seated.
- Moves about excessively during sleep.
- Is always "on the go" or acts as if "driven by a motor."

The multifaceted and uniquely individual way in which ADHD and ADD can be manifested has resulted in continued research and ongoing efforts to define the central problems of these disorders. Attempts to improve on the name and associated symptoms led to a change in name for the 1987 revised edition of the APA's *Diagnostic and Statistical Manual*. DSM III-R renamed this diverse group of symptoms Attention Deficit Hyperactivity Disorder (ADHD). In 1994, in the fourth edition of the DSM, the name was changed again to Attention-deficit/Hyperactivity Disorder with the following symptoms and subtypes noted:

DSM IV Diagnostic Criteria for
Attention-deficit/Hyperactivity Disorder

A. Either (1) or (2) :

(1)   Inattention: At least six of the following symptoms of inattention have persisted for at least six months to adegree that is maladaptive and inconsistent with developmental level:

   (a)   often fails to give close attention to details or makes careless mistakes in school work, work, or other activities

   (b)   often has difficulty sustaining attention in tasks or play activities

   (c)   often does not seem to listen when spoken to directly

   (d)   often does not follow through on instructions and fails to finish schoolwork, chores, or duties in the workplace (not due to oppositional behavior or failure to understand instructions)

   (e)   often has difficulty organizing tasks and activities

   (f)   often avoids, dislikes, or is reluctant to engage in tasks that require sustained mental effort (such as schoolwork or homework)

   (g)   often loses things necessary for tasks or activities (e.g., toys, school assignments, pencils, books, or tools)

   (h)   is often easily distracted by extraneous stimuli

   (i)   is often forgetful in daily activities

(2)   Hyperactivity-Impulsivity: At least six of the following symptoms of hyperactivity-impulsivity have persisted for at least six months to a degree that is maladaptive and inconsistent with developmental level:

Hyperactivity

   (a)   often fidgets with hands or feet or squirms in seat

   (b)   often leaves seat in classroom or in other situations in which remaining seated is expected

   (c)   often runs about or climbs excessively in situations where it is inappropriate (in adolescents or adults, may be limited to subjective feelings of restlessness)

   (d)   often has difficulty playing or engaging in leisure activities quietly

   (e)   is often "on the go" or often acts as if "driven by a motor"

   (f)   often talks excessively

Impulsivity

   (g)   often blurts out answers before questions have been completed

   (h)   often has difficulty awaiting turn

   (i)   often interrupts or intrudes on others (e.g., butts into conversations or games)

B.   Some symptoms that cause impairment were present before age seven.

C.   Some impairment from the symptoms is present in two or more settings (e.g., at school, work, and at home).

D.   There must be clear evidence of clinically significant impairment in social, academic, or occupational functioning.

E.   Does not occur exclusively during the course of a Pervasive Developmental Disorder, Schizo phrenia or other Psychotic Disorder, and is not better accounted for by another mental disorder (e.g., Mood Disorder, Anxiety Disorder, Dissociative Disorder, or a Personality Disorder).

314.01 Attention-deficit/Hyperactivity Disorder, Combined Type: if both criteria A(1) and A(2) are met for the past six months

314.00 Attention-deficit/Hyperactivity Disorder, Predominantly Inattentive Type: if criterion A(1) is met but not criterion A(2) for the past six months

314.01 Attention-deficit/Hyperactivity Disorder, Predominantly Hyperactive- Impulsive Type: if criterion A(2) is met but not criterion A(1) for the past six months

314.9 Attention-deficit/Hyperactivity Disorder Not Otherwise Specified This category is for disorders with prominent symptoms of inattention or hyperactivity-impulsivity that do not meet criteria for Attention-Deficit/Hyperactivity Disorder.

In the most recent edition of the *Diagnostic and Statistical Manual of Mental Disorders*, ADHD is divided into three subtypes:

> **Attention-deficit/Hyperactivity Disorder, Combined Type**
> This subtype is for those individuals who met criterion A(1) and A(2) listed above for the past six months. They are both hyperactive and impulsive as well as inattentive.
> **Attention-deficit/Hyperactivity Disorder, Predominantly Inattentive Type**
> This subtype is for those individuals who met criterion A(1) but not criterion A(2) for the past six months. They exhibit pronounced signs of inattention without significant hyperactivity or impulsivity. Throughout this book we interchangeably refer to this group as the ADD group or the group with Undifferentiated ADD. They are the predominantly inattentive type.
> **Attention-deficit/Hyperactivity Disorder, Predominantly Hyperactive-Impulsive Type**
> This subtype is for individuals who met criterion A(2) but not criterion A(1) for the past six months. They exhibit pronounced hyperactivity and impulsivity, but do not show significant signs of inattentiveness in their daily functioning.
> **Attention-deficit/Hyperactivity Disorder Not Otherwise Specified**
> This category is for disorders with prominent symptoms of inattention or hyperactivity-impulsivity that do not meet criteria for Attention-deficit/Hyperactivity Disorder.

Drs. Shaywitz and Shaywitz, as well as the authors are among those who believe that children, adolescents and adults with predominantly inattentive ADD (undifferentiated ADD/formerly ADDnoH) represent a much more significant percentage of the ADD population and include far more girls than those with ADHD, who may well represent only the "tip of the iceberg" (Shaywitz and Shaywitz, 1988). While they do not manifest the more severe behavioral components of ADHD the attentional and underachievement components of the predominantly inattentive type ADD create significant problems for those affected.

Paul Jaffe, an adult with ADD who has become very active in this area, has described "subtypes of ADD-NH" which all of us working with these children, especially in nonclinic or non-mental-health agency settings, see far more often than hyperactive or conduct-disordered children. They include:

1. *Pass-for-normal*: They're spacey and disorganized, but skilled enough to hide it.
2. *Honorary hyperactive*: They're impulsive, but without the level of motor activation we associate with ADD-H.
3. *Mixed*: At times they're ADD-H, at times ADD-NH.
4. *Hypoactive*: They're passive, physically and mentally listless, and constantly fatigued.. Chances are they're depressed much of the time and anxious. They are shy, withdrawn and conversationally inept. Compared with some who are ADD-H, they're less likely to do things which are impulsive or ill-behaved. Instead of the behavioral explosion typical of ADD-H, the trend is toward behavioral paralysis (Jaffe, 1989)

HISTORY OF TERMINOLOGY

1940's   Minimal Brain Damage
1960   Minimal Brain Dysfunction (MBD)
1965   DSM II
         Hyperkinetic Reaction of Childhood
1980   DSM III
         Attention Deficit Disorder
         with hyperactivity
         without hyperactivity
1987   DSM III-R
         Attention Deficit Hyperactivity Disorder
         Undifferentiated Attention Deficit Disorder
1994   DSM IV
         Attention-deficit/Hyperactivity Disorder,
         Combined Type
         Predominantly Inattentive Type
         Predominantly Hyperactive-Impulsive Type

---

* Although ADHD and ADD are often used interchangeably in the literature, throughout this book ADHD will refer to the predominantly hyperactive-impulsive type and ADD will refer to the predominantly inattentive type.

◆ CHARACTERISTICS OF CHILDREN ◆
AND ADOLESCENTS WITH ADHD/ADD

Before reading this section, you are encouraged to complete, for your child or adolescent, the *Copeland Symptom Checklist for Attention Deficit Disorders* found on pages fifty-two through fifty-four. A Symptom Checklist for adults can be found in Appendix 1. These checklists are included as a guide to greater understanding, especially if you suspect that you or a family member may have an attention disorder. The child and adolescent checklist includes the following areas of difficulty:

- Inattention/Distractibility
- Impulsivity
- Activity Level Problems
- Non-Compliance
- Attention-Getting Behavior
- Immaturity
- Poor Achievement/Cognitive and Visual-
  Motor Problems
- Emotional Difficulties
- Poor Peer Relations
- Family Interaction Problems

The ten areas of difficulty noted on the checklist include the three categories described by the APA and seven developed through our clinical research and practice. They are the most frequently encountered and will be addressed at length in this and subsequent chapters. Most children and adolescents do not have all the symptoms listed, nor do they have difficulties in all the categories identified. They do, however, have many more than their non-ADHD/ADD peers.

The checklist is intended as a way for you to begin observing and evaluating your child's behavior. It is not intended as a definitive diagnosis of ADHD or ADD. Just as no two children are alike, each child, adolescent or adult with an attention disorder will have a unique set of symptoms and characteristics. Only a trained professional can diagnose ADHD and ADD with the degree of certainty necessary for comprehensive care and your peace of mind. If you suspect that you or your child has an attention disorder, we urge you to seek professional assistance from someone thoroughly familiar with this disorder. Only when one is properly diagnosed can treatment interventions be appropriate and effective. An excellent resource for knowledgeable professionals in your community is the local ADHD/ADD support group, a listing of which can be obtained from the national organizations found in Appendix 3.

While our discussion will focus somewhat more on children, many of the symptoms are the same for adolescents and adults as well. As one matures, however, the symptoms become more subtle and are often attributed to problems other than ADHD or ADD. For this reason, many adolescents and adults with attention disorders often go undetected.

♦ *Inattention/Distractibility*

While attention is often discussed as though it were a stable phenomenon, it, in fact, is not. Rather, both attention and inattention are quite variable and dependent upon both internal and external factors, and they are in a constant state of flux. For example, a hungry person will usually attend to the smell of food, while a satiated one may not. A child may have no difficulty attending to video games or TV, but may well tune the teacher out. An adolescent may pay attention to a fun, exciting teacher and ignore one whom he considers boring; an adult may concentrate for hours on a business problem but find listening to his wife's concerns difficult.

While attention is variable in everyone and is very dependent upon motivating factors, inattention and an inability to concentrate are characteristic of almost every child, adolescent and adult with ADHD or ADD. It can be observed as a short attention span, daydreaming, or an inability to focus. Listening to explanations, following directions, and staying on task are major problems. When the child or adolescent has to attend for even a short period of time, problems can occur: explanations may be ignored, parts of directions not read, or important details may be overlooked. Parents and teachers frequently despair: "He doesn't listen." "She doesn't follow directions." The most frequent complaint, however,

---

Before I got married I had six theories about bringing up children; now I have six children and no theories.——John Wilmot, Earl of Rochester

is, "He doesn't pay attention." "Pay attention, *please!*" is the child's constant admonishment—one he hears morning, noon and night. Inattentiveness is a major problem in the classroom and when doing homework. It is present in daily activities as well.

Spaciness, being tuned out or not noticing important stimuli, is another quality of inattentiveness and may also be present. It may be shoes on the floor or the directions for the math homework which the ADHD/ADD child overlooks. Spaciness is noticeable in sports and is especially obvious in the outfield.

An attention disorder can become a major problem when a teenager begins driving. John, a conscientious seventeen-year-old ADD driver, tried very hard to be careful. Accidents, nonetheless, frequently occurred. After one accident, he exclaimed, "I never saw the light turn red; that car came out of nowhere." John, like many ADD drivers, often daydreamed and, unfortunately, drove on automatic pilot much of the time. The many automobile accidents experienced by those with ADHD/ADD can be frightening, frustrating and expensive. ADD deserves treatment if for no other reason than the hazard it poses on the road.

Other kinds of accidents occur as well. John's younger sister, Jessica, who has ADHD, has spent many afternoons in the emergency room with broken bones and bruises as a result of her impulsive behavior and her inattention. Accident proneness is a common characteristic of ADHD and ADD and can be a major source of stress for the family. Serious consequences frequently result because these children and adolescents simply do not pay adequate attention to important information in their world.

Choosing the wrong stimuli to which to respond can cause equal problems. Tony can tell you how many dandelions are in the outfield, but he hasn't caught a ball this season. Angela loves her teacher's bracelets and can tell you all about them, but she doesn't remember what the homework assignment is.

While problems resulting from inattentiveness are frequent, the majority of ADD children, adolescents and adults have the greatest difficulty attending to a task long enough to complete it. It is difficult for them to finish a job quickly and completely whether it is cleaning their room, mowing the yard, writing a book report or doing homework. Adults involved with the inattentive child exclaim in frustration, "Everything he does is only half finished."

Distractibility is a characteristic that contributes to inattentiveness and usually goes hand-in-hand with it. Distractibility is a tendency to become sidetracked by other stimuli which are not relevant to the task at hand. Distractions can be both internal, such as one's own thoughts or fantasies and external—the plane overhead, pencils being sharpened, or noise from another room.

Sarah, a classic example of distractibility, rushes to her room every morning after breakfast with the very best of intentions to dress on time and not miss the bus. Twenty minutes later her mother typically finds her, still in her pajamas, deeply engrossed in playing with a toy. Parents can intervene and help make children focus, but drastic measures may be required.

A child with an attention disorder lacks the ability to concentrate and focus. It is especially difficult for him to stick with long, tedious tasks or ones he considers *boring,* his favorite word. He may sharpen his pencil incessantly or go to the bathroom repeatedly. He generally avoids settling down to work. He does not do these things intentionally; rather, he is physiologically unable to pay attention the way his non-ADHD/ADD classmates can. The activity may also be a way of alerting the sluggish attentional centers. Both teachers and parents must be sensitive to the alerting function of movement and provide for it in ways consistent with the learning or attentional needs of the situation. ADHD/ADD children can become quite sophisticated in both their activity and avoidance maneuvers. Wesley, an appealing first grader, made frequent excursions to the bathroom. When questioned why the teacher let him go so often, Wesley responded energetically and with a twinkle in his eye: "Oh, you have to *look* like you have to go."

When parents and teachers do not understand the problems inherent in ADHD and ADD, they can be unsympathetic and punitive in their responses to these children. Many, in fact, view them as having a selective attention deficit for school and homework. They are understandably confused when they see these children attending for long periods to activities they enjoy. A non-understanding adult at one of our conferences, after looking at some of the information on ADHD/ADD, commented, "Another name for a lazy kid."

Concentration difficulties become most obvious under conditions of familiarity, boredom, repetition and fatigue. By contrast, ADHD/ADD children can concentrate quite well when interest or motivation is strong. The body may, in fact, secrete additional hormones which stimulate increased neurotransmitter release in the brain, thus improving the regulation of the attention centers.

Recent studies have shown that the typical classroom includes many negatives for the ADHD/ADD child: it is often slow-paced; it includes many uninteresting ditto and laborious copying tasks; and periods of concentration, especially those for written work, are not broken by periods of active participation. By contrast, computer instruction, which is novel, interactional, self-paced and visual, can be far more effective than the usual teacher instruction for many easily-distracted children. There are also many positive classroom strategies which decrease inattentiveness and increase the productivity of both the overactive and underactive child.

As frustrating as the symptoms of poor attention can be to the child's teacher or parent, they are equally or even more frustrating to the child himself. Every child wants to succeed, to cooperate and to achieve in his life. The effort which these children must expend to accomplish what non-attention-disordered children do with little effort is extraordinary.

We learn from experience. A man never wakes up his second baby just to see it smile.——Grace Williams

SIGNS OF INATTENTION AND DISTRACTIBILITY

- A short attention span, especially for low-interest activities.

- Difficulty completing tasks.

- Daydreaming.

- Being easily distracted.

- Having nicknames such as "spacey" or "dreamer."

- Engaging in much activity but accomplishing little.

- Beginning enthusiastically but ending poorly.

◆ *Impulsivity*

Impulsivity is the second major characteristic of children with attention disorders. Many consider it to be the most serious and the most enduring problem in adolescence and adulthood. A fifteen-year study of hyperactive children conducted at McGill University revealed that when the hyperactive children they studied grew up, impulsivity was the most problematic and long-lasting of their symptoms (Weiss and Hechtmann, 1986).

Impulse control, i.e., the ability to think before acting, to tolerate delay and to consider the consequences of one's actions, is an essential ingredient for success in life. Very young children characteristically have poor impulse control. By the age of six, however, they have usually learned to delay gratification and to think before acting. The child or adolescent with an attention disorder does not mature in this way. Rather, he frequently becomes upset easily and may vent his frustrations immediately. An angry eight-year-old, for example, may hit his best friend in a moment of confrontation without a thought of his friend's feelings or reactions. When things do not go his way at home, he may scream at his parents, throw a toy, or hit his sister.

The impulsive child is usually not malicious—simply unthinking. It never occurs to him that putting the dog in the dryer after a shampoo might not be the best way to dry his pet quickly, or socking a friend the best way to resolve conflict. He is often genuinely sorry for the problems he has caused. Despite his penitence, however, he often resumes his unthinking behavior immediately following his apology.

Live for the moment could well be the motto of impulsive children. If a match looks interesting, they strike it. If the blue liquid in the bottle under the sink looks appealing, they assume it will taste good too. Big wheels to them were designed for riding down the steepest, most dangerous driveways in the neighborhood. What awaits them around the corner or at the bottom of the hill is a consideration for parents only.

Impulsive children are disorganized and forgetful. One of the most frequent sources of family conflict is their messy rooms. Despite their spending hours attempting to clean it, it is usually considered a disaster by their more organized parents. One mother finally gave up in desperation saying, "I won't come in until bugs start crawling out of your room." Forgotten books and lost assignments, likewise, endear them to neither parents nor teachers. The disorganized child is the one who, after finally completing his homework, loses it on the way to school. Parents and teachers are often ready to pull their hair out—or his.

Staying organized at school is also a problem. Studies have shown that ADHD/ADD children can often be accurately diagnosed by looking in the preschooler's cubby, the elementary school child's desk and the adolescent's locker. After a day of impulsively putting in and pulling out without any organization or planning, their spaces are disasters.

Impulsivity is often the most difficult of all the ADHD symptoms with which to cope. The child or adolescent's unthinking behavior creates constant problems with neighbors, teachers and peers. Broken windows, bloody noses and crying sisters are everyday life with the ADHD child. Often he is the most surprised of anyone when he realizes what he has done. A sense of humor and an awareness that *this too shall pass* can help you avoid total frustration and despondency. Maintaining a sense of equanimity is crucial to the survival of both your child and yourself.

The impulsivity and lack of thought regarding consequences can lead to many skirmishes with adult authorities and later with the legal system as well. Dr. Judith Rappaport at the National Institute of Mental Health has described adolescents with attention disorders, especially ADHD, as at risk for becoming *minor league criminals*. She notes that they often do things which are illegal and foolish, but they rarely possess the organizational ability to plan major criminal activities. Many naive and impulsive adolescents and young adults, nevertheless, face both relatively minor and more serious legal problems because of their unthinking behavior.

The first half of our life is ruined by our parents and the second half by our children.——Clarence Darrow

SIGNS OF IMPULSIVITY

- Excitability.

- Low frustration tolerance.

- Acting before thinking.

- Disorganization.

- Poor planning ability.

- Excessively shifting from one activity to another.

- Having difficulty in group situations which require patience and taking turns.

- Being constantly in trouble for deeds of omission as well as deeds of commission.

- Interrupting frequently.

◆ *Activity-Level Problems*

Problems related to activity level constitute the third major characteristic of attention deficit disorders. Children and adolescents with attention disorders appear to be on a continuum of activity from underactive and lethargic to overactive and hyperactive. There are also those somewhere in the middle— restless and fidgety but not disrupting the class or running down the hall.

That all children with attention disorders are not overactive is perhaps the least understood fact in the whole area. The underactive ADD child is least likely to be recognized and to receive help. When he is identified, parents are often disbelieving because of their assumption that hyperactivity is a necessary feature of attention disorders.   The name *Attention Deficit Hyperactivity Disorder* is, itself, confusing. It is easy to understand why a parent with an underactive, sluggish ADD child may balk at a diagnosis of ADHD.

HYPERACTIVE
* Extremely overactive
* Very impulsive
* No attention span
* Emotionally volatile

OVERACTIVE

Mildly	Moderately
Fidgety	Overactive
Restless	Impulsive
Distractible	Short attention
Impulsive	span
	Very distractible
	Disorganized

UNDERACTIVE
* Daydreaming
* Lethargic
* "Spacey"
* Underactive
* Absent minded
* (Most extreme: Narcolepsy)

Overactivity/Hyperactivity—Clearly, those children who are hyperactive are the first to be recognized. They are constantly on the go, or, when sitting, move some part of their bodies; they also have an unusual amount of energy. As infants they may be restless; they may have feeding problems, especially colic; and they often have trouble sleeping. As toddlers they have boundless energy and often walk early. As one mother stated, "Keith never walked.   He just started running and hasn't stopped since." Mothers are usually exhausted and problems with preschools and peers begin at this time.

In school hyperactive children fidget, drum their fingers, shuffle their feet and appear to be in constant motion. They have difficulty sitting still; they talk non-stop, thus the taunt *motor mouth* by their peers; and they often appear nervous. Disruptive and loud, the hyperactive child is often the class clown. He either amuses the other students, irritates them, or both. Rarely does he delight the adults in his school. He is driven from within, and little external structure or control makes a significant difference.

Even the most well-intentioned teacher becomes annoyed by this child who seems bent on destroying her class. She has usually tried rewards and punishment, criticism and praise. Nothing has worked. His parents are frustrated and so is she. Lost books, forgotten homework, papers she can hardly read and unruliness are par for the day. Her desire to teach is thwarted at best, and the job at the bank has ever increasing appeal.

The hyperactive child is not always overactive, however. When receiving one-to-one attention from an adult or doing something he really enjoys, he will often respond like other children, at least for a while, confounding both parents and teachers. It is understandable why people may perceive his overactive behavior as willfull and defiant.

In general, the research findings indicate that hyperactive children are not necessarily more active than most children in all settings. The more restrictive the environment and the more concentration required, the more likely differences in activity level will be found, especially in restlessness and off-task behavior. In unusual or unfamiliar settings they often behave very much like other children.

This characteristic is frustrating for mothers since the symptoms are notoriously absent when the children visit their pediatricians where they usually behave perfectly. No wonder mothers of these children are often considered neurotic. Teachers too, become frustrated when the pediatrician views the good behavior in his office as typical of that at school.

As hyperactive children become accustomed to an environment, however, their activity level can be expected to increase. After a couple of hours in a *boring* waiting room, your child can probably convince even the most dubious professional that he has ADHD.

In some ways the ADHD child who is hyperactive is the most fortunate, for he is the most likely to be identified and to obtain treatment. As an adult, he can be expected to continue to have an abundance of energy which, if channeled correctly, can be one of his greatest assets. With the assistance of a highly organized and efficient secretary or spouse, many hyperactive adults reach great levels of accomplishment. They are very likely to own their own businesses and to be entrepreneurs as well.

SIGNS OF OVERACTIVITY

- Restlessness—either fidgetiness or being constantly on the go.

- Diminished need for sleep.

- Excessive talking.

- Excessive running, jumping and climbing.

- Difficulty listening.

- Motor restlessness during sleep; kicks covers off and moves constantly.

- Difficulty staying seated at meals, in class, etc.; often walks around the classroom.

Underactivity—In marked contrast to the hyperactive child, the ADD child who is lethargic and underactive is likely to be ignored. This child often has difficulty paying attention and may appear confused and depressed. His major problems are inattention, disorganization and poor planning ability. He has few problems with impulsivity and little, if any, excessive motor activity. He experiences significant problems, however, for even though he often has the best of intentions, he simply cannot seem to get organized and to be productive. Only when the underactive ADD child's poor achievement becomes significant, or the child/adolescent becomes depressed, are parents and teachers alerted to the problem. Even then it may be incorrectly viewed as *laziness, disinterest,* or a *poor attitude.*

John was such a child. He began having trouble in kindergarten and first grade, despite an I.Q. in the 90th percentile. In second grade he was evaluated by the public school system and was found not to have a specific learning disability (SLD). Lack of motivation and inadequate self-discipline were given as the reasons for his poor performance. It was implied that perhaps his parents were being too lenient with him. In reality, John's parents were quite strict with him. Both he and they, in fact, felt that they were badgering him most of the time. The recommended behavior management strategies were temporarily helpful, but the academic problems continued.

Hoping that individual attention would help John, his parents enrolled him in a small private school in third grade. Although he made some progress, his teachers still described him as "not working up to his ability, needing constant reminders to complete assignments," and as "disorganized, forgetful, easily distracted and not paying attention in class." His parents felt frustrated and helpless.

In fifth grade, making C's and D's, John was referred to a psychologist who evaluated him and diagnosed his difficulties as a mild attention deficit disorder without hyperactivity. Treatment included stimulant medication, parent training in behavior management techniques, family counseling and social skills training. As a sixth grader John's report card was all A's in conduct and A's and B's in academic subjects. He now has time to play basketball and has proved to be quite an athlete. Family life has improved greatly and John is now far more successful and feels

---

Of all the animals, the boy is the most unmanageable.——Plato (428-348 B.C.)

more confident. He has become a fun child with whom to be.

While John will have to be monitored closely as he grows up and there will be difficulties to face, his parents are thrilled with his progress. Their family life is much happier now.

SIGNS OF UNDERACTIVITY

- Lethargy.

- Daydreaming/spaciness.

- Failure to complete tasks.

- Inattention.

- Poor leadership ability.

- Difficulty in learning and performing.

Overfocused Disorder—Overfocused behavior is often mistaken for undifferentiated ADD. Those with this disorder are at the opposite end of the cognitive style continuum from the impulsive, hyperactive child. They are excessively deliberate, rather than sluggish, and they have more difficulty changing activities. Unlike those with ADD, they can be compulsive and rigid as well.

Overfocused children work very slowly and excessively check and recheck their work. They often do not complete it because they are so slow and they dislike distraction. It is difficult for them to let go of their immediate task and shift gears to a new activity, even when it is something they prefer to do. These children are very easy to discipline. They are, in fact, too sensitive and responsive to limit-setting and become fearful and upset when faced with harshness or anger. Intense and shy, they tend to avoid others and are overwhelmed by cognitive or emotional stimulation. These children do best in bland, stable, nondemanding situations. The overfocused disorder involves different brain chemicals and requires different medical interventions than those helpful for undifferentiated attention deficit disorder.

◆ *Noncompliance*

Noncompliance is one of the major reasons parents seek professional help for their ADHD and ADD children. Those with attention disorders, especially ADHD, often refuse to mind their parents and teachers and to behave in socially acceptable ways in relating to others.

Noncompliance may result from deficiencies in rule-governed behavior or from unintentional reinforcement of undesirable behaviors by parents. Noncompliance may also result from neurotransmitter imbalances that must be corrected by medication.

Noncompliance, whether active or passive, is a major problem for most children with attention disorders. It creates the most overt negative responses from parents, teachers and others who must deal with the child or adolescent on a daily basis.

Language is very important in the development of compliance. As a child matures linguistically he develops inner language, that is, the internal dialogue that a person has with himself. Instead of impulsively dashing out the door he says, "Let me see, before I go to school I need to check my assignments and my list to make sure I have everything. I don't want to get in trouble today—not with the football game coming on Friday night. I know Dad will ground me if I do."

SIGNS OF NONCOMPLIANCE

- Frequently disobeys.
- Does not cooperate. Determined to do things his own way.
- Argumentative.
- Disregards socially-accepted behavioral expectations.
- "Forgets" unintentionally.
- Uses forgetting as an excuse (intentional).

◆ *Attention-Getting Behavior*

Attention-getting behavior, or the need to be center stage much of the time, is a frustrating characteristic of many ADHD children. It is not characteristic of ADD children who may, in fact, seek to avoid both attention and recognition. Of all the symptoms, attention-getting behavior can be the most exhausting one for parents and the most irritating one to observers. The ADHD child's need for attention appears insatiable despite the fact that he usually receives much more than his siblings or peers. Typical ways the child seeks attention are as follows:

ATTENTION-GETTING BEHAVIOR

Preschoolers and Toddlers

- Whining.
- Repeating forbidden behaviors.
- Challenging authorities constantly.
- Annoying others.
- Using bad language.
- Talking excessively loudly.
- Pulling or tugging at parents' clothing, especially in public situations.

Older Children

- Asking questions constantly.
- Irritating siblings.
- Monopolizing conversations.
- Interrupting frequently.
- Acting the class clown.
- Wearing unusual or different clothing.
- Having exaggerated or different hair styles.
- Identifying with popular groups, especially those considered extreme.

In situations where there is competition, these behaviors worsen markedly. The arrival of company or when mother is on the telephone or cooking dinner may be especially difficult times. In the classroom, where there is much competition, they may blurt out questions, irritate other students, constantly seek the praise or guidance of their teachers, or engage in unacceptable behavior which cannot be ignored.

Most ADHD/ADD children have not been deprived of attention, as one might suspect from their constant demands for more. Just the opposite is often the case. Parents sometimes feel guilty about the problems of their ADHD or ADD children. In their attempts to meet their needs adequately, they may continue to give them too much attention and foster this need even more.

♦ *Immaturity*

Immaturity, including neurological, emotional, social, academic and physical immaturity, is a hallmark of the ADHD/ADD child. Such immaturity is typically evidenced in the following ways:

SIGNS OF IMMATURITY

- Much of the behavior is that of a younger child, with responses being typical of children 6 months to 2-plus years younger.
- Both physical development and neurological development may be delayed.
- Younger children are preferred and relationships are better.
- Emotional reactions are immature.

It often helps in working with the ADHD or ADD child to think of him as a younger child and respond accordingly. When Jason was twelve he wanted desperately to be allowed to ride his bicycle out of the neighborhood and to cross a busy street on the way. His parents, aware that his maturity level was closer to that of a ten-year-old, wisely decided against granting him such a privilege. To the child, his friends, and the parents themselves, the situation seemed unfair. "Why should *I* be the only twelve-year-old in the neighborhood who is not allowed to take off on his own?" he persisted. His mom felt equal frustration as she thought, "Why should *I* be the only mother in the neighborhood who still has to help her twelve-year-old son cross the street?" She, nevertheless, patiently explained that he would be allowed this privilege when he showed her, through agreed-upon goals, that he was responsible.

Experience has shown that maternal instincts are often more valid than scientific instruments or professional opinions. Mothers usually know better than anyone when their children are mature enough to handle certain privileges. Life usually runs more smoothly if you trust your own judgments and do not give in because all your child's friends, who may well be ready, have more freedom. Helpful friends and professionals will respect parents' instinctive knowledge of their child.

It has long been observed that children with attention disorders mature physically later than their peers. While they may walk, talk, roll over and sit up early, fine-motor integration, writing and even the maturation of their teeth are often delayed, especially the development of their permanent teeth. Sometimes affectionately termed *late bloomers*, they may reach various levels of maturity six months to several years later than their peers. For this reason, they may seek out friendships with younger children. If an ADHD or ADD child has a late birthday, especially late spring or summer, it is often advisable to hold him back a year in school, so that he will develop and mature at the same time his classmates do. Determination of school readiness is an important issue for all parents, but it is especially critical for the ADHD/ADD

I think somehow, we learn who we really are and then live with that decision.——Eleanor Roosevelt

child and is addressed in Chapter 7, *Educational Interventions.*

◆ *Poor Academic Achievement/Cognitive
and Visual-Motor Problems*

School is considered by many to be the ADHD/ADD child's worst
affliction. Poor school performance and underachievement are close
to universal problems from preschool to college. There are many
causes of the child or adolescent's poor school performance and
underachievement which can, and usually do, have very serious
negative consequences for self-esteem, long-term academic
accomplishment and later occupational success.

Intelligence *per se* is not affected by attention disorders,
although development of the intellect may be uneven. However, an
attention disorder can cause a child not to reach his potential and
usually by third grade I.Q. scores have dropped significantly.
There appears to be no correlation between ADHD/ADD and
intelligence. It is seen in students of every ability level.

While attention disorders are considered by some to be
learning disabilities, most professionals in the field view attention
disorders and learning disabilities as separate, although frequently
related, difficulties. Learning disabilities will be addressed in
greater depth in Chapter 7.

Even though most ADHD/ADD children do not have coexisting
learning disabilities, their performance is, nevertheless, usually
below their own ability level and that of the class. The child
usually has trouble not because he lacks ability, but because he
cannot concentrate and complete the work. Spontaneous learning
which occurs in the context of social interaction, such as vocabulary, comprehension and general information, is less affected than
academic tasks which require attention to detail, repetition,
memory and problem-solving. To learn, a child must concentrate for
a reasonable amount of time; he must hear some of what is said; he
must have some persistence; and he must lock the information into
long-term memory. All of these abilities are impaired in children
with attention disorders.

These problems do not have to occur, however, as evidenced by
a letter from Sam's parents. Sam was referred at age five for
hyperactivity, noncompliance and very poor preschool performance.

Dear Dr. Copeland,

Now that our relocation has been completed and we are settled in our new home, I wanted to give you an update on Sam. As a preadolescent in the sixth grade, he is something else!

Sam is doing quite well academically and emotionally. At home he is great! However, there have been some mild social concerns. Andy and I have decided to send him to a counselor for a while to help him learn some tips on making and keeping friends. His interpersonal skills have improved greatly during the past six years, but we have lost some credibility with him as he reaches adolescence.

The counselor we have chosen is also quite involved with the local support group and is familiar with the social problems of children with attention deficit. He is an advocate of the medical model in conjunction with psychological support.

Sam has also had a math tutor for two years, but his math average of eighty-nine makes it difficult to convince him that continued tutoring is necessary. We will probably discontinue the tutor on a trial basis and see if he can maintain his grades.

How thankful we are that Sam's problems were recognized early and that help was available. As I think back to our first meeting, when Sam was in Kindergarten and was so overactive and difficult for both his teachers and us, I realize how far we have come together. Your guidance and friendship have meant so much to us over the past seven years. There was a time when I worried that all the hopes and dreams we had for our child might be just that. As time goes by, Andy and I see those hopes becoming reality. We now have no doubt that Sam will become a successful and happy adult.

Thank you for all you have done for us, especially for Sam.

Warmest regards,

Janet

Not only are learning disabilities important in understanding and assisting children to perform successfully in school, but the relationship of language, reading, developmental readiness, overplacement in school and learning style preference are also critical issues.

♦ *Emotional Difficulties*

Many children with attention disorders also experience emotional problems. Some of these are physiologically caused, while others are psychological in origin. Many are the end result of the inevitable frustration and failure which accompany unidentified attention disorders.

One problem frequently seen in children with attention disorders is mood swings. Parents report: "She's happy one minute and miserable the next," or "Some mornings I go up to say 'good morning' and there is an immediate argument. Others, she hops up, throws her arms around my neck and gives me a kiss." Many parents also report good days and bad days. When these are pronounced and when you can tell it is going to be a bad day as soon as the child awakens, allergies may be involved.

Many people with ADHD and ADD are described as *irritable*. This characteristic appears to increase with age. One father of a hyperactive child had been chronically tense, irritable and short-tempered for years. After taking Dexedrine for weight control, he unexpectedly found he was calm, quiet and pleasant to be around. Fits of temper were no longer a daily occurrence, and he was able to concentrate, think clearly and remain patient for long periods of time. It was then determined that he was an adult with an attention deficit disorder. An ADD mother of a hyperactive child with whom we worked was surprised to find that the anti-depressant she was taking not only elevated her mood but helped her organization, planning and efficiency. Neither she nor her doctor was aware that the medication she was taking improved symptoms of ADD as well. Irritability, moodiness, depression or quick tempers can be constant challenges for those who live and work with ADHD/ADD children, adolescents and adults.

The time to relax is when you don't have time for it.——Sydney J. Harris

Because of the many social difficulties encountered, their chronic underachievement, the criticism received and their sense of frustration and failure, it is not surprising that low self-esteem is one of the most common end results of this disorder. Children may think of themselves as mean, dumb, spacey, weird or hyper. Many wish they had never been born. Some withdraw; others fight back. Especially sensitive children inwardly despair and desperately hope for someone or something to help them. The relief experienced by children, adolescents and adults alike is profound when they realize they have a medical problem for which treatment is available.

SIGNS OF EMOTIONAL DIFFICULTIES

- Frequent and unpredictable mood swings.
- Irritability.
- Underreactive to pain/insensitive to danger.
- Easily overstimulated. Hard to stop once "revved up".
- Low frustration tolerance. Excessive emotional reactions to frustrating situations.
- Angry outbursts.
- Moodiness/lack of energy.
- Low self-esteem.
- Immaturity.

◆ *Poor Peer Relations*

Problems in social relationships often come as soon as the child is old enough to walk and can grab a toy that belongs to another toddler. Hyperactive preschool children are often referred to professionals by age three or four because of their problems interacting with peers. Hitting, biting, being too rough and hurting other children are frequent complaints. Teasing is also a common problem and one which alienates them from their classmates and friends. Hyperactive children are often avoided and rejected by peers because of their inappropriate behavior. These children, in turn, feel left out and often accuse others of doing misdeeds to them. The ADD child without hyperactivity, on the other hand, does not usually experience peer problems in preschool.

While peer relations are a serious problem in the early years, they manifest themselves most poignantly in elementary and secondary school. The overactive ADHD child is usually socially assertive and makes friends easily. However, he also loses them easily, for he tends to be bossy; he wants to decide how games will be played; he has difficulty taking turns; and he may be a poor loser. Temper outbursts, impulsive acting out and irritability soon cause peers to avoid or reject him. In elementary and high school the ADHD/ADD child or adolescent may have difficulty making friends and is often left out of group activities. His isolation and loneliness cause all who care to ache for him.

Many ADHD/ADD children, both underactive and overactive, do not appear to notice or respond appropriately to social cues. They frequently have little insight into the cause of their difficulties and may blame others. Some develop humor and become the class clown as a means of having a place in the group, while others retreat into obscurity. They often deny their desire to be part of the group and may actively reject their peers in self-defense—at least in their minds. Specifically teaching social awareness and appropriate social responses is critical as part of the intervention programs for many with ADHD and ADD.

As adolescents, their inappropriate and socially insensitive behavior may continue. By this time many have been rejected so often and lost so much esteem and confidence over the years that they have become withdrawn, depressed, and vulnerable to negative peer groups and substance abuse.

ADD children who are not overactive are more prone to restricted social relationships because of their lack of confidence. Poor school performance, teasing because of their spaciness, and their general difficulty organizing leave them feeling vulnerable and anxious. They may develop one or two best friends or may become isolated and on the fringe of their peer group. While not actively rejected, they may not be included either. Thus, they feel lonely and despondent much of the time. One of the most important jobs of parents and teachers will be fostering positive friendships with appropriate peers.

A few ADHD and ADD children are quite popular. They are usually good athletes, those with innate leadership ability, or those who achieve easily. Those who are well-regarded by their peers fare much better than those who are not. For those children who have problems interacting with peers, long-term prognosis is poor. Positive peer relations, by contrast, are good omens for later success.

The very small boy came home dejectedly from his first day at school:
"Ain't goin' tomorrow," he sputtered.
"Why not, dear?" his mother asked.
"Well, I can't read, and I can't write, and the teacher won't let me talk, so what's the use?"——Coast Guard Magazine

SIGNS OF POOR PEER RELATIONS

- Hits, bites or kicks other children. Generally too aggressive.
- Has difficulty following the rules of games and social interactions.
- Is rejected or avoided by peers.
- Avoids group activities; a loner.
- Bosses other people; wants to be the leader.
- Teases peers and siblings excessively.

◆ *Family Interaction Problems*

There are few disorders which have as profound an effect on the family as ADHD or ADD. This is especially true if the child is hyperactive. The child's unpredictable and often uncontrollable behavior can be both exasperating and exhausting for those in the family who interact with him on a daily basis.

The activity level, the mood swings, the constancy of the hyperactive child's difficulties, and the teacher's weekly calls create a tense situation in the home. There are more slammed doors and hurt feelings, harsh words and tears than in the non-ADHD/ADD household. Parents frequently come to resent the child and then feel guilty because of their feelings.

Those whose children are underactive and disorganized are bewildered and frustrated by their childrens' lack of performance and seeming indifference. Nagging, coercion and continual struggling bring no positive changes. Rather, they increase the growing alienation and helplessness both parents and child feel.

SIGNS OF FAMILY INTERACTION PROBLEMS

- Frequent family conflict.
- Activities and social gatherings are unpleasant.
- Parents argue over discipline since nothing works.

- Mother spends hours and hours on homework with ADD child, leaving little time for others in the family.

- Meals are frequently unpleasant.

- Arguments occur between parents and child over responsibilities and chores.

- Stress is continuous from child's social and academic problems.

- Parents, especially mother, feel: frustrated, angry, helpless, hopeless, guilty, disappointed, alone, afraid for the child, sad and depressed.

While family interaction problems can be a source of much frustration for both parents and child, the family also holds the greatest promise for assuring the long-term positive adjustment of the ADHD/ADD child or adolescent. One study reported that when adults who had been hyperactive were asked what had helped them most to overcome their childhood difficulties, their most common reply was that someone—usually a parent or teacher—had believed in them (Weiss and Hechtman, 1986).

Rebellion against your handicaps gets you nowhere. Self-pity gets you nowhere. One must have the adventurous daring to accept oneself as a bundle of possibilities and undertake the most interesting game in the world—making the most of one's best.——Harry Emerson Fosdick

≡SPI≡

COPELAND SYMPTOM CHECKLIST FOR ATTENTION DEFICIT DISORDERS

Attention Deficit Hyperactivity Disorder (ADHD)
and Undifferentiated Attention Deficit Disorder (ADD)

This checklist was developed from the experience of many specialists in the field of Attention Deficit Disorders and Hyperactivity. It is designed to help you assess whether your child/student has ADHD or ADD, to what degree, and if so, in which area(s) difficulties are experienced. Please mark all statements. Thank you for your assistance in completing this information.

Name of Child _____ Date _____

Completed by _____

Directions: Place a checkmark (✔) by each item below, indicating the degree to which the behavior is characteristic of your child/student.

* denotes ADD with Hyperactivity (ADHD).
• denotes ADD without Hyperactivity (Undifferentiated ADD)

	Not at all	Just a little	Pretty much	Very much	Score	%
I. INATTENTION/DISTRACTIBILITY						
*• 1. A short attention span, especially for low-interest activities.						
*• 2. Difficulty completing tasks.						
• 3. Daydreaming.						
*• 4. Easily distracted.						
• 5. Nicknames such as: "spacey," or "dreamer."						
*• 6. Engages in much activity but accomplishes little.						
*• 7. Enthusiastic beginnings but poor endings.					___ = ___% 21	
II. IMPULSIVITY						
* 1. Excitability.						
*• 2. Low frustration tolerance.						
*• 3. Acts before thinking.						
*• 4. Disorganization.						
*• 5. Poor planning ability.						
*• 6. Excessively shifts from one activity to another.						
* 7. Difficulty in group situations which require patience and taking turns.						
*• 8. Requires much supervision.						
*• 9. Constantly in trouble for deeds of omission as well as deeds of commission.						
*•10. Frequently interrupts conversations; talks out of turn.					___ = ___% 30	
III. ACTIVITY LEVEL PROBLEMS						
A. Overactivity/Hyperactivity						
*• 1. Restlessness — either fidgetiness or being constantly on the go.						
* 2. Diminished need for sleep.						
* 3. Excessive talking.						
* 4. Excessive running, jumping and climbing.						
* 5. Motor restlessness during sleep. Kicks covers off — moves around constantly.						
* 6. Difficulty staying seated at meals, in class, etc. Often walks around classroom.					___ = ___% 18	
B. Underactivity						
• 1. Lethargy.						
• 2. Daydreaming, spaciness.						
• 3. Failure to complete tasks.						
*• 4. Inattention.						
*• 5. Poor leadership ability.						
*• 6. Difficulty in learning and performing.					___ = ___% 18	
IV. NON-COMPLIANCE						
*• 1. Frequently disobeys.						
*• 2. Argumentative.						
* 3. Disregards socially-accepted standards of behavior.						
• 4. "Forgets" unintentionally.						
5. Uses "forgetting" as an excuse (intentional).					___ = ___% 15	

Copyright ©1987 by Edna D. Copeland, Ph.D.

Published by **SPI** Southeastern Psychological Institute, P.O. Box 12389, Atlanta, Georgia 30355-2389

COPELAND SYMPTOM CHECKLIST FOR ATTENTION DEFICIT DISORDERS (Continued)

	Not at all	Just a little	Pretty much	Very much
V. ATTENTION-GETTING BEHAVIOR				
* 1. Frequently needs to be the center of attention.				
* 2. Constantly asks questions or interrupts.				
* 3. Irritates and annoys siblings, peers and adults.				
* 4. Behaves as the "class clown."				
* 5. Uses bad or rude language to attract attention.				
* 6. Engages in other negative behaviors to attract attention.				
VI. IMMATURITY				
*• 1. Behavior resembles that of a younger child. Responses are typical of children 6 months to 2-plus years younger.				
*• 2. Physical development is delayed.				
*• 3. Prefers younger children and relates better to them.				
*• 4. Emotional reactions are often immature.				
VII. POOR ACHIEVEMENT/COGNITIVE & VISUAL-MOTOR PROBLEMS				
*• 1. Underachieves relative to ability.				
*• 2. Loses books, assignments, etc.				
*• 3. Auditory memory and auditory processing problems.				
*• 4. Learning disabilities/learning problems.				
*• 5. Incomplete assignments.				
*• 6. Academic work completed too quickly.				
*• 7. Academic work completed too slowly.				
*• 8. "Messy" or "sloppy" written work; poor handwriting.				
*• 9. Poor memory for directions, instructions and rote learning.				
VIII. EMOTIONAL DIFFICULTIES				
*• 1. Frequent and unpredictable mood swings.				
*• 2. High levels of irritability.				
* 3. Underreactive to pain/insensitive to danger.				
* 4. Easily overstimulated. Hard to calm down once over-excited.				
*• 5. Low frustration tolerance.				
* 6. Temper tantrums, angry outbursts.				
• 7. Moodiness.				
*• 8. Low self-esteem.				
IX. POOR PEER RELATIONS				
* 1. Hits, bites, or kicks other children.				
* 2. Difficulty following the rules of games and social interactions.				
*• 3. Rejected or avoided by peers.				
• 4. Avoids group activities; a loner.				
* 5. Teases peers and siblings excessively.				
* 6. Bullies or bosses other children.				
X. FAMILY INTERACTION PROBLEMS				
1. Frequent family conflict.				
2. Activities and social gatherings are unpleasant.				
3. Parents argue over discipline since nothing works.				
4. Mother spends hours and hours on homework with ADD child leaving little time for others in family.				
5. Meals are frequently unpleasant.				
6. Arguments occur between parents and child over responsibilities and chores.				
7. Stress is continuous from child's social and academic problems.				
8. Parents, especially mother, feel: ☐ frustrated ☐ hopeless ☐ alone ☐ angry ☐ guilty ☐ afraid for child ☐ helpless ☐ disappointed ☐ sad and depressed				

Subtotals (right margin): 18, 12, 27, 24, 18, 24

_____ = _____%

TOTAL _____ = _____%
225

Published by **SPI** Southeastern Psychological Institute, P.O. Box 12389, Atlanta, Georgia 30355-2389

sPI

SCORING THE COPELAND SYMPTOM CHECKLIST
FOR ATTENTION DEFICIT DISORDERS (ADHD/ADD)

(Child/Adolescent Checklist and Adult Checklist)

1. Scores for each category are as follows:

   Not at all = 0;   Just a little = 1;   Pretty much = 2;   Very much = 3

2. Each check receives a score from 0 - 3. Add the checks in each category. That score is placed over the total possible.
   Example:

	0	1	2	3		
* denotes ADD with Hyperactivity (ADHD). • denotes ADD without Hyperactivity (Undifferentiated ADD)	Not at all	Just a little	Pretty much	Very much	Score	%
I. INATTENTION/DISTRACTIBILITY						
* • 1. A short attention span, especially for low-interest activities.				✔		
* • 2. Difficulty completing tasks.			✔			
• 3. Daydreaming.		✔				
* • 4. Easily distracted.				✔		
• 5. Nicknames such as: "spacey," or "dreamer."		✔				
* • 6. Engages in much activity but accomplishes little.				✔		
* • 7. Enthusiastic beginnings but poor endings.				✔	16 / 21 = 76 %
II. IMPULSIVITY						
* 1. Excitability.				✔		
* • 2. Low frustration tolerance.				✔		
* • 3. Acts before thinking.				✔		
* • 4. Disorganization.			✔			
* • 5. Poor planning ability.			✔			
* • 6. Excessively shifts from one activity to another.				✔		
* 7. Difficulty in group situations which require patience and taking turns.				✔		
* • 8. Requires much supervision.				✔		
* • 9. Constantly in trouble for deeds of omission as well as deeds of commission.			✔			
* • 10. Frequently interrupts conversations; talks out of turn.				✔	27 / 30 = 90 %

3. Compute the percentage for each category.

   Significance:*

   Scores between 35-49% suggest mild to moderate difficulties.

   Scores between 50-69% suggest moderate to severe difficulties.

   Scores above 70% suggest major interference.

   (*These scores represent clinical significance. The scale is currently being normed and statistical data should be available soon.)

   Children, adolescents and adults may have difficulties in only one area or in all ten. Those with undifferentiated ADD on the more daydreaming, inattentive, anxious end of the ADD continuum frequently manifest difficulties only in the "Inattention/Distractibility", "Underactivity", and the "Underachievement" categories, while those with overactive, impulsive ADHD will have difficulties in many more areas of their lives.

Published by sPI Southeastern Psychological Institute, P.O. Box 12389, Atlanta, Georgia 30355-2389

When you know a thing, to hold that you know it; and when you do not know a thing, to allow that you do not know it—this is knowledge.

—Confucius

Causes of
ADHD/ADD

Recognizing and diagnosing an attention disorder can often be difficult even when one has a good understanding of the typical symptoms and characteristics. Accurate recognition is often complicated by the fact that symptoms become problematic at different ages in different children. Some children exhibit symptoms before birth, especially overactivity; others become apparent during the preschool years. Most of the characteristics, however, are observable and are recognized during the elementary school years. Sometimes, however, subtle symptoms do not become apparent until the teens; and still other symptoms do not manifest as problems until adulthood. As the community's understanding of attention deficit disorders increases, we can expect these difficulties to be identified at increasingly early ages.

The symptoms of attention disorders also frequently overlap with other conditions, further complicating the process of diagnosis. Tourette Syndrome (TS), for example, is a disorder which sometimes co-occurs with ADHD and ADD. It is characterized by tics, which are involuntary muscle movements in the face, neck and shoulders.   Involuntary vocal sounds, irrelevant comments, distractibility and restlessness may also be present. About half of Tourette Syndrome patients have symptoms of ADHD/ADD as well. Sometimes the presence of the TS gene does not become obvious until after age seven, at which time ADHD is often the first symptom to be recognized.

Another medical problem which occurs frequently with ADHD/ADD and may possibly have an origin in common is ear infections. Many children with attention disorders have a history of chronic ear infections. A recent study of children failing in school found that 69% of the hyperactive children had a history of ten or more ear infections, while only 20% of the nonhyperactive children had more than ten (Hagerman and Falkenstein, 1987). Seizure disorders and attention disorders also co-occur. Research has shown that children with epilepsy have more inattention, impulsivity and many other characteristics of ADHD and ADD (Holdsworth and Whitmore, 1974).

There is also research which suggests that allergies and asthma occur more frequently in children with attention disorders. Other studies, however, have produced contradictory findings. The symptoms are often similar, however, and allergies and asthma should be ruled out if symptoms are present before a definitive diagnosis of ADHD/ADD is made. These conditions may also co-exist with ADHD or ADD.

A medical evaluation of your child is critical to rule out the possibility that other medical disorders are causing the symptoms. These include hypo- and hyperthyroidism, pituitary problems, narcolepsy, hypoglycemia, and seizure disorders, among others. Emotional problems, such as depression, anxiety, bipolar disorders and others, frequently mimic symptoms of ADHD and ADD, and they should be eliminated as causative factors.

Once an accurate diagnosis of ADHD or ADD has been made, "What caused the attention disorder?" is usually the next question. "Is it genetic?" "Was it present at birth?" "Was it caused by the environment in which the child has been raised?" Or "Is it a combination of all these factors?"

The chief function of your body is to carry your brain around.——Thomas Edison

◆ HEREDITY VS ENVIRONMENT AS THE CAUSE ◆
OF ATTENTION DISORDERS

While this debate, *nature vs nurture* or *heredity vs environment,* has been waged for years by scientists attempting to understand the forces which determine man's behavior, increasing evidence strongly suggests that the majority of attention deficit disorders are part of our genetic inheritance. Genes and physiology are believed to be more important in creating attention deficit disorders than are psychological, educational or social factors. However, environmental social factors play a key role in determining how the inherited predisposition to ADHD and ADD actually manifests in daily life.   It is ultimately the influence of all these forces simultaneously acting upon the individual, both during his development and currently, that determines who he becomes and how successfully he manages his life.

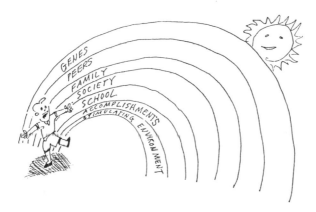

Paying attention is not a simple activity but a very complex process that involves extensive areas of the brain. Each area makes its own special contribution to attention. Characteristics of the stimuli around us and our interest, as well as internal states such as hunger, curiosity, pain and other physiological factors determine, to a large degree, the stimuli which will catch our attention.

◆ *Neurological Studies of Attention Disorders*

There is no single cause of attention disorders, just as there is no single solution. However, at the present time ADHD/ADD are considered by most researchers and practitioners to be physiological problems. Recent scientific studies, especially those of Dr. Alan Zametkin and his associates at the National Institute of Mental Health, have demonstrated quite clearly that there are physiological differences from the norm in the brains of hyperactive adults. The differences noted were primarily in the neurochemistry of the brain in those with ADHD.

One of the first studies, by Dr. Hans Lou (1989), revealed differences between the blood-flow patterns of non-ADHD and ADHD children. Another researcher, a neurologist from Harvard University, found that the prefrontal areas of the brain are important biologic determiners of attention (Mesulam, 1986). He stated that if these areas of the brain are dysfunctional, inattention, distractibility and disinhibition are often present.

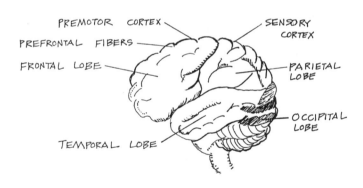

Figure 1. Each side of the brain is divided into four lobes

In addition to neurochemical differences, structural differences may also exist in some people with attention disorders. This is especially true for those who have experienced even minimal brain damage from accidents, infections or epilespy. After frontal lobe injury, Phineas Gage, famous in the medical literature, changed from being an intelligent, pleasant person to one who was impulsive, childlike, inappropriate in his actions, unable to follow through on tasks and socially inept. Other patients with frontal-lobe injury, likewise, often display many of the same behaviors as those with ADHD or ADD.

The majority of the research currently conducted on ADHD/ADD suggests that a deficiency or imbalance of neurotransmitters, or brain chemicals, is probably the cause of most attention deficit disorders. These brain chemicals affect the entire attention network, including the frontal lobes, the premotor cortex, the limbic system, the basal ganglia and the reticular activating system, as well as other frontal and central brain structures important for alertness and attention.

♦ *Neurophysiology of ADHD/ADD*

While the following discussion may be somewhat technical, most readers, we have found, want to understand the neurophysiology of ADHD/ADD, at least as we currently think it to be. Our knowledge will become increasingly precise as new findings emerge.

When a stimulus impinges upon the brain at a level strong enough to reach excitatory potential, the neuron (nerve cell) *fires* and a nerve impulse is conveyed from the nucleus of the nerve body out the length of the axon to varying numbers of dendrites. To pass to another cell, the nerve signal must cross a tiny gap called a *synaptic cleft* at the meeting of the dendrites of one cell with the dendrites of another cell.

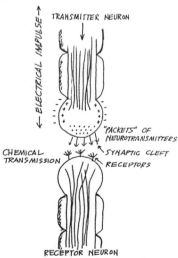

At the synapse, the electrical signal causes the release of a chemical called a *neurotransmitter* which is stored in vesicles, or packets, on the *presynaptic dendrite*, i.e., the dendrite before the synapse.   Once the neurotransmitter has been released and is absorbed by an appropriate receptor on the *post-synaptic dendrite*, i.e., the dendrite after the synapse, the message continues its electrical transmission to the next synapse. It is the neurotransmitters which enable the electrical impulse to be transmitted from one neuron (cell) to another. Without these neurotransmitters, the relay of impulses in the brain would be impossible.

◆ *Neurotransmitters and Neurotransmission*

There are many different neurotransmitters in the brain including norepinephrine, dopamine, choline, and serotonin, among others. Each neurotransmitter seeks a specific receptor on the postsynaptic dendrite and cannot be absorbed by a receptor for another transmitter. For example, norepinephrine can only be absorbed by a norepinephrine receptor. Likewise, dopamine seeks out its own specific receptor.

Many disorders are known to be the result of specific neurotransmitter deficiencies. The level of dopamine, for example, is deficient in Parkinson's disease, while choline has been implicated in Alzheimer's disease. Some disorders result from an excess of a neurotransmitter, others from a deficiency, while still others may result from the neurotransmitters being out of balance.

The neurotransmitters most frequently implicated by the research in ADHD/ADD are norepinephrine and dopamine. Serotonin appears to be the significant neurotransmitter in Tourette Syndrome, obsessive-compulsive disorders and the overfocused behavior sometimes mistaken for underaroused ADD. The neurotransmitters will, in all likelihood, provide the keys to understanding many of man's most perplexing physical, behavioral, emotional and attentional disorders.

Neurotransmission is a complex process and involves both excitatory and inhibitory neurons. Inhibition is equally, if not more, important than excitation. In fact, the more sophisticated

---

The brain is a wonderful organ; it starts working the moment you get up in the morning, and does not stop until you get into the office.——Robert Frost

the organism, the more inhibitory neurons it has. Each physiological response is a complex interplay between all those inhibitory and excitatory neurons being stimulated and transmitting impulses at any given time.

Each neurotransmitter has a specific function and each affects particular nerve cells in particular parts of the brain. ADHD and ADD have, for several years, been considered neurotransmitter disorders. Some medications used to treat attention disorders increase the availability of norepinephrine on the presynaptic dendrites (Ritalin and Dexedrine, for example), while others prevent the re-absorption or re-uptake of norepinephrine, leaving more available at the synaptic clept (Norpramin and Tofranil, for example), while still others prevent the breakdown of norepinephrine (Parnate and Nardil, for example).

Brain functioning is obviously a very complicated process with many potential sources of breakdown. Its complexity renders a search for easy solutions a futile endeavor. A comprehensive understanding of attention disorders is years away. A rudimentary knowledge of the brain does, at least, give us a roadmap. It helps us understand the effect of various interventions, both medical and nonmedical, and have greater confidence in the benefits of these treatments. Until the day that full knowledge of the brain is possible, we must rely upon clinical experience and observable effects for treatment protocols, and we must use that knowledge to develop hypotheses which will assist us in further researching the neurophysiology of this elusive disorder.

New techniques for studying the brain offer great hope for further understanding in the future. Computerized brain scans (BEAMS), blood flow studies, positron emission tomography (PET) and magnetic resonance imaging (MRI) will contribute significantly to our growing body of knowledge about ADHD/ADD. At the present time, however, the known causes of attention disorders can be grouped into the following three major categories: (1) heredity, temperament and genetic makeup; (2) organic factors (brain injury); and (3) environmental toxins.

◆ *Heredity, Temperament and Genetic Makeup*

Heredity is considered by most practitioners working in the field to be the most common cause of ADHD and ADD. Many parents of children with attention disorders relate similar symptoms in their own early years, especially while in school.

The role of heredity in ADHD/ADD is under intense investigation at this time. One researcher studied ninety-three sets of twins and found that identical twins are much more likely than fraternal twins to both have attention disorders (Willerman, 1973). Identical twins have the same genetic make-up, whereas, in fraternal twins, only one of the twins may have the faulty gene.

REMEMBER ME? 17 YEARS AGO IN THE MATERNITY WARD... THERE WAS A MIX UP.

It has also been found that there are four times as many hyperactive parents of hyperactive children as there are hyperactive parents of non-ADHD children (Morrison and Stewart, 1971; Cantwell, 1972). The same investigators found that ADHD is more common in fathers and uncles of children with attention disorders than in the relatives of non-ADHD/ADD children.

◆ ORGANIC FACTORS ◆

Organic factors causing ADHD or ADD include all physiological insults and damage to the central nervous system and/or the brain. Damage may result from injury, from drugs such as cocaine, or from alcohol exposure, especially in utero. More subtle and widespread neurological difficulties can occur from extreme prematurity, or lack of oxygen before or during birth. Only a small percentage of attention disorders is believed to have been organically caused. However, this group is likely to increase in the future.

While some early studies implied that minimal brain injury resulting from difficult pregnancies and deliveries could be the cause of ADHD and ADD, later studies cast doubt on the importance of these factors. It was suggested that unusually short or long labors, very young mothers, distress to the unborn child both before and during delivery, mothers who smoke, and toxemia could possibly contribute to the symptoms of ADHD and ADD. More definitive studies are needed.

Recently there are increasing numbers of babies being born whose parents used and/or abused illegal drugs such as cocaine, crack and heroin either before pregnancy, affecting the sperm or egg, or during pregnancy, harming the developing fetus. There are also increasing numbers of Fetal Alcohol Syndrome (FAS) babies. In states where drug and alcohol abuse are widespread, the problems of organic ADHD/ADD and learning disabilities are especially serious. In addition, premature infants, especially those weighing less than three pounds, are at much greater risk for attention disorders, hyperactivity and learning disabilities.

◆ ENVIRONMENTAL TOXINS ◆

Environmental toxins are another potential source of attention disorders. These toxins include lead, formaldehyde and chemical pesticides among others, and are the cause of increasing concern.

◆ *Lead*

Lead is a highly toxic substance. Recent studies have shown that even "low levels of lead contribute to childhood learning disabilities and high school dropout rates" (Seabrook, 1990). While the exact effects of lead on the brain are not known, studies have surmised that low levels of lead may well produce low levels of attention deficit symptoms. Inattention, impulsivity, and over-arousal are often evident when the lead levels are high.

I have but one lamp by which my feet are guided, and that is the lamp of experience. I know of no way of judging the future but by the past.——Patrick Henry

MOST COMMON SOURCES OF LEAD

- Plumbing
- Cans
- Auto emissions
- Dust and soil
- Paint

According to the Agency for Toxic Substances and Disease Registry, lead pipes and pipes soldered with lead may contaminate water for as many as 10.4 million children. The greatest threat, however, is old paint, especially in deteriorating housing, which endangers about 12 million children. Another 5.9 to 11 million children are at risk from lead deposits in paint and gasoline. About 5 million children live where they may inhale lead from the burning of leaded gasoline, and 1 million children may be exposed to lead from the few cans that are still sealed with lead, which can leach into food. In addition, children's textbooks, library books, and wrapping paper are printed with lead-based ink.

If you suspect that your child has been exposed to lead, you may wish to have your physician check his lead levels. This is typically determined by laboratory tests that measure the lead content in urine samples collected over a 24-48 hour period or by blood tests.

♦ *Chemicals*

It is possible for children with attention disorders to have an allergic reaction to chemicals in their environment or a sensitivity to them. Allergies involve the triggering of the immune system in response to allergens, whereas sensitivities are a result of the body's attempt to incorporate foreign substances into it's biochemistry. Allergists have noticed that a child with fair features, that is, with blue/green eyes and red/blonde hair, is often more likely to have a biochemically sensitive body.

Children with attention disorders are especially sensitive to phenol-based compounds which create a chemical imbalance in the brain that can create ADHD/ADD symptoms. Phenol-based compounds are found in gasoline, paint, perfume, smoke and coal-tar products such as dyes.

Chemicals used to eliminate pests both inside and outside homes create problems for many ADHD/ADD children. The concentration of chemicals applied on the inside of homes tends to be many times higher than the pesticides placed on the outside. Used frequently in homes, schools and office buildings, these chemicals can cause ADHD/ADD symptoms and allergic reactions, as well as life-threatening asthma.

♦ *Formaldehyde*

Children who are sensitive to formaldehyde may react to school dittoes since the purple ink used is made with formaldehyde. In addition, many copying machines produce methanol fumes which the body converts into formaldehyde. If your child is sensitive to formaldehyde you may wish to examine closely other common sources of this substance such as fabric, clothing, carpet, paint, wallboard, and pressed wood in furniture.

♦ QUESTIONS MOST OFTEN ASKED ABOUT ♦
THE CAUSES OF ADHD/ADD

My child appears to be more active when he eats a lot of sugar. Could this be the cause of his hyperactivity and attention problems?

This is a controversial area in the field of attention problems. However, we have found that many children do have a history of food intolerance, dairy products being the most common, followed by chocolate, sugar, corn, dyes, eggs, flavorings and additives, among others. The cause and effect relationship between sugar, food additives or salicylates and hyperactivity was first asserted by Dr. Ben Feingold in 1975 and Dr. Lendon Smith in 1976. During the 1970's many children were put on strict diets that eliminated sugar or the foods to which they displayed a sensitivity. Many parents reported a dramatic reduction in ADHD/ADD symptoms, while others noticed no change at all. Current research has not found an effect significant enough to recommend incorporating changes in diet as a part of the overall treatment plan. However, if you notice a difference when your child eats a certain food, it can do no harm to eliminate it or reduce the amount eaten.

Although the findings of the scientific community are inconclusive at this time, we feel the possibility of food intolerances is certainly worth exploring. If you suspect problems with certain foods, placing your child on an elimination and challenge diet for ten days to two weeks may enable you to determine with somewhat greater certainty whether his symptoms are a reaction to specific foods or to other causes.

> *My husband and I were divorced recently and the children and I relocated to a new city and new school district. My ten-year-old son, who used to be a model student, has been extremely hyperactive at school and is showing many symptoms of having an attention disorder. Could this have all been caused by our move?*

You have described a situation that involves at least four obvious sources of severe stress for your son. Divorce of his parents, moving to a new city, adjusting to a different school and making new friends are all tremendously stressful events for a ten-year-old. Stress is a well-documented source of inattention, disorganization, frustration, inability to concentrate and anger. Stress will often cause symptoms of attention problems in those who do not have ADHD or ADD, and it magnifies significantly the problems of those who do. Your pediatrician and school counselor should be able to evaluate your son and recommend strategies as well as any other professionals needed to assist him during this transition period.

Other common causes of stress in children are neglect for some and, for others, pressure to succeed. Many well-meaning and loving parents who understand the highly competitive world which awaits their children will understandably push them to succeed and do their best. Some parents, however, have begun to question the superkid mentality and to consider the child's temperament, personality, physiology, strengths and weaknesses along with the importance of succeeding in school and outside activities.

> *Most afternoons when my child returns from school he is a wildman. He is extremely active, inattentive and unable to concentrate on anything. Since he is not this way all the time, is it possible that conditions during his school day could be causing his attention problems?*

Your son may not be getting enough physical activity at school to reduce his restlessness and to enhance his attention. In recent years there has been a noticeable decrease in opportunities for physical exercise during the school day. Consequently many children do not get the breaks they so desperately need for releasing energy and modulating tension.

It is also possible that teaching methods incompatible with your son's learning style may be used during the day and may be increasing his difficulties with attention. Some teachers are not aware of their students' preferred modalities for learning and are not incorporating the newest techniques and principles into their teaching methods.

> *Could it be that my child does not have an attention deficit disorder and that school is just too difficult for him?*

It is possible for attentional difficulties to be created when a curriculum is too advanced for a student. For many kindergarten through fourth grade students the curriculum has become too advanced for their level of neurological development. This is largely a result of *curriculum shovedown* which is an attempt to teach more and more material at younger ages, forcing young whole-brain learners without adequate brain specialization to conform to a curriculum which requires much left-brain organization and development and attention spans beyond their neurological maturation.

This problem is receiving widespread attention due to Dr. David Elkind's *Miseducation: Preschoolers at Risk* and due to proponents of developmental placement and a developmental curriculum, such as the National Association for the Education of Young Children (NAEYC). Unfortunately, these changes have not yet been translated into changes in many classrooms.

In addition, significant numbers of children and adolescents are overplaced in school. Neurologically less mature students have shorter attention spans and thus do not perform nearly as well as their neurologically more mature peers. Ask the psychologist or educator on your team to help you assess the appropriateness of your child's curriculum and grade placement for his developmental level.

> *At birth, my ten-month-old son sustained very mild brain injury which I am sure is the cause of his attention deficit disorder symptoms now. Does this mean that he is destined to have ADD problems for the rest of his life?*

Your son is fortunate that you are aware of his problems at an early age and are responding to them immediately. Research studies have consistently shown that the earlier attention disorders are identified and treatment is begun, the greater the possibilities for the child's future success. The most important factor appears to be how well an infant or young child's environment enables him to overcome his early injuries. A positive environment with good sources of support will greatly enhance a child's potential for succeeding. In fact, one study revealed that brain-injured rats raised in sensory-rich environments performed better than normal rats raised in sensory-poor environments (Schwartz, 1964). The significance of the child's early environment in overcoming handicaps has compelling implications for prevention.

Give me the children until they are seven and anyone may have them afterwards.——Saint Francis Xavier

◆ SUMMARY ◆

The exact causes and mechanisms of attention disorders are unknown and may continue to be something of a mystery for many years. To further complicate the picture, ADHD and ADD manifest very differently and may well represent different neurochemical pictures. In addition, as we learn more about the brain and ADHD/ADD, we can expect to define even more subtypes of these disorders.

In our frustration at being unable to find easy solutions to this complex set of problems, it is important that we not "throw out the baby with the bath water." Instead of attempting to deny the existence of the disorder itself, as some have attempted to do, we must carry on tirelessly to find both causes and solutions. To be helpful, all who live and work with ADHD/ADD children must acknowledge and address the uniqueness and complexity of this disorder in each person. Only then can true assistance be provided. Scientific progress has successfully overcome or coped with many of the disorders affecting the body. We must now aggressively address the last and perhaps most exciting frontier of all—the brain itself. It is a challenge and an opportunity unequalled in man's history. Understanding of the intricacies of brain functioning has astounding implications and unequalled potential for benefitting all of mankind.

When you have to make a choice and don't make it, that is in itself a choice.

—William James

Determining If Your Child Has ADHD or ADD

"I suspect that my child has an attention disorder. What should I do?" This question is asked daily in hundreds of cities and communities throughout the modern world. As our knowledge increases and people's awareness is heightened, many more teachers are conscious that the children they teach may have ADHD or ADD. As parents read the news, watch talk shows, and converse with neighbors and friends, they, too, wonder: "Could this be the source of my child's difficult behavior, poor grades and loss of esteem?"

For some, it is a relief to think their troubles may be the result of an attention deficit disorder. After writing in the *New York Times* Magazine about his lifelong experiences with ADD and his newfound hope with its diagnosis and treatment, Frank Wolkenberg received hundreds of letters from people who felt that they, too, might finally have a plausible explanation for their persistent difficulties (Wolkenberg, 1987).

While for some the suggestion of ADHD or ADD is helpful, for others it can be threatening or offensive. Parents may say or feel: *"Perhaps this diagnosis was made too quickly?" "Is it an easy out?" "She just wants him to sit still."* We often receive calls from parents who are irate with a teacher who has suggested that their child might have ADHD or ADD. Others are angry with a professional who, after spending only thirty minutes with their child, has decided the child has an attention disorder.

Deciding whether a child, adolescent or adult has ADHD or ADD is a critical issue and one responsible people cannot take lightly or ignore. But how do parents do that? What plan do they pursue? When should one see a psychologist, psychiatrist, or one's physician? What about teachers....caught in the crossfire between children and parents, rules and regulations, legal considerations, the media, an avalanche of paperwork, and lack of adequate information and direction? What can they do to be of greatest assistance to an ADHD or ADD student? Where do concerned parents begin and who should they contact first?

Our experience has shown the following nine-step plan to be of assistance to parents in determining whether their child or adolescent has an attention disorder.

◆ NINE-STEP PLAN FOR DETERMINING ◆ ADHD/ADD

◆ *1) Decide on a Team Approach*

Perhaps the most important issue to be faced and accepted, first and foremost, is that you are not expected to handle all of your child's problems alone. Even the most capable of *supermoms* cannot single-handedly deal with the full extent of ADHD and ADD. These are complex disorders with physical, psychological, emotional, learning, legal and political overtones unlike few other medical problems of this century. ADHD and ADD deserve thoughtful attention and thorough investigation. They are not labels we can attach lightly to every child who does not do well in school. Nor can we, on the other hand, ignore it.

The diagnosis and treatment of an attention-disordered child cannot be handled by any one parent or professional alone. Our experience has shown that those children who experience the most progress have an effective team behind them. When working smoothly, a carefully assembled ADHD or ADD team is not unlike a football team. With committed members and a carefully chosen captain, the child can reach his goals repeatedly. Without this team effort, a child's progress can be painstakingly slow, or nonexistent, and immensely frustrating for all.

♦ *2) Educate Yourself About the Problem*

As the number one, key member of the team, you possess the most information about your child in the area of ADHD or ADD-related difficulties. Working closely with your spouse, your child and your child's teacher, you will be assembling members of the team.

You are encouraged to sit down, think through, define the immediate problems and organize your strategy. At this point, you may wish to start a three-ring binder labeled: "Understanding: ___(Child's name)___", for you are about to begin a journey of discovery about both you, your offspring, and the many challenges of childhood. By the time he is grown, you will be an expert in child psychology. You may even wish to have another child to benefit from your vast array of knowledge. If not, you will certainly be a good grandparent. At the very least you may finally understand why your own parents, if you had ADHD or ADD, told you, "It serves you right. You were just like him."

Before talking with anyone else, including your spouse, it is recommended that you spend one or two days completing the following exercises:

- Think about and complete the information on:
  "My Child: A Personal Assessment" (Chart 4-1).

- Log your child's behaviors that occur over a
  48-hour period (Chart 4-2). This time should
  be used to gather information and not to try to
  implement changes or get others to understand.
  It is very helpful if your spouse is going through
  the same process independently.

This exercise is important and should be done independently, for people perceive things differently and have different goals. Sometimes the problem is the situation. It may be a problem with an adult and not with the child. Some problems are heightened when parents and children have different temperaments and thus different needs. Assess carefully your needs, especially those your child is thwarting.

◆ *3)   Meet with Your Child*

Now that you have completed these activities and have a good understanding of your concerns, you are ready to meet with your child or adolescent. When your child is relaxed and in a positive mood, sit down with him and tell him that you are trying to understand him better and would like his help. Tell him everything he says is very important. Because you want to remember it, you are going to take notes. Then ask him to discuss the items on Chart 4-3.

As you gather information, ask questions or make comments for clarification only.   You are encouraged not to evaluate responses or try to change opinions at this time, regardless of how you feel about what is being said. As you are meeting, try to organize problem areas and have the child rank them in order of importance. Then discuss solutions he thinks would be helpful.

Nothing, says Goethe, is so terrible as activity without insight. Look before you leap is a maxim for the world.——E. P. Whipple

♦ *4)   Meet with Your Spouse*

Whether living together or apart, it is now time to meet and discuss your mutual findings. With Chart 4-4 as a guide, discuss each area and list the findings.   Indicate who perceives the behavior or characteristic to be a problem. Discuss each and arrive at a determination of whether it is indeed a problem and its rank order. While this sounds easy, often it is not. Mothers are likely to experience the problems more intensely than fathers. They are with the child more, have more calls from and conferences with the teacher, and they usually experience the most difficulties because they spend more time with the child, if for no other reasons. Fathers often are more ego involved and frequently do not understand either the intensity or the meaning of the child's difficulties. Many simply do not fully comprehend the gravity of the situation because of a lack of education in this area.   This attitude was recently brought home when an esteemed publisher of children's educational resources querried, "What's wrong with a little exuberance in children?"   We assured him that we love these children's zest for life.   However, when they are failing academically and are rejected by both peers and adults, there is genuine cause for concern.

Many fathers, on the other hand, are equally knowledgeable and concerned, or perhaps even more so, than mothers. Whenever there is disagreement, parents are encouraged simply to list their concerns and then to seek out knowledge and the opinions of those they trust to understand better the potential problems.

♦ *5)   Meet with the Teacher*

Together, it is now time to meet with the teacher. Fathers are encouraged to attend these meetings. Not only do ADHD and ADD children listen more to fathers than to mothers, but teachers and school personnel do as well. They will be impressed that you care enough to attend the conference.

From preschool through college, the teacher is crucial to your child's diagnosis. She plays an equally important role in treatment as well. Her input is vital because she sees your child in an academic/work environment and the one in which the symptoms are most likely to surface. She has ample opportunity to observe his attention, his ability to settle down and complete assignments, his relationships with peers and authorities, his sense of confidence, his responsibility, and many other aspects of the child which are not observable in the less structured, more relaxed home atmosphere.   A teacher has usually taught and observed numerous children, often hundreds and even thousands, and thus has a better understanding of the typical norms for behavior than do many parents.   Most parents have only one or two children; thus, they have no way to judge normal behavior except through their observations of their own children interacting with family and friends or when they are doing homework or chores at home.

We cannot overemphasize how essential it is that the teacher become a positive part of the team that is assessing whether your child has ADHD or ADD. Both you, your child's physician, and other professionals will be heavily dependent upon both her input and her cooperation. If she is not the captain of this multidisciplinary team, she is certainly the quarterback. Don't try to win this ballgame without her.

Problems in children often threaten parents. When parents feel defensive and struggle with the inevitable feelings of failure that accompany a child's lack of success, they may feel angry and unconsciously look for someone to blame. The school or teacher is often the scapegoat. Resist this temptation. Instead, be as thorough and analytical as possible. Think of the teacher as a partner in your child's life and begin to establish a strong, positive, working relationship with her. Together you must define the problem, and together you will provide solutions. Each working alone is notoriously unsuccessful with an attention-disordered child.

Teachers, too, are often frustrated with this child who seems determined to defy her at every turn, disrupt the class, act silly or threaten her desire to impart wisdom to her twenty-five charges. Just as parents may blame her, she may blame them for the child's lack of discipline and difficult behavior.

Both parents and teachers want to do a good job. The ADHD/ADD child threatens this need. It is important for you and the teacher to avoid an adversarial relationship no matter how frustrated either you or she becomes with the situation or with the child. Openness, respect and mutual goals can make the job rewarding for all.

When you have concerns, it is often helpful to write a note to the teacher (Chart 4-5). Teachers are likewise encouraged to contact parents. Sending the teacher this letter, an ADHD/ADD checklist and checklists for developmental or learning problems (Charts 4-6 and 4-7) prior to your meeting will enable her to begin organizing her thoughts about your child.

At this preliminary meeting with the teacher it is important to firmly establish your mutually cooperative relationship. People are happy only when problems are resolved and the child is successful. Establishing ways to ensure progress is more important than indulging in negative feelings. Next, compare observations and checklists and evaluate all the data on your child. Outline problem areas and note strengths. Hypotheses can be proposed and preliminary prevention strategies discussed. Together, decide upon a two-week strategy to be implemented both at home and school. The methods employed will depend upon the problems defined.

After two weeks, parents and teachers should meet again. At this time, the severity of the problem and whether referral is indicated are usually apparent to all.

It is very much better sometimes to have a panic feeling beforehand, and then be quite calm when things happen, than to be extremely calm beforehand and to get into a panic when things happen.——Winston Churchill

◆ *6)   Schedule a Physical Exam for your Child*

When a child is having significant difficulty in school, further evalution is often needed. Children do not understand why they are not succeeding and usually lack insight into what would be helpful to them. Learning, attending, emotional, physical, social and family problems are so interwoven that it is easy to mistake one for another. A correct diagnosis, nevertheless, is essential for effective intervention and treatment.

Because ADHD and ADD are physiological problems and because they mimic other medical problems, it is essential that a physician be involved in the evaluation of your child. Ideally your pediatrician or family physician will be involved even if you are working with a psychiatrist, psychologist, counselor or neurologist. A physical examination is recommended at which time all other medical possibilities can be ruled out. For example, we recently saw a first-grade child referred by her teacher for ADD. Her protruding eyes, her excessive height and the atypical nature of her symptoms alerted us to other problems. She was, in fact, suffering from acute hyperthyroidism. Treating this child as though she had an attention deficit disorder could actually have been life-threatening.

Your physician will probably request blood studies, including a chemical profile, blood cell count and thyroid functioning tests, in addition to the physical exam. All of this information is essential for two reasons: (1) to rule out other medical causes of the symptoms, and (2) to provide baseline data against which to evaluate any possible side effects of treatment.

The physician's role is crucial and it is important to choose a physician in whom you have confidence. Often it is his role either to be the captain of the team, or to decide who it will be. He will educate you on the range of treatment options available and will help you decide which are most appropriate for you and your child. As necessary, he will refer you to other professionals. These may include: a neurologist, opthalmologist, ENT specialist, psychologist, learning   disabilities   specialist,   speech/language   therapist, developmental psychologist, family therapist, social worker or an occupational or physical therapist. If medication is part of your child's treatment program, your physician should monitor it closely. He will also consult regularly with all the other members of the team to evaluate your child's progress; especially you, the school nurse, the counselor and your child's teacher.

♦ *7) Schedule a Psychological/Psychoeducational Evaluation of Your Child*

A complete Psychological/Psychoeducational Evaluation is also essential for almost every child who is having difficulty in school. Such an evaluation is important, for children with attention disorders often have other coexisting problems, including learning disabilities. Social, behavioral and emotional problems may complicate the overall picture as well.

In addition, some psychological difficulties mimic ADHD and ADD. These include depression, conduct disorders, bipolar disorders, and anxiety. Poor parenting, disorganized environments, and divorce or death in the family may also cause behaviors which mimic ADHD/ADD. Overplacement in school and even giftedness can sometimes be the problem or contribute to it in major ways. Just as a physician would not operate without tests, accurate determination of specific psychological or educational problems is crucial for understanding the total child.

After evaluating your child, the psychologist usually becomes a valued member of your team. She can be most helpful in deciding on the roles of all the professionals involved and in helping them to understand your child's unique strengths and weaknesses. The Psychological/Psychoeducational Evaluation is at the heart of most evaluations for ADHD or ADD.

FIVE BASIC PARTS OF A PSYCHOLOGICAL EVALUATION

1) Developmental Questionnaire
2) Confidential School Questionnaire
3) Learning Strengths/Weaknesses Questionnaire
4) Behavior Questionnaires
5) Psychological and Psychoeducational Tests

The *Developmental Questionnaire*, which is completed by the parents, addresses the reason for referral; family history, including learning, medical and behavioral problems of close relatives; a developmental history which assesses the pregnancy, delivery, post-delivery period, infancy-toddler period, developmental milestones, and coordination. Medical history, school history, peer relationships, home behavior and interests and accomplishments of the child are also addressed.

The *Confidential School Questionnaire* requests the teacher's observations and judgments in the following areas: grades and progress in each of the academic areas; peer relationships and overall adjustment to the class; social/emotional development; cognitive development; and attention span, concentration, impulse control, organizational skills and problem-solving. Lastly, listening skills, speaking skills and gross- and fine-motor development are described. *Questionnaires to determine the learning strengths and weaknesses* of your child are also completed by the teacher. This is an important area which deserves thorough evaluation.

Behavior Questionnaires are also completed by both the parents and the teacher. These questionnaires elicit information on attentional issues, as well as social, emotional and behavioral development.

After gathering and studying all of the information on the questionnaires completed by the parents and the teacher, the psychologist will administer a number of *psychological* and *psychoeducational* tests to your child. These will assist the psychologist in developing a complete picture of your child's capabilities, limitations, and particular learning, attending and performance characteristics.

AREAS EVALUATED BY PSYCHOLOGICAL/ PSYCHOEDUCATIONAL TESTS

1) Intellectual abilities
2) Academic achievement
3) Central nervous system processing
4) Brain dominance and learning style preference
5) Memory—both auditory and visual, long-term and short-term
6) Visual-motor integration and fine-motor ability
7) Attention, concentration, distractibility and impulse control
8) Social, emotional and behavioral development
9) Family interaction patterns

Intellectual Functioning and Academic Achievement—Children with attention disorders show much variability in intellectual development. As indicated previously, ADHD and ADD do not affect intelligence *per se*, and they appear to be normally distributed throughout the population. They do, however, cause unevenness in intellectual development and the underdevelopment of one's potential. For this reason it is important to obtain a good measure of a child's abilities before first grade if possible, or one may never have an accurate assessment of the child's true intellectual talents. After first grade one must rely upon measures of ability and achievement relatively unaffected by ADHD/ADD to have an accurate assessment of potential.

An individually administered intelligence test, often one of the Wechsler Scales, the Stanford Binet Intelligence Scale (4th Edition), McCarthy Scales of Children's Abilities, or the Kaufman Assessment Battery for Children, provides some of the best information

We are not all capable of everything.——Virgil (70-19 B.C.)

on abilities, learning problems and the attention disorder. Certain areas of ability require more concentration and attention than others, and in these areas the child frequently obtains lower scores. These include: short-term auditory memory; short-term visual memory; rote copying tasks requiring speed, concentration, attention to detail and persistence; and oral mathematical problem-solving which requires both concentration and computation.

Many children's I.Q. scores, even by second and third grade, are negatively affected by the attention disorder. It is important to determine the child's current level of functioning and his potential ability as suggested by those measures unaffected by ADHD or ADD and academic achievement. We often see children whose scores on I.Q. tests improve by 10-20 points six months to a year after treatment of the attention disorder. On the other hand, we also see many bright ADHD and ADD children who go undiagnosed until adolescence. They often do very poorly, relative to their ability, on the Scholastic Aptitude Test (SAT) or the American College Test (ACT) necessary for college entrance. Despite being bright and having been exposed, they have not locked in the information, skills and knowledge taught in school because of interference from the ADHD or ADD symptoms and their scores can be quite low relative to ability. Thus, they may seem less capable than they really are.

By third grade, and often earlier, the child is underachieving academically in relation to his potential. His level of *academic achievement* should, therefore, be compared to his *potential ability level* rather than the obtained I.Q. score, *i.e.*, the child's current level of intellectual functioning or his grade placement. Many bright ADHD/ADD students, although achieving at a level significantly below their potential, escape detection and treatment because their work remains at grade level. Others who perform poorly are frequently diagnosed as having learning disabilities when they, in fact, do not have learning disabilities but rather long-standing, undiagnosed attention deficit disorders. Treating these learning disabilities without addressing the ADHD or ADD is only marginally successful and frustrating for all.

It is not best that we should all think alike; it is difference of opinion which makes horse races.——Mark Twain

Having worked with both LD and ADD youngsters for many years, we are convinced that at least fifty per cent of those diagnosed as learning disabled are ADHD/ADD children who are underachieving so dramatically that they appear to have learning disabilities.

Attention disorders, then, can cause underachievement which mimics LD. However, it is important to remember that learning disabilities can and do co-occur with ADHD and ADD in many children. The attention deficit disorder should be distinguished from the learning disability and each independently addressed in the treatment plan.

Central Nervous System Processing—Tests of central nervous system processing evaluate learning strengths and weaknesses and enable accurate diagnosis of any true learning disabilities. They also assess the child's auditory and visual processing, memory, and verbal and written expression. Frequently, children with attention deficit disorders have problems with spatial perception and in learning left and right directionality. It is not uncommon to see auditory processing and auditory memory problems in children with attention disorders. Many of these difficulties are a function of the ADHD/ADD and improve dramatically with treatment of the attention disorder. By contrast, ADHD and ADD are rarely significantly improved by remediation for auditory processing problems.

Memory—Auditory and Visual, Long- and Short-Term— Assessing memory is critical in the evaluation of the child or adolescent. Short-term auditory memory is the most dramatically affected by the attention disorder and most responsive to medical intervention. Visual short-term memory is less affected but certainly can be.

Those with attention disorders also frequently fail to lock information into long-term memory. Thus, measures of general knowledge and of facts learned in school are characteristically much lower than other ability measures. While these do not improve immediately with treatment, long-term retention is greatly improved with continued treatment. Meaningful visual memory appears least affected by attention disorders. This is especially true for the more right-brain visual learner. Kinesthetic learning is usually not impaired at all. Thus, learning by doing continues to be a positive learning approach.

Since memory is a key component of the successful acquisition of new information, it is important that the effect of ADHD/ADD be determined and that appropriate interventions be utilized to eliminate interference or to overcome the deficits with other learning strategies.

*Visual-Motor Integration and Fine-Motor Ability—*These abilities affect handwriting and written expression. Poor eye-hand coordination is a major problem for many ADHD/ADD children and adolescents. As preschoolers they have trouble tying shoelaces, buttoning clothes, cutting and pasting. Coloring within the lines is one of their first encounters with academic failure. Few children with attention disorders can accomplish this feat. As they become older, their poor fine-motor coordination combined with impulsivity and failure to plan ahead leads to disorganized written work, incomplete erasures and precariously aligned math. "Sloppy" and "messy" are routinely displayed in prominent red letters on many an attention-disordered child's work. When the ADHD or ADD is treated, however, these symptoms frequently improve dramatically.

*Attention, Concentration, Distractibility and Impulse Control—*These characteristics are assessed from clinical observations while working with the child, from behavior questionnaire data completed by both parents and teachers, and from specific measures of attention, vigilance, short-term memory and impulse control. These data reveal the unique ways in which the attention and impulse control are selectively affected by the child or adolescent's unique constellation of ADHD/ADD difficulties. Since no two people are ever alike, such understanding is critical for appropriate and effective intervention strategies. After treatment, these measures show the most dramatic improvement. They are, in fact, often utilized as indicators of medication effectiveness.

Social, Emotional and Behavioral Development—Evaluation of these areas reveals aspects important in treating the total child. Low self-esteem, frustration, feelings of failure, depression and hopelessness are widespread among those who have ADHD/ADD. There are frequently behavior problems as well. These symptoms often begin as early as kindergarten and significantly affect the child's life by third grade. Each child adapts to the disorder somewhat differently. Thus it is crucial to identify the child's emotional strengths and weaknesses, his maturity level in a variety of areas, and the other adaptive and maladaptive behaviors he has learned in order to cope. His social relationships with peers and adult authorities are also important to assess.

Family Interaction Patterns—Understanding the family interaction patterns of the ADHD or ADD child is crucial to developing an effective treatment program. Customary parental interventions are often not effective. To complicate their interactions further, ADHD and ADD children often have attention-disordered parents. Many have ADHD/ADD siblings as well. The entire family system must be addressed to ensure success.

♦ *8) Schedule Appointments with Related Professionals*

Referrals will often be made by the physician or psychologist based on the findings of their evaluations. We encourage you to follow through on these suggestions. Other professionals frequently recommended for the treatment of the ADHD/ADD child or adolescent include psychiatrists, neurologists, allergists, ophthalmologists, social workers, counselors and family therapists, and speech, occupational and physical therapists. The pharmacist, too,

---

Education is helping the child realize his potentialities.——Erich Fromm

is often quite involved. When needed, these professionals play an important role in the overall assessment and treatment program of your child.

Since the body functions as a whole, problems in one area can adversely affect the functioning and efficiency of other parts of the body. Even a child with a very efficient neurological attention system, for example, will have difficulty attending in school if his vision is poor and he is not able to read accurately information on the blackboard. We have seen many children with auditory discrimination problems who could not understand what the teacher was saying and eventually tuned out. Likewise, a hungry child will have difficulty putting forward his best efforts in school. It is important to include evaluations from other professionals recommended by the captain of your child's team.

♦ *9) Enjoy Your Child*

Confident that you have thoroughly researched your child's difficulties and assembled the best team possible to assist him, you may now relax somewhat and enjoy your offspring's childhood. We hope you can avoid being frantic and stressed, even though you will be busy for several years coordinating the efforts of the many professionals involved and helping your child through the exciting but bumpy path to adulthood. You will be required to devote more time, energy and caring to parenthood, perhaps, than other parents do. But, you have the opportunity to experience a closeness with your child and a joy in parenting that is far greater than most. Attention disorders do not have to be handicaps; instead, they can be challenges and opportunities. They will, however, require more patience, optimism, perseverance and love from parents than is required to raise a non-ADHD/ADD child. Erma Bombeck's comments about mothers of handicapped children are perhaps equally applicable to mothers of ADHD/ADD children and adolescents:

Most women become mothers by accident, some by
choice, a few by social pressures and a couple by habit.
This year, nearly 100,000 women will become mothers
of handicapped children. Did you ever wonder how

mothers of handicapped children are chosen? Somehow I visualize God hovering over earth selecting His instruments for propagation with great care and deliberation. As He observes, He instructs His angels to make notes in a giant ledger.

'Armstrong, Beth, son, patron saint Matthew.'

'Forrest, Marjorie, daughter, patron saint Cecelia.'

'Rudledge, Carrie, twins, patron saint ... give her Gerard, he's used to profanity.'

Finally He passes a name to an angel and smiles, 'Give her a handicapped child.'

The angel is curious, 'Why this one, God? She's so happy.'

'Exactly,' smiles God. 'Could I give a handicapped child to a mother who does not know laughter? That would be cruel.'

'But has she patience?' asks the angel.

'I don't want her to have too much patience or she will drown in a sea of self-pity and despair. Once the shock and resentment wears off, she'll handle it.'

'I watched her today. She has that feeling of self and independence that is so rare and so necessary in a mother. You see, the child I'm going to give her has his own world. She has to make it live in her world and that's not going to be easy.'

'But, Lord, I don't think she even believes in you.'

God smiles. 'No matter. I can fix that. This one is perfect. She has just enough selfishness.'

The angel gasps, 'Selfishness? Is that a virtue?'

God nods. 'If she can't separate herself from the child occasionally, she'll never survive. Yes, here is a woman whom I will bless with a child less than perfect. She doesn't realize it yet, but she is to be envied. She will never take for granted a "spoken word." She will never consider a "step" ordinary. When her child says "Momma" for the first time she will be present at a miracle and know it! When she describes a tree or a sunset to her blind child, she will see it as few people ever see my creations.'

'I will permit her to see clearly the things I see ... ignorance, cruelty, prejudice ... and allow her to rise above them. She will never be alone. I will be at her side every minute of every day of her life because she is doing my work as surely as she is here by my side.'

'And what about her patron saint?' asks the angel, his pen poised in the air.

God smiles, 'A mirror will suffice.' [4]

---

[4]Reprinted with permission from Erma Bombeck and <u>Their World Magazine</u>, 1989.

◆ SUMMARY ◆

Determining if Your Child Has ADHD/ADD

1) Decide on a team approach.

2) Educate yourself about the problem.

3) Meet with your child.

4) Meet with your spouse.

5) Meet with the teacher.

6) Schedule a physical exam for your child.

7) Schedule a psychological/psychoeducational evaluation.

8) Schedule appointments with related professionals.

9) Enjoy your child.

To assist you in understanding the roles of each member of the team, they are outlined on the following pages.

◆ ROLES OF THE MEMBERS OF THE TREATMENT TEAM ◆

◆ CHARTS UTILIZED IN ASSESSING THE ◆ CHILD'S DIFFICULTIES

PARENT'S ROLE

1. Identify problems and strengths at home.

2. Consult with child. Identify his sources of frustration and gratification. Enlist his help in thinking of solutions.

3. Complete checklists and write down lists of:

   a. Academic strengths and weaknesses.
   b. Behavioral strengths and weaknesses.
   c. Child/adolescent's concerns about school.
   d. Child/adolescent's concerns about home.

4. Meet with teacher.

5. Implement two-week program at home. If significant problems are identified: refer to Special Education Services, the School Counselor, or . . .

6. Consult a professional.

7. Educate yourself.

8. Seek out a support group.

9. Coordinate efforts of family, child, teachers and professionals.

10. Educate those important for your child's well-being.

11. Implement programs at home recommended by professionals.

CHILD/ADOLESCENT'S ROLE

1. Identify the problems as he perceives them at home and school.

2. Identify his strengths as he sees them at home and school.

3. Identify his goals, both realistic and unrealistic, at home and at school.

4. Provide insight into why he's doing what he's doing: Example:

"Why did you hit Susie?"	"Because she destroyed my room."
	"I'm ashamed of her."
"Why did you not turn in homework?"	"Can't get organized—Just can't seem to keep it all together."

5. Offer possible solutions.

6. Help decide on a plan of action.

7. Agree to try to implement the plan.

8. Help problem-solve when he cannot.

TEACHER'S ROLE

1. Identify child/adolescent's problems and strengths at school:
    (a) Academic   (b) Social/Emotional/Behavioral

2. Consult with the child. Identify his sources of frustration and gratification. Enlist his thoughts about solutions.

3. Outline problem areas. Complete checklists:

    a. Academic
    b. Behavioral
    c. Attention and concentration (ADHD/ADD checklists).
    d. Learning strengths/weaknesses; brain dominance;
       Central Nervous System processing (Symptom
       Checklists for Developmental Disabilities).

4. Meet with parents. Decide on problems, goals and strategies.

5. Implement two-week program at school that is coordinated at home. If significant problems continue . . .

6. Discuss with principal and/or other appropriate personnel.

7. Refer to Special Education and/or School Counselor.

8. Complete information requested by physician and other professionals. If not contacted, phone or write a letter indicating your interest and willingness to help.

9. Meet with professionals and parents and decide on a strategy as a team.

10. Implement programs recommended at school.

11. Work closely with the School Nurse or Counselor who will coordinate the administration of medication and serve as school liaison with the physician and often the parents.

12. Complete checklists on a regular basis as agreed by the team.

    a. Behavior charts.
    b. Medication checklists for benefits and side effects.

SCHOOL'S ROLE

(Counselor, School Nurse, Special Education
Personnel and Administration)

1.   Provide consultation and support to teacher.

2.   Establish liaison between school, professional and parents.

3.   Communicate interest in child and parents.

4.   Help parents understand school's strengths and limitations in assisting with the problem.

5.   When problems are identified:

    a.   Refer to Special Education or Student Support Service.
    b.   Obtain psychological/psychoeducational evaluation.
    c.   Refer to School Counselor.
    d.   Provide special education.
    e.   Assist parents in obtaining independent professional assistance, including psychological, medical and educational.
    f.   Refer parents to support groups.

Where Available:

    a.   Offer parenting groups for special needs.
    b.   Provide social skills training, esteem-building, and other counseling activities for child.

6.   Provide educational information to parents and teachers on:

    a.   Learning disabililties and attention deficit disorders.
    b.   Behavior management strategies at home.
    c.   Classroom management strategies.
    d.   Discipline, responsibility and encouragement.
    e.   Self-esteem.
    f.   Brain dominance and learning style preference.
    g.   School readiness/overplacement in school.

7.   Provide seminars and training programs for parents, teachers and local professionals. Involve PTA/PTO.

PHYSICIAN'S ROLE

1. When appointment is scheduled for school-related problems, send appropriate questionnaires/checklists to be completed by parents and teachers before the appointment.

2. Meet with parents.

   a. Discuss concerns and review information.
   b. Obtain thorough medical history.
   c. Review developmental and school history.
   d. Review family, medical, learning and attending problems.

3. Meet with child/adolescent. Review concerns and solicit his views of problems at home and school. Informally assess his social/emotional status.

4. Give thorough physical examination.

   a. Physical exam - include vision and hearing screening.
   b. Blood tests: Complete Chemical Profile, Thyroid Functioning Tests, Heavy Metals Testing, and others indicated.

5. As appropriate, refer to other professionals:

   a. Neurologist.
   b. Opthalmologist.
   c. ENT Specialist.
   d. Allergist.
   e. Psychologist.
   f. LD Specialist; Developmental Specialist; Speech and Language Pathologist.
   g. Family Therapist/Social Worker.
   h. Occupational Therapist or Physical Therapist.

6. After diagnosis of ADHD or ADD:

   a. Educate parents on the range of treatment options available and help them decide which are most appropriate for their child and themselves.
   b. Begin treatment.
   c. Decide on captain for the team.
   d. Monitor your part of the treatment closely. Consult regularly with all other members of the team.

CHILD/ADOLESCENT PSYCHOLOGIST'S ROLE

1. Evaluate child thoroughly:

    a. Psychological/emotional/esteem.
    b. Intellectual strengths and weaknesses.
    c. Educational:

        1. Learning strengths and weaknesses.
        2. Potential vs. achievement.
        3. Learning disabilities.

    d. Attention, concentration, impulse control.
    e. Family relationships.
    f. Peer/social relationships.

2. Send findings to physician and school with parents' permission.

3. Confer with physician and teacher by phone or in person regarding the findings and recommendations.

4. Help decide with physician on roles of each team member and who will be captain. Determine with parents and professionals who will be responsible for coordinating the team's efforts. Decide on and implement appropriate treatment plan.

5. Provide relevant and current educational information to parents and teachers on particular problems.

6. Provide psychotherapy/counseling to child and/or parents.

7. Offer or refer to a support group.

8. Refer to appropriate professionals for academic intervention, whether tutoring, LD remediation, family counseling, etc.

9. Be knowledgeable about legal issues, special education resources and special schools. Make specific recommendations.

10. Be actively involved in community education.

CHILD PSYCHIATRIST'S ROLE

1. Evaluate for ADHD/ADD. Differentiate from other psychiatric disorders, including oppositional defiant disorder, conduct disorder, depression, bipolar disorder and thought disorder, among others.

2. Provide medical and psychological interventions for ADHD or ADD simultaneously.

3. Treat more severe emotional problems which may coexist with attention disorders.

4. Treat family members whose emotional problems are negatively impacting child, especially those requiring medical intervention as well as psychological.

5. Usually becomes captain of team when involved.

6. Consult with teachers and school.

7. Provide group therapy experiences for parents and child.

8. Hospitalize child, if necessary, when problems are unmanageable or threatening to child's welfare or welfare of others.

9. Become actively involved in community education.

OTHER PROFESSIONALS' ROLES

NEUROLOGIST:

1.   Rule out seizure disorders, including complex partial seizures, narcolepsy, and others, as contributing factors. EEG and BEAM evaluations if indicated.

2.   Monitor medication for seizures. May monitor medication for ADHD or ADD.

ALLERGIST:

1.   Determine presence of allergies, asthma and food intolerances.

2.   Treat any problems found.

ENT SPECIALIST:

1.   Evaluate hearing and middle-ear fluid problems when child has history of chronic ear infections. Be aware of auditory processing problems and language-based learning disabilities sometimes resulting from chronic ear infections. Advise parents.

2.   Assess presence of allergies. Evaluate or refer.

3.   Treat any problems noted.

OPTHALMOLOGIST:

1.   Evaluate vision and visual perception, depth perception, etc., thoroughly, especially when child presents with blurring words, slow copying from board, reading problems, family history of visual problems, clumsiness or poor coordination. Usually needed by second grade at the latest.

2.   Treat any visual problems diagnosed.

FAMILY THERAPIST/SOCIAL WORKER:

1. Educate parents on ADHD/ADD and their effect on the family. Treat dysfunctional interactions in family.

2. Promote positive relationships and teach effective parenting interventions.

3. Provide psychotherapy for child and/or parents.   Refer to appropriate professionals for specific interventions needed to promote overall family health: support groups, including CH.A.D.D.(Children with Attention Deficit Disorders), ADDA (Attention Deficit Disorders Associations) and LDA (Learning Disabilities Association), among others.

CHART 4-1

MY CHILD/ADOLESCENT: A PERSONAL ASSESSMENT

A. Things Or Behaviors That Concern Me:

(1) _____

(2) _____

(3) _____

(4) _____

(5) _____

B. My Child's Strengths/Assets As I Perceive Them:

(1) _____

(2) _____

(3) _____

(4) _____

(5) _____

C. My Child's Weak Points As I Perceive Them:

(1) _____

(2) _____

(3) _____

(4) _____

(5) _____

CHART 4-2

MY CHILD/ADOLESCENT'S BEHAVIOR

Negative Behaviors

	Date	Time	What Happened	Possible Goal of Behavior	My Reaction
1.					
2.					
3.					
4.					
5.					
6.					

Positive Behaviors

	Date	Time	What Happened	Possible Goal of Behavior	My Reaction
1.					
2.					
3.					
4.					
5.					
6.					

DESIRED BEHAVIOR FOR:

Negative Behavior #1: _____

Negative Behavior #2: _____

Negative Behavior #3: _____

Negative Behavior #4: _____

Negative Behavior #5: _____

CHART 4-3

CHILD/ADOLESCENT'S ASSESSMENT
OF HOME-SCHOOL

A. School:

(1)   Tell me about school.

(2)   What do you like?

(3)   What do you dislike?

(4)   Any problems?

(5)   What changes would make things better at school?

(6)   How would you solve your problems?

B.   **Home:**

Things I like:

Things I don't like:

Things I feel are fair:

Things I feel are unfair:

What changes would make things better at home?

Ways To Solve The Problems:

Home:

School:

CHART 4-4

OUR CHILD/ADOLESCENT'S BEHAVIOR

Problem Areas

<u>Rank Order</u>   <u>As Perceived By Whom?</u>
(#1 = Greatest
 #6 = Least)

                                 <u>M</u>   <u>F</u>   <u>C</u>   <u>T</u>*

___   1._____ __ __ __ __

___   2._____ __ __ __ __

___   3._____ __ __ __ __

___   4._____ __ __ __ __

___   5._____ __ __ __ __

___   6._____ __ __ __ __

Strengths

___   1._____ __ __ __ __

___   2._____ __ __ __ __

___   3._____ __ __ __ __

___   4._____ __ __ __ __

___   5._____ __ __ __ __

___   6._____ __ __ __ __

_____

*M = Mother; F = Father; C = Child; T = Teacher.

CHART 4-5
LETTER TO TEACHER

Dear _____:

My child,_____, appears to be having difficulty at _____ (home/school/both). I am especially concerned about the following.

1. _____
2. _____
3. _____
4. _____
5. _____

I would like to request a meeting with you as soon as possible. To make our time together most helpful, I am doing the following and would appreciate your doing so as well:

1) Please list the behaviors which concern you, and when they occur, on the enclosed form. Also note positive behaviors and strengths.
2) Please complete the ___(Preschool or Elementary) Symptom Checklist enclosed. Also complete the Symptom Checklist for Attention Deficit Disorders.
3) Please comment on _____'s academic development on the attached and bring a copy of the achievement and ability test scores, if available.

I appreciate your assistance immensely. While truly understanding _____'s problems may take some extra time, in the long run it will save both your time and energy and mine. More importantly, we can save him much frustration and failure by addressing his difficulties now. I do appreciate your extra time and effort and know that together we can define ____'s problems and strengths and then efficiently and effectively provide solutions.

I look forward to hearing from you soon.

Sincerely,

Mr. or Mrs. Parent

CHART 4-6

PRESCHOOL CHECKUP

Southeastern Psychological INSTITUTE

PRESCHOOL CHECK UP

A SYMPTOM CHECKLIST FOR DEVELOPMENTAL DISABILITIES

Edna D. Copeland, Ph.D., Director
Child/Clinical Psychologist

Southeastern Psychological Institute
P.O. Box 12389
Atlanta, Georgia 30355-2389

Dedicated to Prevention through Early Intervention sm
©Copyright, Edna D. Copeland Ph.D., 1984, 1987

NEED FOR EARLY RECOGNITION OF DEVELOPMENTAL PROBLEMS IN PRESCHOOLERS

The years from 4 through 6 are critical years in the intellectual, visual-motor, psycholinguistic and personality development of the child. Although often treated as an in-between age, this age period constitutes a well-defined landmark in the young child's mental, language, visual, perceptual and motor development. It is also the period when he/she is exposed for the first time to some type of formal education and is brought into wider social contacts with children of his/her own age. By age 4 a child's intellectual, psycholinguistic, visual-motor and personality characteristics are developed sufficiently well to determine deviations, both positively and negatively. By age 5 almost every precursor of learning, attention and behavior problems is apparent. Likewise, giftedness and accelerated capabilities are also easily recognized. *All* children have individual patterns of relative assets and weaknesses. It is important to understand these even in the child without special needs or gifts so that his assets can be realized to the fullest.

Approximately 27% of the preschool population has been described as "At Risk" for Developmental Disabilities. For preventive reasons, it appears expedient to recognize developmental delays in children between the ages of 4½ to 6. Careful evaluation, planning and remediation can preclude or minimize, as much as possible, learning, attention, and behavior disorders at the elementary school level. Likewise, plans can be made to provide for the gifted or talented child's special needs. Relatively individualized programs for all children can be established to capitalize upon their assets.

The **SOUTHEASTERN PSYCHOLOGICAL INSTITUTE** is especially concerned with identifying and remediating Developmental Disabilities. It is far easier to treat and remediate difficulties at an early age before children have experienced failure, frustration and subsequent academic, social, and emotional problems.

The Symptom Checklist for Developmental Disabilities was developed by Dr. Edna D. Copeland after 15 years of clinical practice to help parents and teachers determine whether their children or the children they teach have Developmental Disabilities.

SYMPTOM CHECKLIST

This checklist was developed from the experience of many specialists in the fields which comprise Developmental Disabilities. The questions asked are warning signals of conditions which may interfere with your child's academic, emotional and social adjustment now and in the future.

If you answer "Yes" to as many as 20% of the questions, it may mean that your child has a Developmental Disability. A Developmental Disability does *not* mean that a child is lacking in intelligence or capability. Rather, it means that a child might have difficulty achieving academically and/or socially at his/her level of ability.

Directions: Place a checkmark (✓) by those questions to which your answer is "Yes". Do not mark questions to which you answer "No".

SYMPTOM CHECKLIST FOR DEVELOPMENTAL DISABILITIES

I. ATTENTION / CONCENTRATION / IMPULSE CONTROL / BEHAVIOR

___ 1. Does your child interrupt frequently?

___ 2. Is your child easily distracted?

___ 3. Is your child up and down frequently during meals?

___ 4. Is your child's work often sloppy although it can be neat if he/she really tries?

___ 5. Does your child move from activity to activity without settling down to any one thing for long?

___ 6. Is there inconsistency in your child's performance, i.e., one day he/she performs a task well; the next day, he/she performs the same task poorly?

7. Does your child have difficulty playing alone?
8. Was your child not cuddly as an infant?
9. Did your child require little sleep as an infant?
10. Is your child more demanding than other children?
11. Is punishment ineffective with your child?
12. Is your child rejected by peers and/or adults?
13. Is your child always better in a one-to-one situation?
14. Is your child beginning to think of himself as "mean" or "dumb"?
15. Does you child "fidget" a lot?
16. Does your child often fail to finish things he/she starts?
17. Does your child have difficulty concentrating on tasks requiring sustained attention?
18. Is your child excitable and impulsive?
19. Does your child deny mistakes or blame others?
20. Is your child immature for his/her age?
21. Does your child's mood change quickly and drastically?
22. Does your child have temper tantrums?
23. Is your child more active than his/her peers?
24. Does your child become frustrated easily?
25. Does your child have poor self-control?
26. Is your child extremely daring?
27. Is your child a discipline problem?
28. Does your child find it necessary to touch everything he/she sees?
29. Does your child bother other children — either by touching them or intruding into their activities and conversations?
30. Does your child have difficulty waiting his turn in games or group situations?
31. Do birthday parties and situations with a lot of stimulation cause your child to become overly excited and lose control?
32. Is your child consistently less active than other children?
33. Is your child afraid of heights?
34. Does your child bully other children?
35. Is your child purposely destructive or hurtful of others?

II. HEARING/AUDITORY PERCEPTION/AUDITORY PROCESSING

1. Does your child have trouble remembering things?
2. Does your child seem to "tune-out" or day-dream at times?
3. Was your child's speech late or abnormal in any way?
4. Did your child have chronic ear infections during any time from birth to age 6?
5. Was your child late in learning his/her colors, numbers or alphabet?
6. Does your child continue to have speech substitutions, e.g. "f" for "th", ("free" for "three"), "w" for "l", ("bawoon" for "balloon"), etc.
7. Do other people have difficulty understanding your child's speech?
8. Do you often have to repeat directions for your child?
9. Does it seem that your child pays very little attention to you?
10. Is your child unable to modulate his/her voice, i.e. speak softly when in quiet situations and louder when needed to be heard?
11. Does your child talk very loudly, even during normal conversations?
12. When called from another room, does your child frequently not respond?
13. Does your child frequently turn the same ear in the direction of sound?
14. Does your child complain that his ears hurt or ring?
15. Is there a history of hearing or auditory problems in your family?

III. VISION/VISUAL PERCEPTION/VISUAL PROCESSING/VISUAL-MOTOR SKILLS

1. Does your child have little interest in puzzles, legos, and visual toys?
2. Did your child have difficulty learning to recognize colors, shapes, letters and numbers?
3. Does your child confuse letters, numbers, shapes or words which are similar?
4. Are your child's drawings immature and lacking in detail?

5. Does your child have difficulty putting toys or games together?
6. Does your child have trouble producing letters, numbers and words on demand even though he can recognize them?
7. Does your child have difficulty recognizing letters, numbers, shapes, words or objects if parts are missing?
8. Does/did your child reverse letters (b/d), numbers (6/9), or words (saw/was)?
9. Did your child have difficulty learning right and left?
10. Does your child get lost easily or seem confused about directions?
11. Does your child have a poor concept of time?
12. Are your child's verbal abilities much better than written expression? Does he/she dislike writing?
13. Does your child have difficulty coloring within lines or writing as well as his peers?
14. Does your child avoid games or activities involving catching or throwing a ball?
15. Does your child squint when looking at the board or far away objects?

IV. MEDICAL

1. Does your child get frequent headaches?
2. Is your child often tired?
3. Did your child have difficulty establishing bowel and bladder control?
4. Does your child still have relapses in bowel or bladder control either day or night?
5. Does your child have a poor appetite?
6. Does your child have a history of anemia of any type?
7. Is your child irritable before and/or shortly after meals?
8. Does your child crave sweets?
9. Was your child colicky as an infant?
10. Was your child an unusually cranky baby?
11. Was your child an unusually passive baby?
12. Does your child have a history of allergies?
13. Is there a history of allergies in the family?

Name of Child: _____
Date: _____
Completed by: _____

Southeastern Psychological INSTITUTE

A CHECK UP for ELEMENTARY SCHOOL CHILDREN

A SYMPTOM CHECKLIST FOR DEVELOPMENTAL DISABILITIES

Edna D. Copeland, Ph.D., Director
Child / Clinical Psychologist

Southeastern Psychological Institute
P.O. Box 12389
Atlanta, Georgia 30355-2389

Dedicated to Prevention through Early Intervention

©Copyright, Edna D. Copeland, Ph.D., 1984, 1987

PREVENTION OF LEARNING, BEHAVIOR AND EMOTIONAL DISORDERS THROUGH EARLY IDENTIFICATION, REMEDIATION, TREATMENT AND EDUCATION.

It is becoming increasingly apparent that school failure, behavioral problems, juvenile delinquency, drug and alcohol abuse, and problems of social and work adjustment in adolescents and adults have their origins very early in life. Some estimate that as many as 70% of both the learning and emotional problems encountered in adolescents and adults began in unrecognized problems of childhood. Many of these difficulties can be detected by age 6, and younger, as developmental disabilities. These disabilities include learning disorders; communicative disorders; visual-perceptual, visual processing and visual-motor integration deficits; disorders of attention, concentration and perseverance; delayed emotional development; behavioral disorders; and hyperactivity. Subtle physical, visual and hearing problems can also contribute to early school failure and subsequent behavioral and emotional difficulties.

It is the belief of the SOUTHEASTERN PSYCHOLOGICAL INSTITUTE that early identification followed by careful planning, treatment and remediation can eliminate, or significantly minimize, learning, attention, academic, emotional and behavioral problems at the elementary school level when the problems are milder and more amenable to intervention. It can save the child from facing years of school failure which, in turn, can lead to frustration, loss of self-esteem, acting-out, and other emotional difficulties. Early identification and intervention, likewise, spare families the pain and frustration of feeling they are responsible but helpless to change things. In addition, improvement occurs rapidly at younger ages.

Parents are the first to recognize that something is not "exactly right" with their child. However, they frequently do not know whether their concerns are really significant, which things the child will "grow out of", and which warrant professional consultation.

The Symptom Checklist for Developmental Disabilities was developed by Dr. Edna Copeland, after 15 years of clinical practice, to help parents and teachers determine whether their children or the children they teach have developmental difficulties that are either learning, attentional, behavioral, social or emotional in nature.

If you have checked many items and have concerns after completing this questionnaire, you are encouraged to discuss your child's development with his/her teacher and/or pediatrician, or a child psychologist. Addressing even mild developmental delays early is crucial for the child's ultimate welfare. Determining strengths is, likewise, important.

SYMPTOM CHECKLIST

This checklist was developed from the experience of many specialists in the fields which comprise Developmental Disabilities. The questions asked are warning signals of conditions which may interfere with your child's academic, emotional and social adjustment now and in the future.

If you answer "Yes" to as many as 20% of the questions, it may mean that your child has a Developmental Disability. A Developmental Disability does not mean that a child is lacking in intelligence or capability. Rather, it means that a child may have difficulty achieving academically and socially at his/her level of ability.

Directions: Place a checkmark (✓) by those questions to which your answer is "Yes". Do not mark questions to which you answer "No".

SYMPTOM CHECKLIST FOR DEVELOPMENTAL DISABILITIES

I. ATTENTION/CONCENTRATION/IMPULSE CONTROL/BEHAVIOR

1. Does your child interrupt frequently?
2. Is your child easily distracted?
3. Is your child up and down frequently during meals?
4. Is your child's work often sloppy although it can be neat if he/she really tries?
5. Does your child move from activity to activity without settling down to any one thing for long?
6. Is there inconsistency in your child's performance, i.e., one day he/she performs a task well; the next day, he/she performs the same task poorly?
7. Does your child have difficulty playing alone?
8. Was your child not cuddly as an infant?
9. Did your child require little sleep as an infant?
10. Is your child more demanding than other children?
11. Is punishment ineffective with your child?
12. Is your child always better in a one-to-one situation?
13. Does your child "fidget" a lot?
14. Does your child often fail to finish things he/she starts?
15. Does your child have difficulty concentrating on tasks requiring sustained attention?
16. Is your child excitable and impulsive?
17. Is your child immature for his/her age?
18. Does your child's mood change quickly and drastically?
19. Is your child more active than his/her peers?
20. Does your child become frustrated easily?
21. Does your child have poor self-control?
22. Is your child extremely daring?
23. Is your child a discipline problem?
24. Does your child find it necessary to touch everything he/she sees?
25. Does your child bother other children — either by touching them or intruding into their activities and conversations?
26. Does your child have difficulty waiting his turn in games or group situations?
27. Do birthday parties and situations with a lot of stimulation cause your child to become overly excited and lose control?
28. Is your child consistently less active than other children?

II. SOCIAL/EMOTIONAL

1. Is your child rejected or ignored by peers and/or adults?

2. Is your child beginning to think of himself as "mean" or "dumb"?
3. Does your child deny mistakes or blame others?
4. Does your child's mood change quickly and drastically?
5. Does your child have temper tantrums?
6. Does your child show many fears or one unreasonable fear?
7. Does your child bully others?
8. Is your child purposely destructive or hurtful of animals or people?
9. Is your child withdrawn, apathetic, or "off in his own world"?
10. Does your child seem sad or worried much of the time?
11. Does your child have frequent nightmares or other sleep disturbance?
12. Does your child seem irresponsible, undependable, or disorganized?
13. Does your child have a precocious interest in sex or seem to have sexual identity problems?
14. Is your child resistant to discipline or directions; is he/she defiant, resentful or uncooperative?
15. Has your child lost interest in activities with his/her friends and family?

III. HEARING/AUDITORY PERCEPTION/AUDITORY PROCESSING

1. Does your child have trouble remembering things?
2. Does your child seem to "tune-out" or daydream at times?
3. Was your child's speech late or abnormal in any way?
4. Did your child have chronic ear infections during any time from birth to age 6?
5. Was your child late in learning his/her colors, numbers or alphabet?

6. Does your child continue to have speech substitutions, e.g., "f" for "th", "free" for "three") "w" for "l" ("bawoon" for "balloon"), etc?
7. Do other people have difficulty understanding your child's speech?
8. Do you often have to repeat directions for your child?
9. Does it seem that your child pays very little attention to you?
10. Is your child unable to modulate his/her voice, i.e., speak softly when in quiet situations and louder when needed to be heard?
11. Does your child talk very loudly, even during normal conversations?
12. When called from another room, does your child frequently not respond?
13. Does your child frequently turn the same ear in the direction of sound?
14. Does your child complain that his ears hurt or ring?
15. Is there a history of hearing or auditory problems in your family?

IV. VISION/VISUAL PERCEPTION/VISUAL PROCESSING/VISUAL-MOTOR SKILLS

1. Does your child have little interest in puzzles, legos, and visual toys?
2. Did your child have difficulty learning to recognize colors, shapes, letters and numbers?
3. Does your child confuse letters, numbers, shapes or words which are similar?
4. Are your child's drawings immature and lacking in detail?
5. Does your child have difficulty putting toys or games together?
6. Does your child have trouble producing letters, numbers and words on demand even though he can recognize them?

7. Does your child have difficulty recognizing letters, numbers, shapes, words or objects if parts are missing?
8. Does/did your child reverse letters (b/d), numbers (6/9), or words (saw/was)?
9. Did your child have difficulty learning right and left?
10. Does your child get lost easily or seem confused about directions?
11. Does your child have a poor concept of time?
12. Are your child's verbal abilities much better than written expression? Does he/she dislike writing?
13. Does your child have difficulty coloring within lines or writing as well as his peers?
14. Does your child avoid games or activities involving catching or throwing a ball?
15. Does your child squint when looking at the board or far away objects?

V. ACADEMIC/ACHIEVEMENT

1. Is your child's academic achievement below the level you had expected based on ability? Do the teachers say, "He/she is not working up to potential?"
2. Is your child's daily performance in school inconsistent, remembering things he/she has learned one day and not the next?
3. Is your child having difficulty reading or understanding what he/she reads?
4. Does your child seem afraid or embarrassed to ask questions at school?
5. Does your child follow academic directions poorly?
6. Does your child dislike school?
7. Does your child have difficulty with math but enjoy reading and spelling?
8. Does your child have difficulty completing class assignments within the allotted time?
9. Has your child's teacher expressed concern about any area of academic performance?
10. Has your child had difficulty adjusting to classroom routine and discipline?

VI. MEDICAL

1. Does your child get frequent headaches and/or stomachaches?
2. Is your child always tired?
3. Did your child have difficulty establishing bowel and bladder control?
4. Does your child still have relapses in bowel or bladder control either day or night?
5. Does your child have a poor appetite?
6. Does your child have a history of anemia of any type?
7. Is your child irritable before and/or shortly after meals?
8. Does your child crave sweets?
9. Was your child colicky as an infant?
10. Was your child an unusually cranky baby?
11. Was your child an unusually passive baby?
12. Does your child have a history of allergies?
13. Is there a history of allergies in the family?

Name of Child: _____

Date: _____

Completed by: _____

WHAT DO WE
DO NOW?

There are only two lasting bequests we can hope to give our children. One of these is roots; the other, wings.

—Hodding Carter

Treating the Whole Child

Perhaps the most important information to surface from the last few years of intensive investigation of attention disorders is that no treatment approach is successful alone. Neither medical, educational, behavioral, cognitive nor psychological intervention is, by itself, adequate. Rather, both research and clinical experience present one compelling truth, that is, parents must seek treatment for the whole child. Medications must be considered and are often necessary to alter the neurochemical imbalances causing the problems. Educational needs must be identified and programs tailored to individual strengths and weaknesses. The structure and order lacking because of a deficient attentional and organizational system must be provided. Loving guidance and firm support must be constantly given to children who internalize rules and expectations less well than their peers. Diet must be addressed, allergies unmasked, and toxins eliminated. Friends must be actively cultivated, while successful activities are diligently pursued. Social skills must be concretely taught, while special gifts are recognized and developed. Psychological conflicts must be resolved and self-esteem enhanced. Through it all, you must simultaneously be an ardent champion of your child, a diligent taskmaster, and a devoted friend.

Successfully parenting a child or adolescent with an attention disorder requires orchestration of the highest degree. You must become a skilled conductor bringing the many facets of your child's life into harmonious symphony.

In addition, you must become an advocate for your child, vigorously pursuing his best interests and constantly reminding him of who he is. On his behalf, you must become a strategist, an attorney, a peacemaker and a soothsayer. While this task is difficult, these goals are possible and have been accomplished by many like you who have traveled the ADHD/ADD road.

♦ WHAT PARENTS NEED ♦

"Raising a confident and competent ADHD or ADD child who will become a successful, cooperative and contributing adult ... is this really possible?" you ask yourself.

It is our firm belief that it is. During the last twenty years we have seen the children we began working with as preschoolers now going off to college. They have done well; they feel good about themselves; and their futures are bright with possibilities. They are, for the most part, a sensitive and caring group. Many want to help others like themselves. Early detection and intervention by loving, responsible parents enabled them to succeed.

You hold the key to your children's future successes. You are their most important teacher. You influence their lives more than anyone else. Home is the first schoolhouse and parents are the first teachers. Whether we wish it or not, how we raise our ADHD/ADD children will significantly determine their futures.

Unfortunately, most of us have little or no education on how to raise children successfully. Our most important job in life is left to chance, i.e., how our parents raised us. Even if we are lucky and are pleased with our parents' methods, they rarely work with ADHD/ADD children. In addition, times and circumstances have changed. Our parents' strategies and rules, goals and values often seem to have little relevance in today's world.

Even though raising children with attention disorders is not easy, nevertheless, most parents are devoted to meeting their children's needs, to giving them emotional nourishment, and to providing the skills and opportunities to help them live productive and fulfilling lives. All of the parents we have worked with, both rich and poor, educated and uneducated, happy themselves or unhappy, want the best for their children. They want to raise confident, capable and cooperative children.

What are the characteristics of such children and adolescents?

Children who are confident have positive self-esteem. They feel secure in their abilities, and they can withstand setbacks and disappointments. Capable children have skills and knowledge, creativity and initiative. They are successful in activities they undertake, whether interpersonal or work and school related. Cooperative children are those who can interact well with others to accomplish goals.

What do you, as a parent, need to enable you to become the parent who can raise a successful, happy ADHD/ADD child or adolescent?

As I grow older, I pay less attention to what men say. I just watch what they do.——Andrew Carnegie

To be of greatest assistance to their children, parents need several important things.

♦ *Knowledge*

When we first embark on our parenting odyssey, most of us know very little about those things which will vitally affect the development and future of our children.   Despite this lack of information, most parents can raise a child without an attention disorder reasonably successfully based on their own experiences. Easy children, in fact, can often almost raise themselves. Trying to raise an attention-disordered child without knowledge, however, can be notably unsuccessful.   To parent an ADHD/ADD child effectively requires knowledge and understanding in all of the following areas:

- Attention deficit disorders
- Learning styles and preferences
- Learning disabilities
- Behavior disorders
- Medical disorders.
- School readiness
- Correct school and class placement
- Behavior modification
- Discipline
- Limit setting
- Training in responsibility
- Encouragement
- Organization and structure
- Social skills training

You are encouraged to begin a journey of discovery about those things which will dramatically affect your ADHD/ADD child. Doing so will give you the best possible chance of achieving your parenting goals.

♦ *Skills*

Just as most of us have little knowledge in those areas which so dramatically affect our children's lives, we likewise have little knowledge of how to raise children successfully. Children with attention disorders, unintentionally, but nontheless, rarely make life easy for you. To cope successfully you must be armed with the latest cornucopia of parenting skills that work—and work with ADHD/ADD children. Most treatment programs for children with attention disorders have parent education and training programs. You are encouraged to participate in one of these or to review other programs which have been successful with children like yours.

Parenting, like most things, is a skill which can be learned. Both you and your children will benefit from your concerted effort to become an expert in the field. Knowledge is power, and skills are the tools for implementing it.

◆ *Support*

Those parents who are supported by their families, their children's teachers, their professionals and their communities will have the best chance of doing their job well. A parent's multiple roles of teacher, visualizer, encourager and role-model requires not only personal strength, but much support from others.

Sometimes, however, neither parents nor their children receive this understanding and acceptance. It is, therefore, crucial that you seek out others who have similar concerns and form a support network. Support groups are therapeutic; there is virtually no expense involved; and they serve as one of the best sources of current and relevant information.

Parents of ADHD and ADD children are fortunate that two strong support groups exist throughout the United States and Canada. These include CH.A.D.D. (Children with Attention Deficit Disorders) and ADDA (Attention Deficit Disorders Association). LDA, the Learning Disabilities Association, is also an extremely helpful group for those whose children have learning disabilities as well. These groups are listed in the Appendix. Support groups not associated with national groups meet in many communities. The names can usually be obtained from local professionals.

The benefits of involving oneself in a support group cannot be overestimated. No problem is insurmountable if it is shared with and by others. Support groups also offer valuable assistance in helping parents obtain knowledge, learn effective skills and develop plans for action. Such groups usually offer bi-monthly and monthly programs as well as regional conferences which often feature nationally recognized experts in the fields which affect your child. Local resources have usually been well-researched as well as the latest information on school issues or legislation which may affect your ADHD or ADD child. The most helpful books and articles are usually known and are often available through these groups. This network of friends and compatriots can be the ADHD/ADD parent's saving grace in a time of stress, confusion or lack of direction.

♦ *Plans For Action*

Now that you are bolstered by support and armed with knowledge and skills, we are ready to address treatment approaches for your ADHD/ADD child or adolescent. Research overwhelmingly suggests that one approach alone will not be sufficient. For some children every intervention may be needed. For most, at least two or three will be required. In the following chapters, each of the treatment approaches most commonly utilized in treating attention disorders will be addressed.

It is important to assess your child holistically. Only then can a multimodal treatment strategy be determined which will benefit

---

Even if you're on the right track, you'll get run over if you just sit there.——Will Rogers.

not only the child or adolescent's many-faceted personality but will assist family members as well. *Wholeness*—academic, emotional, social and spiritual—is the ultimate goal of any successful program for you and your child. Do not settle for less.

◆ PUTTING IT ALL TOGETHER ◆

Once an attention disorder has been diagnosed, there are many treatment options for you to consider and many decisions to be made. The range of treatment approaches includes: medical management; educational intervention; attention to diet, nutrition, allergies and environmental toxins; behavior management strategies; counseling and family therapy; cognitive therapy; and social skills training, among others.

This section on treatment approaches is not intended to replace professional assistance. Its goals, rather, are to assist you in becoming more knowledgeable and prepared to take whatever appropriate actions make sense to you. We encourage you to acquire as much information as possible on these disorders, and to seek assistance from your child's school, private physicians, private professionals, your local mental health center, child care agencies, organizations funded by United Way, and other appropriate agencies.

Once thoroughly educated on attention disorders, trust your judgment based on both your knowledge and your parental intuition. We sincerely believe that you, and you alone, with an understanding of the options available, can choose the treatments which will work best for your child or adolescent and your family. In the process we believe you can find the strength to continue, the optimism to remain hopeful, and the faith to believe in your child.

Healing is a matter of time, but it is sometimes also a matter of opportunity.

—Hippocrates

Medical Interventions

Most of us would prefer a nonmedical intervention to manage the symptoms of an attention disorder. Nevertheless, the use of stimulant medication at the present time is the most common treatment for children and adolescents with ADHD and ADD. At least 750,000 of the U. S. school-age population take stimulant medication annually for management of their ADHD/ADD symptoms and the number is expected to increase to more than a million by the early 1990's (Safer, 1988).

While the exact mechanisms are not completely understood, it is widely accepted in scientific circles that physiological ADHD and ADD are the result of deficiencies and/or imbalances in neurotransmitters, or brain chemicals, which have important roles in regulating attention and inhibition. Dr. H. C. Lou and his associates reported in *Archives of Neurology* (1989) the findings of their investigations which indicated that striatal regions in the brain are not receiving an adequate blood supply. Dr. Alan Zametkin and his associates at the National Institute of

Mental Health found that hyperactive adults who had been hyperactive since childhood and also had hyperactive children, had decreased glucose metabolism rates in areas of the brain responsible for attention, impulse control and motor inhibition, among others, as well as a more global decreased rate of glucose metabolism (Zametkin et al, 1990). These decreased rates are believed to be a factor of impaired neurotransmitter regulation.

Current evidence suggests that stimulant medication alters neurochemical imbalances and blood flow to particular regions, resulting in improved functioning in the frontal and central brain structures important for alertness and attention. Dr. Lou's findings, for example, showed that methylphenidate increased blood flow to the structures which mediate high forms of attention. As medication improves brain functioning, there is a corresponding improvement in the child's ability to attend and in his impulse control, behavior, cooperativeness, reasonableness, and sensitivity to social cues and expectations. A positive change in alertness is noted in the underactive, daydreaming ADD child, while increased attention and decreased activity and restlessness are noted in the overactive ADHD child or adolescent. Academic improvement is almost always noted, as well as improved behavior, peer relations and family interactions. Sports, music and other nonacademic activities are also positively affected.

One of the most immediate and dramatic changes frequently noticed when ADHD children begin taking medication is an improvement in their fine-motor skills, especially handwriting. The following handwriting sample of an eight-year-old off medication one day and on medication the next graphically illustrates this point.

Before Medication

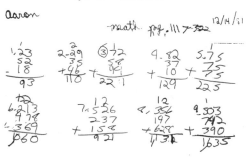

After Medication

aaron   12-13-87

math   pgs. 112-113   1-47

1. 8 x 2 = 16	13. 9 x 8 = 72
2. 9 x 3 = 27	14. 8 x 5 = 40
3. 6 x 0 = 0	15. 8 x 8 = 64
4. 7 x 3 = 21	16. 8 x 6 = 48
5. 5 x 6 = 30	17. 9 x 9 = 81
6. 5 x 5 = 25	18. 7 x 7 = 49
7. 5 x 9 = 45	19. 7 x 9 = 63
8. 6 x 3 = 18	20. 6 x 7 = 42
9. 8 x 4 = 32	21. 6 x 9 = 54
10. 8 x 7 = 56	22. 5 x 7 = 35
11. 4 x 9 = 36	23. 7 x 4 = 28
12. 6 x 6 = 36	24. 3 x 8 = 24

Very Neat! Thanks!

For the last fifty years professionals and parents have been treating children with attention disorders with a variety of approaches. While each approach has offered some assistance, the one which appears consistently to have been the most helpful is the use of stimulant medication. Research shows that for a great percentage of those accurately diagnosed with ADHD or ADD, medication is an appropriate and effective treatment choice.[5]

Even though medication is effective, it is our belief that, unless the child is in crisis and the school is requiring that something be done immediately, or the family is desperate, non-medical interventions should be tried first, or at least concurrently with medication. Treatment is an individual matter, however, and each professional has a somewhat different approach and philosophy for treating the problems of an attention disorder. One's choice is usually based on experiences, education and interests. We know that changes in lifestyle, diet, stress and the support of groups of people with similar difficulties can result in major improvements in cancer, heart disease, arthritis and diabetes,

---

[5]The use of medication in the treatment of attention disorders is such an important topic and one which creates so much anxiety in parents that Medications for Attention Disorders: A Comprehensive Handbook (Copeland, 1991) has been written to guide parents in understanding and making a decision regarding this treatment option.

among others. It is very reasonable, therefore, to believe that these interventions may have the potential for assisting those with attention disorders as well. While very hopeful, we do not, however, recommend awaiting the day that treatment for the root causes, rather than the symptoms, comes.

Before using medication we encourage you to educate yourself on behavior management strategies; to check for allergies, food intolerances, and environmental toxins; to make certain that your child is not inappropriately placed in his grade or academic program at school; to determine his learning strengths and weaknesses; to assess the presence of learning disabilities or gaps in his acquired knowledge; and to learn effective parenting methods. These approaches are addressed at length in Chapters 7 through 9. After investigating and/or trying other treatment approaches, you may be ready to consider trying medication as part of the child's overall treatment program. Consultation with your child's physician will greatly assist your decision-making process.

Of all the treatment approaches available for ADHD and ADD, choosing to use medication is often the most difficult decision for parents to make. When given adequate information, however, many parents decide that treating the whole child, i.e. treating him medically, socially, psychologically and educationally, will ultimately result in promoting the self-esteem, competence, organization and cooperative spirit necessary to ensure their child's success for a lifetime. We asked one father of an ADHD teen, who struggled intensely with the issue of medication, to share his story with us.

> *When my son was six he was diagnosed as having ADHD and medication was recommended. My initial reaction was one of anger and hurt. I found it difficult to believe that the world could not accept and tolerate this delightful boy. After all, he looked just like me and was clearly bright, articulate, and full of energy. I loved him and expected the world to do the same. As time progressed, however, I came to realize that no matter how much my wife tried to work with teachers and other parents to help them understand our son's abundance of energy and his short attention span, his world was still not a happy one. He was constantly falling short of the expectations everyone placed on him. He began to feel badly about himself. He even began to think of himself as "dumb" and thought that people did not like him.*

> *Reluctantly I agreed that we should try medication. The results with him were immediate. He was able for the first time to sit still, pay attention, listen and follow directions. Not only his teachers, but his friends as well, started to relate more positively to him. Even when he was with me, he seemed to be more relaxed and in control of his thoughts and actions.*

> *I am glad now that medication was available and that we agreed to use it for our son. As I look back on my own childhood, I am realizing that had medication been available at that time, it would probably have benefitted me as well.*

◆ GOAL OF MEDICATION ◆

The goal of all medications used to treat ADHD and ADD is to help the brain function efficiently and effectively. Just as glasses correct vision, medication alters the neurochemical imbalances causing the ADHD or ADD symptoms. Some doctors have compared the use of medications for attention disorders with the use of insulin for diabetes. Medication for ADHD and ADD allows the child to function with a more normal *brain* chemistry, while insulin helps a diabetic function with better *blood* chemistry. The analogy to vision also applies: glasses help thousands of people to see better. Without glasses or contacts, many cannot even function. Efficiency and happiness then quickly plummet.

Contrary to some parents' fears, medicine does not change the child's basic nature. Children treated with medication are simply better able to accomplish what they want to do. Treatment does not force a child to be good, to change his consciousness or to diminish his freedom of expression. Whatever the child's goals, he will simply accomplish them more successfully on medication than off. Our experience shows, however, that ADHD/ADD children and adolescents desperately want to be successful, to have friends and to be in charge of their lives. To be out of control most of the time is devastating to their internal sense of stability, predictability, self-control and confidence.

Even though medication is the most widely used treatment for ADHD and ADD and is appropriate under many conditions, there are many problems inherent in trying it first:

Words are, of course, the most powerful drug used by mankind.——Rudyard Kipling

1) If the medicine is successful, there is often little incentive to try other interventions which are necessary for the long-term benefit of the child.

2) Research has shown that those children treated with medication *alone* have no better outcome by late adolescence than those who were not treated at all (Cantwell, 1985; Weiss et al., 1975).

3) Many times the amount of medication can be reduced when food-related problems and allergies are alleviated. Reducing stress and implementing structure and routine also reduce the need for medication.

4) Parents are much more content with medication after they have exhausted other alternatives first.

5) After six weeks of other interventions, those children who do not really need medication are usually very apparent.

6) Parents and teachers who may want an easy way out are usually discouraged.

◆ IMPORTANT FACTS TO REMEMBER ◆

During the past ten years there has been an unprecedented amount of research on the effects of various treatment approaches for ADHD/ADD, including medication. As Josephine Elia, M.D., at the National Institute of Mental Health says, "We're trying to understand the effects of stimulants on some of the neuro-transmitters and their metabolites (chemicals in the brain that appear to be somehow associated with ADHD). We know the drugs work—they're very effective—but we don't know how they work" (Elia, 1989). Various institutions and investigators have clearly established the ability of medicine to alter the symptoms of attention disorders. They have also revealed other equally important aspects of this treatment method.

♦ *Medicine alone is not enough.*

Research has shown that medicine alone is not adequate for long-term changes. Likewise, psychological, behavioral and educational interventions have been found relatively unsuccessful without medication. It appears that *medicine enables the child to benefit from interventions which are ineffective without it.* In fact, the Food and Drug Administration requires that the label on drugs used for ADHD/ADD state that they be used "as an integral part of a total treatment program which typically includes other remedial measures (psychological, educational, social)" (*Physicians' Desk Reference*, 1991).

These findings were confirmed in a follow-up study of older adolescents, conducted by Dr. Jim Swanson, who has studied ADHD/ADD for fifteen years. He found that only those adolescents who received psychological and educational treatment in addition to medicine were significantly better adjusted than those without any treatment at all (Swanson, 1988).

Another study reported in 1987 in *The Journal of the American Academy of Child Psychiatry* compared two groups of ADHD/ADD children, ages six to twelve. The first group was treated with medication only, while the other received psychotherapy, cognitive therapy, behavior modification, family counseling and medication. After two years the group receiving multimodal treatment showed marked academic improvement, while the group receiving medication alone did not. A follow-up ten years later showed that none of the boys in the multimodal treatment group had been institutionalized, while twenty-two percent of those who had received medication alone had been hospitalized (Satterfield, 1987).

While most acknowledge the need for a multifaceted treatment program, it does not always occur. One physician from California commented on the frustration that physicians feel when parents do not seek counseling when it is recommended. He found that among his patients who had been referred for counseling only forty percent actually followed through (Kwasman, 1989).

Children are our most valuable natural resource.——Herbert Hoover

◆ *Medication must be monitored properly.*

It is important to determine which member of your team will be supervising the medication and stay in touch with him on a regular basis. Most physicians recommend follow-up at least every three to four months after the appropriate regimen for the medication has been established. Even though the child appears to be doing well, follow-up is not an *unnecessary medical expense*, as parents may sometimes think. Professionals often report seeing children who are believed to be doing well, when in fact they are significantly over- or under-medicated. With a little questioning of the child, it is often apparent that the wrong medication is being used even though improvement may have been significant. When the medication is correct the child should not report feeling *sick* or in *slow motion*, as they sometimes do. Children must often be asked appropriate questions, since they frequently do not volunteer pertinent information. In addition, as rapidly as children's bodies are changing during the growing years, it is not unrealistic to expect that the proper dosage of medication, or the type of medication used, may need to be changed or adjusted on a regular basis.

Parents may sometimes need to initiate close follow-up. A questionnaire for monitoring behavioral and educational changes with different dose levels and for different medicines is included at the end of this chapter. A *Side-Effects Checklist* is also included to assist you in determining any adverse responses.

♦ *Parents must be educated about medication.*

It is often quite difficult for parents to continue the recommended treatment unless they have received adequate education about the medicine—both its benefits and its side effects. Often a combination of interventions is tried until the most effective options, or the ones most agreeable with the child and his family, are determined. Since ADHD or ADD may well be, for many, a lifelong disorder, it is important to expend the necessary energy in the initial stages of treatment to ensure long-term compliance and benefit.

♦ *Medication should not be used to treat learning disabilities.*

Recent research has expressed a concern that growing numbers of learning-impaired students are being treated with stimulant medications. Drs. Shaywitz and Shaywitz (1988), both physicians at the Yale University School of Medicine, have concluded that it is improper to treat learning disorders with stimulants and "only attention-deficit disorder...can be ameliorated by a treatment program incorporating stimulant therapy." For this reason, it is important that a thorough psychological/psychoeducational evaluation of the child be done to determine if there is a learning disability, a conduct disorder, or other problems that must be treated through different measures. (*Learning disabilities* are discussed in Chapter 7. A *conduct disorder* is a psychiatric disorder which includes vandalism, fighting, lying or stealing.) Both of these can, and often do, co-occur with attention disorders, especially ADHD.

♦ UNDERSTANDING MEDICATION ♦

Deciding on a particular medication is largely a trial-and-error procedure. Professionals who have worked with ADHD and ADD children for a long time usually have a conceptual framework as well as an intuitive sense of what will be effective. The most commonly used medications are methylphenidate hydrochloride

(Ritalin) and dextroamphetamine HCL (Dexedrine), with Ritalin being prescribed far more frequently than Dexedrine. Dexedrine has been used since 1937, while Ritalin was approved for use with children in 1961.

Cylert is another stimulant medication that is the most recently available. It was approved for use in the United States in 1975 and has been utilized with some success for fifteen years. A much less commonly used stimulant medication is methamphetamine (Desoxyn). Little information exists on the long-term effects of Cylert and Desoxyn. By contrast, both Ritalin and Dexedrine have been used for many years with studies showing no apparent long-term problems with use. In fact, these medications have been tested with children far more than many other medications which are prescribed for them daily with little question.

It is important that medicine be started in low doses and increased gradually by the physician on your team. Dr. Paul Wender cautions in his book, *The Hyperactive Child, Adolescent, and Adult,* that all too frequently the dose never reaches the therapeutic level, or the child is started on too much medication, has an adverse initial response and the medicine is discontinued (Wender, 1987). If a child does not respond to one medicine, he may well respond to another. It may take several weeks to establish the optimum medication, time intervals and dosage taken.

The following case of an adolescent referred to us the summer before his junior year in high school, demonstrates this point.

> *Despite being extremely bright, Mike had never done well in school. He was not active or disruptive—he simply did not perform. When criticized, however, he became defensive and angry. Thus, he had more than one argument with his teachers. It was apparent to both his parents and his teachers that he was bright and was exceptionally creative and enterprising. During the summers he often started businesses which were quite successful for a person his age. His grades, however, remained unsatisfactory, and family life was stressful despite his parents' devotion to him. His father questioned whether his divorce from Mike's mother had created his son's problems. Schools were changed often to find just*

the right place. Despite being in a small, structured class, little improvement was noted.

By seventh grade, things were deteriorating drastically. Something had to be done. Family counseling was recommended and that helped some at home. However, there was no improvement at school. His parents became discouraged after six months and decided that counseling was not the answer. Testing only confirmed what they already knew: Mike was very bright, he was under-achieving, he was an independent thinker, and he hated school. His only pleasure came from the business ventures he continued to conjure up, and his job at the golf club. The owner was impressed by Mike's intellect and his creative problem-solving ability. He looked to him often for assistance. This was the first adult authority who respected Mike. He blossomed in the summers under his tutelage. There was little carry-over, however, and the next school year was a repeat performance of the many before.

For eighth grade a boarding school was advised. Mike had no friends at school and was becoming increasingly isolated from his family. His creativity was now spent on sardonic comments to teachers and open hostility to peers. With his family he was angry and rebellious, although still thoughtful and sensitive at times. He felt no one understood or cared. His parents did not understand Mike, but they certainly did care!

Boarding school was really no better or worse. Mike continued to alienate both his teachers and his peers with his attitude. He failed to turn in his classwork and homework, and school was described as "boring". He remained at boarding school until his sophomore year, when a change seemed needed. At the new boarding school his parents chose, he seemed somewhat more satisfied, although his adjustment continued to be marginal. He did become more concerned about his grades and managed to make C's for the most part. He became interested in sailing, but there was no club for that. He pursued his interest in photography by working on the yearbook. He continued, however, to feel lonely and isolated.

After Mike's sophomore year, his parents were feeling desperate. At the recommendation of a friend they decided to have a psychological evaluation. The findings were similar to those of previous evaluations, except that they were advised that Mike probably had an attention deficit disorder. It was subtle but his history was classic. He was significantly underachieving despite his I.Q. which was found to be in the gifted range. Mike did not have learning disabilities but had a classic ADD profile. Counseling was recommended for both Mike and his family. However, they were advised that it would probably be only minimally helpful if the ADD were not treated as well. It was recommended that they consult with a physician, in their case, a psychiatrist.

After exploring all possible medical causes, including allergies and depression, among others, the psychiatrist concurred with the diagnosis of ADD. He suggested stimulant medication and psychotherapy. Mike's parents were tremendously relieved to know that their son's difficulties could be helped. True to his nature, Mike would not acknowledge that anything could be wrong with him. However, he was intrigued by the possibility of improvement. He was very motivated at this time to go to college and realized it would be impossible under the present conditions.

Mike was tried on both Ritalin and Dexedrine. Neither was helpful but instead made him tired and irritable. Norpramin was tried next and was effective. Within a few days, Mike's irritability and anger had decreased, and the improvement was dramatic in a few weeks. He was no longer aloof, but began to participate with the family. He seemed to attend better. However, it was difficult to determine his level of concentration for certain during the summer. Medication was continued in the fall with good results.

Mike is now a senior. He has been on medication for one and a half years. He is happy with himself, and his grades are A's and B's. He started not only a sailing club but managed to wheel and deal and get an alumnus to donate four old sailboats which the boys have repaired and are enjoying immensely. He has a best friend for the first time in his life and is even dating. He is very pleased with himself. He still does not acknowledge to his parents that anything is wrong, but he now takes the medicine quite willingly.

Needless to say, his family is happy at this point. Their only regret is that Mike experienced sixteen years of frustration and failure before his problem was diagnosed. They are glad that people are more aware of ADD and that other families can get help sooner.

♦ FIRST-CHOICE MEDICATIONS: ♦
STIMULANTS

♦ *Ritalin*

Ritalin (Methylphenidate Hydrochloride), manufactured by Ciba-Geigy Pharmaceutical Company, is the most commonly used stimulant medication and the one frequently tried first. Ritalin is effective with a great percentage of those with whom it is tried.

Ritalin is available in a short-acting tablet form which lasts approximately three to five hours, depending upon individual metabolism. The short-acting tablet form is the easiest to titrate, or adjust dosage, because it comes in three sizes: 5 mg., 10 mg., or 20 mg. The 5 mg. tablet may be split for even smaller doses needed by a few children. Some children are undermedicated on 5 mg. and overmedicated on 10 mg., and this allows 7.5 mg. to be an option. The more precise the dosage based on need, the more successful are the benefits.

Ritalin is also available in a long-acting, time-release 20 mg. tablet (SR-20) that lasts approximately seven to ten hours, depending on individual metabolism. It is the approximate equivalent of a 10 mg. tablet taken twice daily. The long-acting form can be of major benefit for those who do not wish to take medicine at noon at school and for those who desire a consistent level of medication throughout the day. However, the SR-20 may not produce the same benefit as two 10 mg. tablets given at breakfast and noon. It needs to be monitored very carefully since it may metabolize unevenly in some children, causing an overmedicated response initially followed by an undermedicated response later in the day.

Research has shown that the average dose of Ritalin is 10 mg. twice daily. Lower doses (.3 mg. per kilogram of weight) result in the best improvement in cognitive skills and learning abilities, while the greatest improvements in behavior and social skills are obtained with doses of approximately .6 mg./kg. (1 kg. = 2.2 pounds). Higher doses can result in a decrease in cognitive skills, but they may sometimes be required for very severe behavior problems.

The appropriate amount of medication for any child must be determined on an individual basis with much feedback from parents and teachers to the physician. Checklists are the most efficient and objective way for you and your child's teacher to monitor medication benefits and side effects and to share them with your child's team manager or physician.

The Ritalin short-acting tablet is usually effective within thirty minutes after ingestion. While there has been some concern that food interfered with the metabolism of the medication, most physicians currently recommend taking the medication after meals to avoid loss of appetite and/or stomachaches if the child is prone to them (see section on *Side Effects of Ritalin, Dexedrine and Cylert*). Since the Ritalin tablet lasts only three to five hours, a second dose is usually needed four hours later, and for many children a third dose in the afternoon is helpful.

Some children experience increased hyperactivity and/or sensitivity and moodiness when the tablet form of Ritalin wears off. This is called a *rebound effect*. When severe, parents can switch to a long-acting form of medicine or they can give one-half the usual dose a few minutes before the medicine should wear off, thus significantly decreasing the rebound effect. Most of the side effects which occur can be overcome with patience and appropriate titration and timing of medication administration.

The long-acting form of Ritalin, the Sustained Release (SR-20), takes somewhat longer to become effective. The effects should then be consistent throughout the day, although it may not be, wearing off more gradually than the tablet form.

Parents rightfully worry about the amount of medication their child is taking. The dosage required depends on many variables, including the severity of the child's symptoms and his general sensitivity, among others. Allergic children are usually quite sensitive and require less than typical doses. *High-dose responders*, on the other hand, may take more than 60 mgs. per day without adequate symptom relief. Body weight is not necessarily a good indicator of dosage required even though it is a helpful baseline parameter. For example, a two hundred pound father of one of our patients received immense benefit from 5 mgs. of Ritalin four

---

Mankind owes to the child the best it has to give.——U.N. Declaration

times a day, while his forty-five-pound, hyperactive son required 10 mgs. of Ritalin three times daily.

A child or adolescent may take one, two or even three doses of Ritalin per day. The third dose is often necessary for very active children or those with academic assignments, especially tests, which require study after three o'clock.

◆ *Dexedrine*

Dexedrine (Dextroamphetamine Sulfate), manufactured by Smith, Kline and French, is not used as commonly as Ritalin, but some children, adolescents and adults respond better to it than to Ritalin. It is available in 5 mg. short-acting tablets that last approximately three to five hours, depending upon the person's metabolism. Long-acting spansules are also available. They are time-release and last approximately seven to twelve hours. The Dexedrine spansule releases consistently throughout the day and is often preferred over Ritalin when a long-acting form is needed.

The effective dose of Dexedrine is usually between half to two-thirds of the Ritalin dose. It is initiated and managed in much the same way as Ritalin. It usually requires approximately one hour for the benefits of Dexedrine Spansule to be obtained, after which time they appear to remain evenly distributed over the day. Dexedrine Spansule wears off slowly and usually does not cause the rebound effect which sometimes occurs with the tablet form.

While the response to medication is determined primarily through trials on each medication, some indications for preferring Dexedrine are:

1) A history of tics or depression. Dexedrine's neuro-transmitter effects are sometimes more helpful than Ritalin's effects in these cases.
2) A spansule is absolutely essential and the child/adolescent cannot take 10 mgs. of medication twice daily. The dosage level of Dexedrine Spansule is far easier to adjust than the Ritalin-SR since it is available in three sizes: 5 mg., 10 mg., and 15 mg.
3) As children enter adolescence, Dexedrine Spansule is often more effective. The increased potential for misuse of stimulants (giving to friends, selling, using

inappropriately) must be carefully weighed against the benefits.

4) Dexedrine is available in a liquid and has been approved for children, usually very hyperactive ones, five years of age and younger. It is possible to give doses as small as 1.25 mg. of the elixir. Dexedrine is approved by the FDA for use in very young children.

◆ Cylert (Pemoline)

Cylert is a relatively new medication, having been used in the United States for about fifteen years.   Of the stimulants, researchers know the least about its potential long-term effects and benefits. It is manufactured by Abbott Laboratories and is available in 18.75, 37.5, and 75 mg. tablets. It is generally tried after Ritalin and Dexedrine have been found unsuccessful. For some children, however, it appears to be a very effective medication.

Cylert is different from both Ritalin and Dexedrine in that it builds up in the bloodstream and must reach a certain blood level before it is optimally effective. While some improvement occurs within two or three days, it generally requires two to three weeks of continuous administration of this medicine before optimum therapeutic benefit is achieved. For this reason, it must be given on weekends and holidays. If it is given on weekdays only, it will be only marginally effective. Periodic evaluation of liver enzymes is recommended when a child is taking Cylert.

◆ *Side Effects of Ritalin, Dexedrine and Cylert*

Almost every medicine does have side effects. Whenever there is a medical problem, each person must make a choice between living with the medical disorder or living with the potential side effects of treatment. This decision usually involves deciding upon the least negative option. Many parents of ADHD/ADD children have decided that the side effects of medicine are far less negative than the academic failure, social and emotional problems, and family stress created by untreated attention disorders.   It is a more positive option for many if a correct diagnosis has been made and medicine is started at low doses and increased systematically with close monitoring. It is the improper use of stimulants, whether through misdiagnosis or overdosage, that has caused most of the problems so prominent in the adverse publicity surrounding this issue.

Appetite Suppression—This is the most frequent side effect cited for both Ritalin and Dexedrine, and Cylert to a lesser extent. However, many parents have found that it can be managed. Giving the child breakfast before he takes the medicine will generally cause the morning meal not to be affected. The noon meal is more often a problem than not. The child should be encouraged to eat something, even if he must make himself. Even a little food will prevent a headache or the irritability that can occur with hunger. Parents can make this meal as enticing as possible to promote cooperation.

Children are usually ravenous by three or four o'clock in the afternoon. At this time, they should be given nutritious foods, such as fruit, cheese, nuts, and whole grains instead of the usual snack foods. Some parents even have the evening meal ready or serve leftovers from the night before.

If medicine is not taken after noon, hunger is rarely affected in the afternoon and evening. If a third dose is necessary in the afternoon, dinner may also be affected. Often the bedtime snack becomes dinner for the child.

While attention-disordered children as a group may be slimmer than their peers, they are also frequently healthier, especially after they outgrow the ear and throat infections of their early years. Many American chidren eat far more than is needed for optimum health; ADHD/ADD children on medication generally do not. For the ADD child who is eating hyperactively and thus overweight, appetite suppression can be a benefit. The stimulants, however, are not recommended for weight control. If parents are concerned about their child's eating patterns and wish to be certain that he is receiving sufficient nutrients, they may wish to consider adding vitamin and mineral supplements, under the direction of their child's physician, to the child's diet. Special milkshakes used to increase weight gain can also be beneficial to the child who becomes overly thin.

Some concerns have been raised over the possibility of growth suppression due to the loss of appetite. This area has been carefully investigated by many. Drs. Klein and Mannuzza (1988), compared the growth rates of young adults treated with methyl-phenidate hydrochloride in childhood because of hyperactivity and nontreated adults, and found no difference in height between the group that was treated and the population in general. Interestingly, they found that if growth is slowed down at all during the time children are taking the medication, there appears to be a *growth rebound* effect that occurs when it is discontinued.

Despite the fairly limited real danger, most physicians check height and weight three to four times a year and obtain an annual CBC and chemical profile. If problems are noted, the stimulants are discontinued. Other medications are usually tried in their place if still needed.

Sleep Disturbance—The majority of children with overactive ADHD have difficulty falling asleep. However, most are reported to *sleep like logs* once they do. The stimulants sometimes cause or increase difficulty falling asleep. When they do, they must be adjusted to avoid this negative effect. Some children actually fall asleep more easily when on small doses of stimulant medication. The most difficulty seems to occur when the child is coming off medication, especially if rebound occurs, about the time he should be falling asleep. Fine-tuning the medication regimen can usually avoid these problems.

One intervention that is effective with many ADHD/ADD children who have difficulty concentrating and focusing long enough to go to sleep is to use a *sleep machine*. These are available in inexpensive models with only one noise, such as rainfall, to expensive ones with multiple noises and multiple volumes. We discovered the positive effect of sleep machines after noting repeatedly that many of these children wanted to sleep with fans on, even in the winter. It was not cool air they wanted, but rather the noise the fan made.

The keys to sleep are stimulating the attention centers adequately to allow the calming necessary for sleep to occur, and blocking out episodic distracting noises. Otherwise, the body may be still, but the mind remains in high gear. Dr. Marcel Kinsbourne found in his work with high dose responders, who were hospitalized as part of a research project, that a bedtime dose of medication was essential for sleep.

Increase In Pulse Rate Or Blood Pressure—Stimulants may cause a mild increase in heart rate. It is important to determine whether this is a side effect for your child. When it does occur, it is often a minor increase and does not warrant discontinuation of medication. However, there have been a few cases in which it necessitated a different therapeutic intervention.

Studies on heart rate and blood pressure have yielded conflicting and inconclusive results. However, an Emory University research study measured the blood pressure of black male adolescents taking methylphenidate. Because a significant increase was shown in diastolic blood pressure, it may be especially important to monitor carefully this group of adolescents on medication (Brown and Sexson, 1989).

Headaches And Stomachaches—These are frequent complaints when a child first begins medication. When the medication is started at low doses, however, these negative effects are usually minimal and subside after a few days. If they continue, a change of medication is usually warranted. For very sensitive children, especially very allergic children, medication may simply not be a workable part of the solution. Dealing with the allergies and food intolerances may provide the best treatment for this child.

Lethargy, Depression, Becoming "Glassy-Eyed" Or A "Zombie"—These symptoms are not side effects of the medication. Rather, they indicate that the dosage of medication is too high, the child is on the wrong medication for the attention disorder, or that the diagnosis is incorrect. It is crucial that neither parents nor teachers believe that these are side effects which must be tolerated to gain the benefit of the medicine. Children and adolescents on appropriate medication do not have personality changes nor become depressed. Rather, they are very much themselves, but have the ability to concentrate, contain their impulses, and have a more appropriate activity level. Children who experience depression with the attention disorder often respond better to antidepressants than to stimulants, however.

Development Of Tics Or Tourette Syndrome—A few children will develop tics or involuntary muscle movements such as eye-blinking or grimacing when placed on stimulant medication. When this occurs, medication must be reduced or discontinued. There is some evidence that children with a family history of tics may be more likely to develop them. In these cases, use of stimulant medications should be approached even more cautiously.

Tourette Syndrome (TS), a disorder characterized by involuntary motor tics or motor movements such as eye-blinking or coughing, is not caused by stimulant medication. An underlying or subclinical Tourette Syndrome, however, may be precipitated by it. For this reason, it is very important to evaluate the family history for Tourette Syndrome before using stimulant medication. Many children with TS may also have ADHD or ADD.   In fact, more than half of Tourette Syndrome patients exhibit these symptoms. Usually, the more pronounced the Tourette Syndrome, the more pronounced the attentional disorder.   One study of children between the ages of five and twelve who had TS found that sixty-nine percent of them had listening and attention problems (Jagger, et al., 1982).

Because children with Tourette Syndrome often have an increased sensitivity to the possible negative effects of stimulant medication, many pediatricians are reluctant to use medication with them. Studies have also shown that stimulant medication increases the severity of the tics in as many as half of TS children (Golden, 1988).

◆ SECOND-CHOICE MEDICATIONS: ◆ ANTIDEPRESSANTS

◆ *Tricyclic Antidepressants*

Tricyclic antidepressant may be a misnomer for this group of medications used to treat a number of disorders including depression, bedwetting, migraine headaches and attention deficit disorders. Like the stimulants, tricyclic antidepressants affect the neurotransmitters. They appear to prevent the reuptake or re-absorption of selected brain chemicals, leaving more available to stimulate those parts of the brain which control attention, inhibition, vigilance and alertness.

The two most commonly used are *Tofranil* (Imipramine Hydrochloride) and *Norpramine* (Desipramine Hydrochloride.) Norpramine is a derivative of Tofranil and produces fewer side effects. However, most pediatricians are more knowledgeable about Tofranil because of its extensive use in bedwetting and may be more comfortable prescribing it. Only Tofranil has been approved for children under the age of twelve. Caution is urged with the use of Norpramin in prepubertal children because of its uncertain effects on cardiac functioning in some young children (Riddle, 1991).

The antidepressants are slower-acting medications that build up in the blood stream and produce behavioral, attentional and learning effects similar to those of stimulants in ADHD/ADD children, adolescents and adults. They are frequently the medicine of choice for those who have ADD, who are also depressed and/or moody and irritable. Since depression is a common symptom of

ADD and is often a byproduct of the undifferentiated ADD child's chronic underactivity, constant negative feedback, and poor peer and family relations, antidepressants are often used to assist with both problems simultaneously.

These medications are frequently used when the stimulants are either ineffective or contraindicated because of side effects or other medical reasons. One advantage they have over stimulants is that their effects are longer lasting, so that control of symptoms occurs consistently throughout the day and evening and on weekends. In addition, they tend to enhance sleep rather than increasing sleep disturbance, and appetite is not suppressed. Usually there is a positive effect on mood and self-image along with a decrease in irritability and lability.

Despite having been used for over twenty years, many questions remain about their overall effects and long-term benefits, however. Many patients respond positively to the tricyclics at first but will develop a tolerance to them and will receive no benefit after several weeks or months.

Headaches are a potential side effect, even at low doses. At higher doses, children, adolescents and adults may experience drowsiness, constipation, dry mouth or blurred vision. Tofranil, in larger doses, may impair memory and fine-motor coordination as well.

As with all medications, precautions must be observed and periodic check-ups carefully enforced. Monitoring heart rate and blood pressure, as well as EKG monitoring, is essential. Periodic blood tests approximately every six months should be obtained to check liver functioning as well.

It is important to be aware of the extreme danger should a child overdose. Tricyclics can be fatal with only a few pills because of the cardiac arrhythmias caused by these medications. All medicines should be kept securely out of the reach of young children and carefully controlled and administered for older ones.   This precaution is imperative with tricyclics.   Should a child or adolescent become depressed or suicidal, these medications should be removed from your home entirely.

♦ *Other Antidepressants*

Monoamine Oxidase Inhibitors (MAOI's)—MAOI's, such as Parnate and Nardil, have been very effective with ADHD adolescents and adults who exhibit severe impulsivity and more acting-out behaviors. However, they are considered "a medication of last resort" because they have acute negative reactions with a number of tyramine-containing foods such as cheese and chocolate, among others, and some drugs as well.

Prozac—Newer antidepressants such as Prozac are currently being investigated. Prozac offers the potential of equal benefit for depression with fewer potential negative effects. It affects the neurotransmitter, serotonin, instead of norepinephrine and dopamine. Some concerns have been raised over the possibility that it may interfere with the inhibition of aggressive impulses, however. Its use should be approached with caution and careful evaluation of the personality dynamics of the potential user.

Despite their potential risks, most experts consider tricyclic antidepressants a valuable tool in our medicinal arsenal against ADHD/ADD and depression. The risk:benefit ratio, however, must be carefully assessed to determine quite definitively that the benefits clearly outweigh the risks.

♦ MEDICATIONS FOR SPECIAL SITUATIONS ♦

In certain situations neither first- nor second-choice medications are appropriate or effective. While the following medications are not used as frequently as those in the first or second groups, there are instances where they are beneficial in the overall treatment program of the ADHD/ADD child or adolescent.

♦ *Clonidine*

Clonidine, marketed as Catapres among others, has been found useful for overfocused children. Stimulant medication, on the other hand, worsens their symptoms markedly. Behavior management strategies, education, and environmental manipulation are also extremely helpful for the overfocused child.

Dr. Robert Hunt, Director of Research and Training at Vanderbilt Child and Adolescent Psychiatric Hospital, has treated perhaps the most children with clonidine and believes that there are certain children who respond better to clonidine than to methylphenidate (Ritalin). These include ADHD children who are very energetic, have low frustration tolerance levels, and who show signs of aggression, conduct disorder, oppositional behavior or explosiveness (Hunt et al., 1990).

Clonidine has also been found to be helpful in treating children with tics or Tourette Syndrome, although the research in this area is somewhat inconclusive.

♦ Tegretol

Tegretol (Carbomazepine), an anticonvulsant, is used for treating ADHD/ADD children with seizure disorders, especially complex partial seizures, which may manifest primarily in outbursts of aggressive behavior. Children with other seizure disorders may require a combination of anticonvulsants and stimulants to manage adequately both sets of problems simultaneously.

Other anticonvulsants, such as phenobarbital and Dilantin, may increase attention deficit symptoms. Rather than stimulate the reticular and attention systems, they slow them down, increasing the child's inattention, activity and impulsivity.

♦ Caffeine

Caffeine, either in the form of coffee or caffeinated colas, has been reported by some parents to have a calming effect on their child.

An equal number of parents report that it increases activity and the symptoms of ADHD/ADD. Studies of caffeine treatment for attention disorders have failed to find any consistent beneficial effects of caffeine for either ADHD or ADD. However, some research has reported positive effects. If you believe caffeine is helpful to your child, it is unlikely to be harmful to allow it in moderation.

♦ *Major Tranquilizers*

Major tranquilizers or neuroleptics, such as the phenothiazines (Mellaril, Thorazine) and haloperidol (Haldol), are used primarily to treat more severe psychiatric disorders such as schizophrenia, the manic phases of bipolar disorder, or psychotic states. They are rarely used with attention disorders unless they co-occur with one of the above disorders, and they are generally much less effective than stimulants. Small doses of Haldol, however, are often utilized successfully in the treatment of Tourette Syndrome.

These medications are currently used primarily by psychiatrists when the symptoms are severe and all other interventions have failed to be effective. Hospitalization is often a necessary part of the treatment as well.

Children need love, especially when they do not deserve it.——Harold S. Hulbert

◆ QUESTIONS MOST OFTEN ASKED ◆
ABOUT MEDICATION

If we give medication to our children to control behavior and attention, aren't we teaching them that drugs are a solution to problems?

This is a valid concern and one most parents express. Dr. Josephine Elia of the National Institute of Mental Health, however, has reported that ADHD/ADD children on stimulant therapy do not become addicted to stimulants. She states, "They don't get the euphoric effect that abusers do, and they don't experience withdrawal symptoms when they stop taking the drug." (Elia, 1989). Some studies have suggested that ADHD/ADD children and adolescents who receive treatment that includes medication with other appropriate therapies have a reduced risk of substance abuse (Collins, Whalen and Henker, 1980).

Drug and alcohol addiction are far more common in untreated ADHD/ADD adolescents and adults than in those properly treated by a physician. Many people with attention disorders are quite angry and frustrated and have intense feelings of failure and lack of esteem. These are the conditions most likely to lead to substance abuse of any kind.

In fact, one study in Long Island of hyperactive adolescents found that children with ADHD are at a high risk for developing substance abuse problems (Gittelman, 1985). A similar study of fifty-seven adolescents, forty boys and seventeen girls, who were referred to an inpatient facility for treatment of substance abuse, found that twenty-one percent had an attention deficit disorder, hyperactivity, or impulse disorder (DeMilo, 1989).

Often adolescents and adults will experience some relief of symptoms when they try drugs and alcohol experimentally. They may then begin to self-medicate. They often take too much and they may use other medications to offset these effects.

It is important to remember, however, that ADHD and ADD are physiological problems and not behavioral or learning problems. The reticular formation, the prefrontal cortex, the limbic system, and other attention centers are not being stimulated properly and thus are not organizing and integrating information appropriately. Medication alerts the entire attention network so that the brain functions efficiently and effectively. If medication is taken by a child, adolescent or adult without an attention disorder, it will overstimulate the attention system producing tension and overfocused behavior. Those with physiological ADHD and ADD do not experience these effects unless given too much medication.

Some physicians seem uneasy about prescribing stimulant medications. Why is that?

Medicine is less likely to be over-utilized or abused if safeguards are followed. The Drug Enforcement Agency (DEA) is so carefully monitoring stimulant medications that many physicians have become concerned about prescribing them. If medication is not given judiciously and within carefully monitored guidelines, there is a risk that the use of stimulant medication will become so controversial that it may not be available to those who truly need it. Thus, precaution is well-founded. However, there is some danger, less so now than previously, that those who need it may not receive it because of an overly cautious attitude.

My child seems to have negative feelings about taking medicine? What should I do?

A child's attitude about taking medication usually mirrors that of his parents. If you are uncertain about medication as a treatment approach for your child, you may be subtly communicating your hesitation to him. Examine your own feelings first and then talk openly with your child. If, after talking with your physician, you genuinely believe that medication is needed, then explain to your child that this is a medical issue and not a philosophical one. Ask him to try the medicine and evaluate for himself its effectiveness.

Sometimes children are embarrassed about taking medication, or they are teased by their peers. Every effort should be made under these conditions to ensure the child's privacy. Long-acting medicines are often necessary to avoid the *tell-tale* visit to the nurse or office at noon. Some children, especially adolescents, have very strong feelings about their bodies and may be adamantly opposed to taking medication of any kind. If this is the case, we do not believe you should force your child to take medication. It remains important to educate your child on the benefits so that he completely understands the overall pros and cons.

> *My child is going off to school next year. How should I handle medication there?*

If your child is going to college, he should be responsible enough by this time to handle his own medicine. It is crucial that he understand that this and all medications should only be used by the person for whom they were prescribed. He should plan to keep his medicine securely out of the reach of other students, and under no circumstances should he share it with another student. You should impress upon him that Ritalin and Dexedrine are Schedule II drugs, *i.e.*, they are classified as *narcotics* by the FDA, and there could be severe medical and legal consequences if they are used by anyone other than himself. This fact cannot be overstressed to independent thinking ADHD adolescents.

If your child is going away to school or to camp, it is important for you to talk with the school nurse and explain his medication to her. She should keep the medication in her office and make arrangements for him to pick it up at appropriate times during the day. Under no circumstances should a school or camp allow a child to keep medicines such as these in his room. While your child may be extremely responsible and understand the appropriate use of his medication, other students may not. Having medication in the room may be a temptation to another student and place an unnecessary burden on your child.

> *I have heard that by adolescence ADHD/ADD children outgrow their need for medicine. Is that true?*

While it was previously believed by the professional community that children would outgrow attention disorders, it is now clear that ADHD and ADD symptoms persist for many people into adulthood. A fifteen-year study conducted by four Canadian psychiatrists found that about half of the children in this study seemed to outgrow the symptoms, while the other half did not (Weiss et al, 1975).

In the 1970's follow-up studies of hyperactive children first became available. They have shown that, even though ADHD adolescents may have a somewhat diminished activity level, they continue to be restless, distractible, emotionally immature and unable to maintain goals; they usually have poor self-esteem as well. For many, medication continues to be of great benefit. One study at the University of Rochester found that not only was stimulant medication helpful in managing the adolescent's symptoms, but that side effects were rare, and there were no instances of abuse (Klorman, et al., 1987).

Does insurance help cover any of the costs of stimulant drugs and psychotherapy?

Almost all health insurance plans cover prescription drugs and some cover psychological and psychiatric treatment. Mental health agencies often base their fees on the family's ability to pay. It is also possible that a local service agency may be willing to help you with the costs. ADHD/ADD are also now included as conditions eligible for SSI assistance from Social Security and for Medicaid.

◆ SUMMARY ◆

While our understanding of the physiological mechanisms that cause ADHD and ADD is incomplete, and the exact mechanisms of the medications utilized are not precisely known, researchers have found some answers for the thousands of children and adolescents facing these problems daily. All indications are that future scientific studies will continue to search diligently for greater understanding of the causes of and treatments for attention disorders. In the meantime, caring parents will continue to evaluate and employ the treatment options currently available. We hope all families can report happy endings like the one related in the following essay, written by Mike, whose story was reported earlier in this chapter, for his college application. We are happy to report that he was accepted by a good college. We have reproduced it here as he wrote it.

MY MOST DIFFICULT OBSTACLE TO OVERCOME

As my academic career became more demanding, I became severely frustrated, for it seemed I could never maintain the par of excellence that my brother did. It didn't make sense. I was a very bright child passing all the diagnostic and IQ tests with amazing margins. In fact, the tests showed I was one of the brightest students in the school, yet my grades did not correspond to these findings. I always understood my work and would try with unlimited energy, but it seemed I never would be able to make the deadlines. In between my burst of enthusiasm for my given task and the final draft, I would get distracted. Somebody would then herd me back into the same direction with which I started. Life was frustrating. Tension would build at home, and my self-esteem would shrink. Life appeared miserable when it was forecasted to be grand.

As the roller coaster of my grammar school years continued, my mother sought professional help. This disturbed me. I felt that there was nothing wrong with me. Everything was in order inside my mind; it was just the rest of the world that wasn't comprehending my sporadic output. My parents and teachers always thought I was not giving my best effort because I would do great one day and lousy the next. It didn't occur to me that there could be a problem with my mental functioning.

I was told that I had a learning disability—the Attention Deficit Disorder. All the tests had confirmed that I was a victim of this disorder and it explained why, for all these years, I had been labeled as one who just didn't care. The barrier had just begun to crack. I was excited with the idea that I wasn't a lazy goof-off who just did what he pleased whenever so motivated. I began to receive counseling for my disorder and life began to blossom into all sorts of different paths all leading away from the despairing ones of the past. I could now be aware of my problem and strategically take measures to compensate for its effect.

One of the best solutions to my problem was my

decision to go to boarding school. It allowed me to escape the stained and confining reputation of my grammar school years and start on a clean slate. Furthermore, boarding school allowed me to mature at an accelerated rate while being conscious of my problem.

Shortly thereafter, I was faced with the decision of taking medicine for my disorder. I was told the medicine had showed overwhelming results in other people with the same problem as mine. It was an experimental drug[6] and I was reluctant to take any foreign substances that would not allow me control of my actions. At first, there was not much of a change, but as the dosage increased, there were significant results. From my point of view, there was not much of a change, but as I was told by those around me, they could see a drastic difference in my behavior and production. Things became different now that I could work along side people without having the interference of a short attention. Besides some mild constipation as a side effect of the drug (Norpramin), life was getting better everyday. Foreign languages and small details were not as burdensome. Consistency and organization were becoming my more prevalent attributes. I could continue with the same bursting enthusiasm as I always did, but now, I wouldn't stray from my project thirty minutes later. To make a long story short, my self-esteem was much higher, and I was on top of the ball. After conquering a major barrier between myself and the rest of the world, I felt confident and could accomplish much more in my new state of mind.

---

[6]The medication Norpramin was not an experimental drug. Mike's thinking so was a miscommunication and highlights the need to have children and adolescents openly discuss their understanding, concerns and feelings about taking medication.

COPELAND MEDICATION FOLLOW-UP QUESTIONNAIRE
FOR MONITORING OF MEDICATION
(Parent/Teacher)

Copeland Medication Follow-Up Questionnaire

Teacher/Parent

Weekly Record Form

Copyright ©1991 by Edna D. Copeland, Ph.D.

Child's Name _____

Date _____ to _____
month/day   month/day

Completed by _____ Date _____

Please Indicate E — excellent; G — good; F — fair; P — poor

Day		Medication Schedule (specify (1) Name of medication; (2) Dose; and (3) Time medication is to be taken)	Attention / Ability to Focus	Impulse Control	Activity Level (Over/Under)	Compliance / Cooperation	Organization	Peer / Sibling Relations	Completing and Turning in School Work	Grades	(Weekly or periodic comments to be written out)
Mon.	a.m.										
	p.m.										
Tues.	a.m.										
	p.m.										
Wed.	a.m.										
	p.m.										
Thurs.	a.m.										
	p.m.										
Fri.	a.m.										
	p.m.										
Sat.	a.m.										
	p.m.										
Sun.	a.m.										
	p.m.										

Please put any additional comments on the back of this sheet.

MEDICATION SIDE-EFFECTS CHECKLIST

Child/Adolescent's Name_____Date_____Medication_____
__Tab __Spansule_____   Dose A.M._____ P.M._____
Evening_____ Completed by (Name)_____

Side Effects

When medication is used, side effects sometimes occur. If any of the side effects listed below is observed, please indicate which one(s) occurred and the severity of it.

	Not at All	Just A Little	Pretty Much	Very Much	Don't Know
Decreased appetite	___	___	___	___	___
Weight loss	___	___	___	___	___
Difficulty falling asleep	___	___	___	___	___
Fitful sleeping	___	___	___	___	___
Difficulty awakening	___	___	___	___	___
Nightmares	___	___	___	___	___
Headaches	___	___	___	___	___
Stomachaches	___	___	___	___	___
Tics	___	___	___	___	___
Dizziness	___	___	___	___	___
Rashes	___	___	___	___	___
Bedwetting	___	___	___	___	___
Irritability	___	___	___	___	___
Feeling anxious	___	___	___	___	___
Restlessness	___	___	___	___	___
Tenseness	___	___	___	___	___
Heart racing	___	___	___	___	___
Socially withdrawn	___	___	___	___	___
Sadness	___	___	___	___	___
Other	___	___	___	___	___
_____	___	___	___	___	___

What we want is to see the child in pursuit of knowledge, and not knowledge in pursuit of the child.

—George Bernard Shaw

Educational Interventions

School is one of the child's primary sources of self-esteem and fulfillment. It can also be a primary source of frustration and failure. There is rarely much a parent can do to offset the damaging effects of a negative school experience. It is, therefore, critical that the learning and educational needs of the child be addressed in the classroom, as well as his social and emotional needs. Teachers have a profound influence on children's lives, perhaps even more than parents once they enter school. Children are thrilled with every sign of interest and responsiveness from their teachers. They are equally crushed and distraught at every sign of disinterest or perceived rejection. Comments such as "You're not trying," or "This assignment is unacceptable. It is so sloppy. You'll have to do it over," secretly devastate the child.

Equally powerful, but in a positive way, is a light touch on the arm, a smile and "Hi, I'm glad to see you today." Anne Ortlund, in her book *Children Are Wet Cement*, comments, "How impressionable children are! They are really helpless in the hands of those around them. They're so easily convinced, so pliable; they believe whatever they're told." This may be especially true of the ADHD or ADD child. Teachers have powerful *hands* and can be instrumental in helping to mold an ADHD/ADD child into the competent, happy adult he can, with encouragement, become.

Not all ADHD/ADD children are fortunate enough to have knowledgeable and informed teachers and parents during their school years. Although intended to prepare and inspire a child for greater accomplishments in life, the elementary and high school years can often serve to discourage him from establishing and pursuing future goals. The following story related by Tim, a nineteen-year-old with ADHD, is similar to other stories we have heard from older students.

> *When I was two, my Mom enrolled me in a preschool so I could, as she says, "learn to relate to other children." I don't remember much about preschool, but when I see those teachers now they seem surprised that I'm in college. I guess I must have been pretty bad.*
>
> *I remember that my Kindergarten teacher was really nice. I sat on her lap a lot because I couldn't sit still for story time. I was always wiggling or crawling under the table. We worked in small groups and everything was so slow; I just wanted to finish and go outside. It was all pretty boring. It seemed like I was always waiting for something—and always in trouble.*

The worst part of school was first through third grades. Everything was hard—I couldn't hold a pencil, I couldn't color or write well...I couldn't even sit still in my chair. I was happy and enjoyed playing with my friends, but it seemed that all I did was disappoint my teachers. They were forever telling me to "be still," "pay attention," and "stop doing such sloppy work." I was frustrated and felt like a failure.

By third grade I had had enough of school and told my mom I wasn't going back ever again. Each day was torture for me since I was constantly being corrected and called down. I felt so humiliated. The kids got mad at me too. I can't remember anything that I did in school during those years that was considered good. I loved to read, and understood everything, but the tests always required writing which I just couldn't do. On more than one occasion I felt like throwing in the towel.

Math was even worse. There were so many things to remember and each problem took an eternity to complete. Lots of times I got the right answer but the steps weren't there, so it was counted wrong. It all seemed so unfair.

The rest of elementary school wasn't any better. Prison couldn't be worse than the way my daily routine felt. Sitting still for six hours each day and then coming home to do more written work was awful. I would have run away but I had no place to go.

There were a few bright spots—P.E., lunch and recess. No matter how hard I tried to do things right and please my teachers, I don't think I turned in even one assignment on which I made an "A." I looked forward to the end of the day when I could get in bed and read novels. I would gladly have stayed in my room forever.

In middle school I had one teacher who told me that I was "extremely creative and gifted with words." She actually gave me an "A" on a play that I wrote and read it to the class. That day was probably the happiest day of my entire school career.

High school was a little better since I could type all my papers and the books we read were interesting. I was still always in trouble for not paying attention or for getting out of my seat too often.

In spite of the traumas of school, I decided to give college a try. I started a few months ago and hope that I will graduate. Being in class only four hours a day is great—especially with breaks between classes. I schedule as many of my courses as I can for the afternoon, so I can stay up late at night to read and then sleep in the morning. Some of the coursework is really interesting, but I often wonder if I'm capable of doing college-level work.

Such despair and insecurity can be partially, if not completely, eliminated if an alert, informed and caring teacher recognizes that a child is having difficulty and contacts his family to initiate a coordinated effort to assist him. On the other hand, the child's parents may be the first to contact the school. In either case, the goal is to establish a strong sense of teamwork between school and home.[7]

◆ IMPORTANT EDUCATIONAL ISSUES ◆

To ensure a child or adolescent's success in school, several important educational issues must be considered. In this chapter

---

[7]While the educational issues discussed in this book are intended primarily to increase a parent's understanding, a corresponding discussion of these issues from the teacher's perspective, including classroom management strategies, may be found in the book Attention Without Tension: a Teacher's Handbook on Attention Disorders (ADHD/ADD) (Copeland and Love, 1990).

we will highlight the major concerns that must be addressed by the child's ADHD/ADD team as they evaluate and guide him.

♦ *Developmental Readiness*

For all students with attentional problems, developmental readiness is an essential issue to be considered. It is especially important to assess whether your child is developmentally, not *chronologically,* ready for kindergarten or first grade. To be successful in school a child must be able to act appropriately, control his impulses and to concentrate. To avoid difficulty he must have developed maturity in the areas of auditory and visual processing, short- and long-term auditory and visual memory, sequencing, visual-motor integration, and fine- and gross-motor skills. You may wish to give special consideration to this issue if your ADHD/ADD child has a late spring or summer birthday. Studies have shown *Summer Children,* as they are called, to be especially at risk for later academic and developmental difficulties.

To determine readiness, and also the potential presence of learning disabilities, you may wish to complete the *Preschool Checkup: A Symptom Checklist for Developmental Disabilities,* on pages 106 and 107. Then answer the following:

	Yes	No
1) My child is a girl.	____	____
2) My child's birthday is:		
Boy: Before May.	____	____
Girl: Before June.	____	____
3) My child has good verbal skills.	____	____
4) My child has good attention, concentration and impulse control.	____	____

	Yes	No
5) My child has above-average intellectual ability.	____	____
6) I answered *Yes* to less than 20% of the questions in any of the categories on the *Preschool Checkup: A Symptom Checklist for Developmental Disabilities.* (*No* means you answered *Yes* to more than 20% of the questions in any category.)	____	____

If you answered *No* to as many as four of the questions above, your child may be at risk for academic problems. You are encouraged to consult your teacher or pediatrician or the audioprogram, *First Grade Readiness* (Copeland, 1987). Determining a child's developmental readiness for kindergarten and first grade could easily be the most critical educational decision you make for your child. Unfortunately, it is also the one parents must make with the least knowledge and insight since they are uninitiated travelers on their child's educational journey.

♦ *Appropriate Grade Placement*

Appropriate grade and school placements are extremely important issues for the child or adolescent with an attention disorder. Benjy had the benefit of the correct school placement, while Tracey did not. A school with two thousand students, or even one thousand, can be overwhelming to the child who is easily overstimulated and disorganized, even with treatment. Attending a small private school or even moving to a smaller community may sometimes be necessary to meet your child's needs. One precious, undiagnosed ADD child with whom we worked performed well and longed for the quiet of her Chapter 1 math class which had only four students. As the stress of school intensified her behavior became increasingly difficult and explosive at home. Her behavior and loss of emotional control prompted the referral—not suspected ADD. With her sluggish processing and disorganization school had become so stressful for this shy, somewhat perfectionistic child that she could no longer cope. Smaller classes are often needed in addition to medical and behavioral treatment of the attention disorder.

Appropriate grade placement is equally important. Readiness for many tasks, whether writing with a pencil or understanding *Hamlet,* requires neurological maturation which is far more developmental than chronological. Since most ADHD/ADD children are neurologically immature, their ability to handle many aspects of academics, peer relations and organizational skills may develop later than those of most children.

If your elementary ADHD or ADD child is experiencing difficulty, you are encouraged to complete *A Checkup for Elementary School Children: A Symptom Checklist for Developmental Disabilities* on page 108. Then answer the following:

Appropriate Class/School Placement

	Yes	No
1) My child is a girl.	___	___
2) My child is one of the older students in his/her class.	___	___
3) My child has good verbal skills.	___	___
4) My child is above the 50% when compared with peers (academic and ability measures).	___	___
5) My child has good attention, concentration and impulse control.	___	___

<u>Yes</u>   <u>No</u>

6) I answered *Yes* to less than
20% of the questions in any of
the categories on *A Checkup for
Elementary School Children.* (*No*
means you answered *Yes* to more
than 20% of the questions in any
category.)   ____   ____

If you answered *No* to as many as four of the above questions,
you are encouraged to consult your child's teacher, counselor or
student support team for assistance and advice. Your pediatrician
or family physician can also be helpful.

Many children with attention disorders have had to repeat a
grade because of their delayed neurological, academic, social and
emotional development. While certainly not an easy decision, and
one for which you may find little support, it is frequently helpful
to *bite the bullet,* as we often tell parents, and do what is in the
long-term best interests of your child. This decision is much easier
if the child can change schools to repeat the grade. It is frequently
recommended, especially for the chronologically younger ADHD/
ADD student who began school at a somewhat earlier age, to say,
"I'm so sorry. I made a mistake. You were too young to go to
school. By staying back school will be much more fun and you'll
be more successful."

Children are sometimes relieved by this decision and
sometimes distressed. Regardless, you must have faith that you
are making the best decision for your child and continually
communicate that to him. You can share with him the results of
studies of professional athletes. One of these showed that the
majority of those who made it to the Pros had birthdays in the first
two quarters of the year and were larger than their peers (Horn,
1989). They presumably entered school at a later age. Likewise,
the majority of school leaders, both athletically and socially, are
the more mature students. If all else fails, you can tell him that he
will be the first in his group to drive. While not easy, it is a
decision with which the child can come to terms. Later he will

understand and be appreciative as well.

Retention, we stress, however, *cannot* be the primary solution for a problem. Rather, it must be viewed as a part of the solution, which also includes attention to all the academic, social and attentional needs which are usually present as well. *All* of the child's difficulties must be addressed if he is to succeed.

◆ *Learning Disabilities*

Retaining a child should not, of course, be a substitute for diagnosing and treating any learning disabilities that coexist with the attention disorder. Approximately 20% to 40% of ADHD and ADD children are believed to have a coexisting learning disability.

The distinction between ADD/ADHD and LD is often confusing for parents. Attention disorders and learning disabilities are considered by most professionals to be separate difficulties; however, they frequently co-occur and each may produce symptoms of the other. Both their distinctiveness and their overlap need to be understood.

As reported in *The Proceedings of The National Conference on Learning Disabilities*, 1987, The Interagency Committee on Learning Disabilities recommended in its report submitted to Congress in August, 1987, that a new definition of learning

---

I have never let my schooling interfere with my education.——Mark Twain

disabilities be adopted.   The modified definition is as follows
(changes to previous definition in italics):

> Learning disabilities is a generic term that refers to
> a heterogeneous group of disorders manifested by signifi-
> cant difficulties in the acquisition and use of listening,
> speaking, reading, writing, reasoning or mathematical
> abilities, or *of social skills*. These disorders are intrinsic
> to the individual and presumed to be due to central
> nervous system dysfunction.   Even though a learning
> disability may occur concomitantly with other handicap-
> ping conditions (eg, sensory impairment, mental
> retardation, social and emotional disturbance), *with
> socio*environmental influences (eg, cultural differences,
> insufficient or inappropriate instruction, psychogenic
> factors) *and especially with attention deficit disorder, all
> of which may cause learning problems, a learning dis-
> ability* is not the direct result of those conditions or
> influences.

While attention disorders and learning disabilities are
considered separate entities, many children with ADHD and ADD
also have learning disabilities. A much larger percentage of those
with learning disabilities have coexisting attention disorders.
When an ADHD/ADD child has a coexisting learning disability, it
is frequently one or more of the following:

> *Auditory perception and auditory
> processing problems,* including poor
> auditory discrimination, delayed auditory
> reception, and verbal comprehension
> problems, among others.

> *Auditory memory problems,* especially
> short-term memory.

> *Visual perception and visual processing
> problems*, including poor visual reception,
> delayed visual association, poor visual

organization and planning, and delayed figure-ground discrimination, among others.

Visual memory problems, especially short-term memory.

Fine-motor problems—trouble tying shoes, buttoning clothes, cutting, coloring, sloppy handwriting.

Visual-motor integration delays and poor eye-hand coordination—poor copying from the board or from books.

Space and time—poor sense of time; trouble learning left and right.

Reading disorders—(Dyslexia).

Spelling disorders—(Dyslexia).

Math disorders—(Dyscalculia).

Selected fine-motor control disabilities — (Dysgraphia).

Written language problems.

Problems of work rate.

One of the worst problems for children with attention disorders, especially ADHD, is that of handwriting. The great majority of ADHD children especially do work that is described as *messy* or *sloppy*. The combination of poor fine-motor coordination, impulsivity and failure to plan ahead makes handwriting a real chore for these children. Typically their words will overrun the lines; erasures will be incomplete or so vigorous there are holes in the paper; and math numbers will not be lined up correctly. Many ADHD/ADD children find cursive much easier than printing because it requires less fine-motor control and because each letter has a distinctive kinesthetic motor pattern that assists with locking in recognition of the letter configuration. Others, however, will continue to prefer printing because it is neater.

Writing is a major source of frustration for those with attention disorders. The following statement made by a third grade boy, says it all: "Mrs. Smith is really mad at me this week. We've been learning cursive, and she says I'm just not getting it right. Today we worked on *e's* and mine looked awful. I really hate cursive. Why can't I just print?"

Another major difficulty for ADHD/ADD children is work rate. Impulsive, overactive children rush through their work without regard for neatness or accuracy. They usually finish assignments and tests first but often must do them over or make failing grades.

More underactive ADD children and adolescents often have a very slow work rate. Their assignments and tests are usually neat, but the laboriousness of the task becomes a major obstacle. These are children who rarely complete their classwork and often spend hours on homework. By fourth grade the volume of work has usually increased to the point that their rate has become a major source of frustration and failure for both the child, his parents and the teacher. Those with slow work rates often cannot speed up and become anxious and panicked when pressed to do so.

A third style is the child who alternates between a fast and slow work rate depending upon the instructions. "Please finish your work!" results in fast, inaccurate and messy work. When neatness is emphasized the child slows down, often to a snail's pace. He may have no middle ground. Both teachers and parents must often decide whether they want quantity or quality. Many children with attention disorders simply cannot accomplish both simultaneously. Work rate is an extremely important issue for both ADHD and ADD children and adolescents but is one of which both parents and teachers often have little awareness or understanding.

♦ *Learning Style Preference*

To maximize a child's potential for learning in the classroom it is essential to understand the brain and how it functions. Scientific research has described the brain as being composed of three sections which some writers have termed the *Doing Brain*, the *Feeling Brain* and the *Thinking Brain* for simplicity (Clark and Clark, 1989). The Doing Brain regulates the basic functions of the body such as breathing and blood pressure. The Feeling Brain is where emotions are found and is only seen in higher mammals. All information must pass through the Feeling Brain first before progressing on to the Thinking Brain. This explains why a child's learning is enhanced when he feels comfortable at school and likes his teachers and classmates. It also means that those learning experiences which have strong emotions attached will be remembered for a much longer time than those which are exclusively cognitive. Positive emotional experiences in the classroom promote learning; negative ones produce aversion to the academic experience.

The Thinking Brain is divided into hemispheres, often referred to as the *right* and *left* brains. The brain of an infant functions as a whole. During childhood the two hemispheres grow and increasing specialization takes place. By age four or five, most children have established a preference and operate more comfortably out of either the right or left side of their brains.

Yes, we have a community outreach program, but not for right-brain people.

While these divisions are somewhat arbitrary and all people use both sides of their brains, in general those whom we describe as *left-brain* tend to be more analytical, explicit, concrete and sequential. They have good verbal skills and are articulate and goal-oriented. They may not necessarily talk more, however. People we describe as *intellectual* or *thinkers* are talking inside their heads. These children often enjoy school because most schools are more left-brain in their approach to teaching, especially after first or second grade.

Right-brain people are more intuitive, spontaneous, visual, playful, artistic, creative, nonverbal, emotional and diffuse. They tend to be imaginative, fantasy-oriented, and more random in their thinking processes. Solutions to problems appear, as if by magic, to right-brain people while they are in the shower or riding in a car.

It is possible for either a right- or left-brain child or adolescent to also have an attention problem. School is frequently more difficult, however, for right-brain ADHD/ADD children as they tend to experience lack of focus and disorganization from both causes.

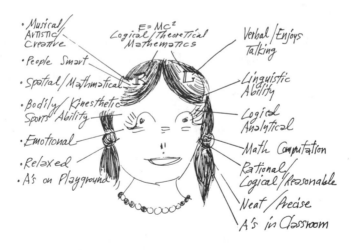

Research in the field of brain specialization has shown that brain dominance affects a child's approach to all areas of learning. Based on this new understanding of the brain, it is generally accepted among educators that children have three learning styles: kinesthetic/tactile, auditory and visual. *Kinesthetic* learners learn by doing. They need to feel the information and use their entire bodies as much as possible in the learning process. The good athlete is the best example of the kinesthetic learner. Children and adolescents who prefer this modality often have difficulty learning information presented visually and especially auditorially. They often intuitively say, "Just *show* me how to do it." The kinesthetic learner is often described as *good with his hands.*

Visual learners learn best by seeing and by vivid emotional experiences. They often remember information in colors and learn best when school work is color-coded on flash cards or highlighted in their books. *Auditory learners* remember best what they read and hear. They usually perform best with the academic curricula currently utilized by most American schools.

Understanding your child's learning style can provide valuable information for both you and him. Once your child's preference is determined, learning strategies can be developed to build on his strengths and help him compensate for any weaknesses. It can also be extremely helpful for a teacher to understand her own learning style preference since differences in style can dramatically affect how a child and a teacher relate.   Most children love the spontaneity and vivaciousness of an extroverted right-brain teacher. Often she can best tolerate and understand the antics of the ADHD child.

On the other hand, the structure and organization of the more left-brain teacher are usually necessary to keep the ADHD/ADD child focused and successful.   Whole-brain teachers who have organized, predictable classrooms, but are also emotionally warm and even somewhat charismatic, provide the best of both worlds.

They can be especially good with ADHD/ADD students.

♦ *Language and Reading Disorders in Preschoolers*

Recent research has revealed a strong connection between early oral language skills and later reading ability. It has also been shown that attention significantly affects language development and that language, memory and attention dramatically affect reading ability. One study found attention to be one of the highest predictors of subsequent reading ability (Butler, 1988).

Young children with attention disorders do not pay attention to the words that they hear and thus do not lock language into their long-term memory. This, among other things, may result in language-based learning disorders later on. Young children with attention disorders, especially ADHD, also have great difficulty organizing their thoughts, so much so that what they say may sound like gibberish. Or they may perseverate and say the same thing over and over, unable to progress further with their thought process.

To prevent later difficulties with reading it is important to identify attention problems in young preschool children and begin appropriate treatment. This usually includes management of diet and allergies, training in listening skills, behavior management

---

The direction in which education starts a man will determine his future life.——Plato (428-348 B.C.)

programs, specific speech and language therapy, and increased attention to language development. The importance of attention for language and reading has resulted in reconsideration of the use of medication for preschool children who have a co-occurring attention disorder and language delay/disability.

♦ *Legal Issues*

Since social and educational awareness and understanding of attention disorders are relatively new, there are currently no federal laws that directly address the ADHD and ADD child. Two laws, however, indirectly address the needs of children with attention disorders.

Public Law 94-142 guarantees special education services to those children and adolescents with learning disabilities and other health impairments (OHI) who *qualify*. Different states have adopted somewhat different qualifying criteria but most require, for LD assistance, a discrepancy between ability, as measured by an I.Q. or ability test, and academic achievement of approximately two grade levels or a standard score difference of 20 points. Only about 20 percent of students with ADHD/ADD who are referred will qualify for services as learning disabled. However, ADHD/ADD are considered eligible under OHI with proper diagnosis. While P.L. 94-142 was designed to meet the needs of students with learning disabilities, and has previously not been well suited to assist students with attention disorders, the situation is currently being reviewed by the Department of Education and new guidelines for the schools are expected soon.

Section 504 of the Rehabilitation Act of 1973 (P.L. 93-112) also provides assistance. It states that no person with a handicap (including a *hidden handicap)* can be excluded from or denied benefits of any program receiving federal financial assistance. Section 504 has recently been tested as it applies to ADHD and ADD children. Parents in almost every state who have voiced complaints have won special education assistance or appropriate classroom modifications and accommodations. To learn the most recent status of the laws affecting children with attention disorders you may wish to contact the U.S. Department of Education, Office of Civil Rights, Washington, D.C. 20202.

◆ INVESTIGATING EDUCATIONAL OPTIONS ◆

If your ADHD or ADD child has special needs beyond those the public school setting is able to accommodate, you may wish to consider the alternative of a private school. Many parents have found that the smaller classes and individual attention offered by private schools are of great benefit to their child. Visiting those schools in your community and observing their classes and facilities will acquaint you with their strengths and weaknesses and enable you to decide which setting offers the best fit for your child.

Another alternative being considered by growing numbers of parents is home schooling. For some ADHD/ADD children this is a workable alternative. Coordinating your instruction with your local school district will ensure that your child receives the required number of instruction hours and the appropriate courses to enable him to progress academically. You will need to contact either your state or county board of education to determine which group oversees homeschooling in your state. Of course, it will be necessary for you to schedule appropriate afternoon and week-end activities with other children to help your child maintain his socialization skills. Home schooling associations can be found in many communities. Information on the one closest to you can be obtained by contacting your state or county board of education.

◆ SUMMARY ◆

The educational experience consumes a great portion of a child's life from age four through college and is often a key source of the child's successes and failures in life. There are many educational issues which must be addressed as well. Parents are urged to consider these needs as one of the ADHD/ADD child's highest priorities and to give them the thoughtful and energetic attention they deserve.

The growth of the human mind is still high adventure, in many ways the highest adventure on earth.——Norman Cousins

There are no extraordinary people...only ordinary people who do extraordinary things with what they've been given.

—K. Bradford Brown

Psychological Interventions

Psychological interventions are equal in importance to medical and educational treatments if optimum benefit is to be achieved for both the child and his family. It is these interventions which enable the child to overcome the behavioral and emotional manifestations of the attention disorder and the family to understand and unite adequately to deal effectively with it.

The psychological therapies most commonly utilized with ADHD/ADD children and adolescents include:

- Parent education and training
- Family counseling
- Behavior modification
- Cognitive therapy
- Social skills training
- Individual psychotherapy

◆ PARENT EDUCATION AND TRAINING ◆

Attention deficit disorders can have profoundly negative effects on the family. As discussed in Chapter 2, this is especially true if the child is hyperactive. Those whose children have ADD without the hyperactivity are perhaps not as exhausted, frustrated and angry as the parents of the ADHD child, but they, too, are bewildered and exasperated much of the time.

We sometimes ask parent audiences, "How many of you would have had children if you had known then what you know now?" In audiences with non-ADHD/ADD children, often fewer than half the parents' hands are raised, despite the fact that they truly love their children. Those with ADHD or ADD children are even more overwhelmed by the demands and responsibilities of parenting. Few of these parents raise their hands. Guilt and pain are evident as they examine their feelings.

Parent education is essential to understanding what both the child and his family are experiencing. Though still intense, once understood, the problems are more comprehensible for all. With education, training, guidance and support, most *can* learn to cope effectively. Thus, parent education is the first and perhaps the most critical component of a successful intervention plan.

◆ FAMILY COUNSELING ◆

Family counseling is also an essential adjunctive therapy in the treatment of the ADHD/ADD child, especially for the family of a child or an adolescent with a long-standing, undiagnosed attention disorder.

Because of their behavior, their lack of success, their seeming indifference, and their imperviousness to discipline, ADHD/ADD children and adolescents tend, over the years, to generate much psychological tension between themselves, their parents and their siblings. They often have disruptive and divisive effects on the parents' relationship as well. Each parent, in his or her frustration, may hold the spouse in some way responsible for their mutual failure in childrearing. Many a marriage has ended in divorce because of the constant stress created by the ADHD/ADD child. Even when the child is on medication, the benefits are generally worn off by the time the child reaches home. If medicine is not taken in the afternoon and on weekends, disruptive and inappropriate behavior may continue unabated—and family problems will as well. The *dysfunctional family*, about which much is written in the current psychological literature, is often created by the ADHD/ADD child and not vice-versa, as it may appear to the naive observer. However, with knowledge and skills, the family can become a primary source of strength for all of its members.

♦ *Mothers of ADHD/ADD Children and Adolescents*

In general, a mother spends more time with the child, even if she works outside the home, than the father. She is usually the one who deals with the unpleasant interactions the most—limit-setting, discipline, enforcing rules, and punishment. It is she who is likely to feel extremely ineffective when the child does not seem to learn. Hours and hours of homework at the kitchen table leave everyone frustrated and unfulfilled.

Mothers often grow to resent the child and then feel guilty for doing so. They frequently give in to the child's unreasonable and often destructive behavior out of exhaustion and defeat. They may come to resent the father who may be unavailable to help on the one hand or who may take an overly permissive or harsh approach to discipline on the other.

♦ *Fathers*

Fathers of ADHD/ADD children often handle their frustrations with the child by withdrawing or blaming the mother:

"If you would discipline that child, he wouldn't cause so many problems. Why can't you make him mind?"

Mothers defensively respond:

"Well, if you were ever home you could help. And, for the record, he gets away with a lot with you, too. However, it's okay for you to give in to him . . . but not me. You're just not being fair."

Fathers often become intensely absorbed in their work, working late and on weekends as well. They may avoid the responsibility of discipline, even when with their child, not wanting to ruin the little time they have to spend together. Often the child is very much like the father. He may, therefore, not see his offspring's behavior as a serious problem. Since children with attention disorders, especially ADHD children, are usually better with their fathers and in novel situations, the father may truly not understand and may believe his wife is the cause of his child's negative behavior because she lacks the ability to control him. Instead of offering help, he may criticize her handling of the child; or he may be angry because so much of her time and energy are invested in the child and not in him. Most fathers, if they are honest with themselves, blame their wives' *inadequate discipline* for much of the problem and secretly resent the drain the child is on the family.

One of the tragedies in the ADHD/ADD child's family situation is the parents' arguments and the divisiveness that his behaviors create. He feels responsible for his parents' difficulties, for the turmoil and stress, and for the conflicts that occur. Family counseling is necessary for understanding one's emotional response to the disorder; for understanding the family's dynamics and how the child's difficulties accentuate existing problems; for learning how to express one's feelings effectively and appropriately; and for working through the many years of inevitable tension and conflict. This process is essential for the family if they are concerned with everyone's ultimate well-being.

One parent frequently has ADHD or ADD as well. Often this is the father, since it seems to be a disorder that affects males more than females. Home life, in fact, is smoother if the father, not the mother, has an attention disorder. When the mother has ADD, she experiences much stress trying to organize and manage the very complex workings of the family. Family counseling may include treating the ADHD/ADD parent as well.

♦ Siblings

The siblings of ADHD/ADD children also suffer. Many, especially younger siblings, become quiet and overly compliant; they withdraw to avoid the horrendous conflict they observe on a daily basis. Other siblings resent the ADHD child because of the time and attention he receives for being *bad*. Still others copy the ADHD child's behavior, leaving the family with two, not one, uncontrollable children.

Parent training in behavioral methods, is also essential to bring order, unity and common purpose to the household. We find that when parents understand the problem and have effective strategies with which to deal with the child, they cohese again quickly and can work together on the real problem, that is, the behavioral and attentional difficulties of the child. As one mother stated, "It is such a relief to have a name for it. I've spent six years feeling like an inept parent. Even though my husband loves me and our relationship is still good, I know he has secretly blamed me. We are both grateful to know what the problem is and have ways we can now help our two ADD children, our other children, and ourselves."

In seeking family counseling, parents must find a psychiatrist, psychologist, social worker or counselor thoroughly familiar with ADHD/ADD, family systems, and behavior management strategies. While psychotherapy is an extremely beneficial treatment for many psychological disorders and conflicts, research data have shown it to be of little benefit as a primary treatment of the ADHD or ADD child. Play therapy and individual counseling are also notably

---

Experience is a name everyone gives to their mistakes.——Oscar Wilde

unsuccessful with this child without other treatment interventions in place as well.

◆ BEHAVIOR MODIFICATION ◆

Behavior management techniques have been effectively used in child-rearing for the past twenty years. After medication, behavior modification is perhaps the single most effective program utilized for those with both ADHD and ADD.

The goal of most parents is to teach their children the behavior, values, goals and interpersonal skills which seem worthy to them, and to discourage those of which they do not approve. They do so by reinforcing those things they desire through positive reinforcement and incentives, and discouraging those things not wanted in their children through lack of attention, negative reinforcement or punishment. Most parents intuitively follow behavioral principles when they are successful. Those who are not successful often are using behavioral principles as well; however, they are inadvertently reinforcing the wrong things—that is, behaviors and attributes they do not want in their children.

Children with attention disorders, especially hyperactive children, do not respond as readily to the positive and negative reinforcers effective with most non-attention-disordered children. Physical punishment is especially problematic and typically only makes their behavior worse. Almost every parent we see says, "I've tried every discipline and nothing works." Systematic intervention with behavioral methods under the supervision of a trained professional is usually helpful in alleviating many of the ADHD/ADD child's inappropriate and unwanted behaviors and in eliciting positive ones.

Professionals utilizing behavior management approaches have as their goal to teach parents how to selectively reinforce in their children impulse control, self-discipline, organizational skills, and conformity to parental, school and societal expectations through the use of both positive reinforcement for approved behavior and negative consequences for undesirable ones.

Behavior follows certain principles that must be understood if one is to successfully mold the character, personality and behaviors of children and adolescents with attention disorders. These are discussed at length in Chapter 11, *Using Discipline Effectively.* Discipline is possible only when one has a good understanding of the universal principles of behavior, and especially how those principles are affected by attention disorders.

◆ *Practical Behavior Management Programs*

Two behavioral programs utilized successfully in our practice are the *Thinking Room* for negative behavior, and the *Chip* or Point Reinforcement System for positive accomplishments and behaviors. These are discussed in Chapter 11, and also in Chapter 12, *Teaching Responsibility.*

To begin thinking in behavioral terms and to understand how important it is for you to recognize and reinforce the correct responses in your child, and to ignore or negatively reinforce incorrect ones, you are encouraged to read *Parents Are Teachers* by Dr. Wesley Becker. This simple but effective book highlights, in a straightforward, helpful manner, the everyday mistakes that parents make.

◆ *Developing Organization and Planning*
   Abilities For Home Responsibilities

Another area effectively addressed by behavior modification programs is that of helping parents establish the structure which will help their ADHD/ADD children and adolescents establish routines and develop organizational skills.

The attention network in the brain, especially in the motor and frontal cortex and central brain structures, is responsible for organization, planning, judgment, and generally "*keeping one's act together.*" Since these are deficient in most children and adolescents with attention disorders, those with ADHD and ADD are notably disorganized, forgetful, and unable to plan ahead and decide upon priorities. Establishing structure, routine and organization are essential, for only in this way do they internalize the structure they will need for future success. ADHD/ADD

Anyone can hold the helm when the sea is calm.——Publilius Syrus (First century B.C.)

children and adolescents must be taught organization and self-discipline.

In our work, one of the first things we teach parents to do is to establish the structure, routines and responsibilities expected of a child. Structured programs of responsibility, planning, time management and accountability are helpful for every child. They are critical for the ADHD/ADD child or adolescent and his family, for these skills do not come as easily as for those with very alert attention systems. They also provide tremendous security for the child, as well as a sense of being in control and accomplishing his goals.

◆ *Organizing the ADHD/ADD*
Child/Adolescent for School

Organization and self-discipline are essential ingredients of success at school, as well as at home, for they are the cornerstones of efficiency and productivity. Organizing the ADHD/ADD child and adolescent for school are addressed in Chapter 13, *Handling the Homework Hurdle*. A structure for dealing with the many and complex demands of school is an important part of any behavioral program.

◆ *Summary of Behavior Modification Approaches*

The importance of effective behavior management strategies cannot be overstated. Utilizing these methods, it is possible to facilitate the development of neuronal pathways for behaviors which will become good habits with sufficient practice. Once daily activities are habitual patterns of response, and with the mechanisms of order firmly in place in one's mind, the ADHD/ADD child or adolescent is free to expend his intellectual, emotional and creative resources on developing his potential rather than trying to get through the day. This is a goal worthy of every parent's efforts, for these are the abilities that will serve their children well, both presently and throughout life.

Reasoning with a child is fine, if you can reach the child's reason without destroying your own.——John Mason Brown

◆ COGNITIVE THERAPY ◆

Noncompliance was discussed in Chapter 2 as a major reason why parents seek professional assistance for their ADHD/ADD children. Not minding their parents and disregarding socially accepted behavioral expectations create major family and school stresses. Their children's poor self-control and inadequate problem-solving skills are also of great concern. Many of these difficulties are believed to be a function of language deficits and problems with *rule-governed behavior*.

Rule-governed behavior, according to Dr. Russell Barkley, requires: (1) language; (2) neurological processes for acquiring language, generating language and converting linguistic stimuli into motor behavior; and (3) the training of the child in the rules of his community, in self-control and in problem-solving (Barkley, 1981).

Dr. Barkley, Dr. Jane Healy and other researchers believe that the mediation of behavior by language is crucial in the development of higher-level functioning and behavior. Current research reveals that the brain is not fully matured until late adolescence. At this time, the frontal lobes enlarge and connect with the reticular formation which directs arousal and alertness. This circuit passes through a part of the limbic system, forming a loop which works as a gating system to select and direct attention.

One of the most important functions of the prefrontal cortex is that of being an inhibitor of excitement.   Once the entire feedback system is in place, adolescents have an ongoing means of checking their behavior.   It helps them with organization and planning—with remembering what they are supposed to be doing and how. By contrast, those with poor feedback systems do not seem to notice when they have made a mistake; they may be disorganized and forgetful; they may get distracted while doing a job at home; or they may be unable to concentrate in school (Healy, 1987).

Language is very important in the development of the frontal lobes—especially *inner language* or mental dialogue with oneself. Children who talk through a problem mentally before acting do better in school and gain higher-level thinking skills sooner than those who do not.   Parents serve as powerful models for such thoughtful behavior. Children copy the problem-solving strategies they see their parents employing.

This growth of the brain in adolescence and the completion of the feedback loops which make up the attention system may be one explanation why an estimated one-third to one-half of ADHD/ADD children outgrow their symptoms by the end of adolescence. Once the feedback loop is in place, the prefrontal cortex with its role in judgment, planning and inhibition takes over and a mature young adult emerges.

The goal of cognitive therapy is to help children and adolescents utilize language for problem-solving rather than impulsively responding to various stimuli. Internalizing the rules for behavior, learning self-control and using mental dialogue for problem-solving are the foundations for later emotional maturity, good judgment and appropriate responding.

Those who have worked with hyperactive and ADD pre-schoolers especially are aware of the many auditory processing, auditory memory and language deficits which exist. Stimulant medication improves attention. Improved language usually follows soon afterward and, in turn, assists in improving attention and impulse control. Children who understand and who can verbalize their thoughts and needs are usually much less active than those who cannot but desire to do so and are frustrated by their inability to communicate and to solve problems. Children consciously taught alternative behaviors to their inappropriate responses do much better than those who are only punished or negatively reinforced.

It is important that cognitive approaches which utilize social problem-solving skills mediated through language be included in the treatment of ADHD/ADD. Cognitive therapy has experienced much success in the treatment of many disorders. It has been found an effective adjunctive therapy for ADHD and ADD as well.

Parents are combining the best of both approaches when they utilize behavior management strategies and combine them with verbal understanding of the process. The goals of both positive and negative reinforcements and alternative, cognitively-determined new approaches to problematic situations are also stressed. Very successful, this approach has now been named *Cognitive Behavior Modification (CBM)*. Crucial to the success of Cognitive Behavior Modification is parents' willingness to spend time discussing behaviors and solutions with their ADHD/ADD children in a positive emotional climate of helpfulness, teaching and collaborative problem solving. Like all of us, those with attention disorders appreciate the respect, trust and regard this approach conveys.

◆ SOCIAL SKILLS TRAINING ◆

Perhaps the most heartrending experience parents face is the social isolation and rejection their ADHD/ADD children experience. Overactive ADHD children are recognized immediately by their peers and often are perceived negatively within two hours of interaction . . . or even two minutes. Their aggressiveness, bossiness and boastfulness, coupled with off-task, disruptive, impulsive and immature responding, make them poor candidates for positive social interactions. Those with undifferentiated ADD are usually not actively rejected, but their spaciness, disorganization, sluggishness and poor performance often result in their being passed over by peers in the friendship-selection process as well.

Since one of the best predictors of positive outcome in adulthood is peer relations in childhood, social competence and the development of specific social skills to improve social competence are essential for both the short- and long-term adjustment of ADHD

Change your thoughts and you change your world.——Norman Vincent Peale

and ADD children and adolescents. Thus, they should be an essential part of their overall treatment programs.

Social competence is defined as the effectiveness of a child/adolescent's behavior in a specific social situation. Social flexibility, i.e., the ability to adapt one's behavior to the changing demands of different social situations is one example of social competence. Children with attention disorders can interact quite well in one social situation, that is, one-on-one with an interested adult, but they have great difficulty in other social situations such as the classroom where their need for constant teacher and peer attention can create major problems.

Social skills, on the other hand, are specific strategies used in social situations which promote positive social goals. Social skills are necessary precursors to social competence.

Social Skills Training Programs typically identify the skills a child or an adolescent lacks and then systematically introduce these skills one at a time and teach the child how to utilize them successfully. Learning each skill is accomplished through discussion, modeling, role-play, positive reinforcement and practice. Generalization to home and to school are encouraged by involving parents and teachers in the encouragement and reinforcement process. Typical behaviors addressed include making eye contact, beginning a conversation, listening, joining a group, seeking help from others appropriately, giving a compliment, and working cooperatively.

Positive human interaction is essential to a person's sense of well-being and fulfillment. Behavior management and cognitive therapy assist the ADHD/ADD child or adolescent at the level of thinking and behavior. His emotional well-being, determined most often by his relationships with the significant others in his life, is greatly assisted by approaches which teach him to interpret social situations correctly and to respond appropriately, ensuring positive interactions.

◆ INDIVIDUAL PSYCHOTHERAPY ◆

Individual psychotherapy, often called *talking therapy*, has been notoriously unsuccessful with children and adolescents with attention disorders as a primary treatment. Until one addresses root physiologic, educational and behavioral problems, psychotherapy can at best help the child become comfortable with his failures, and at worst lull parents into a false sense that they are addressing the problem.

Psychotherapy can, however, play an important adjunctive role in the treatment of attention disorders when medical, educational, behavioral and social skills interventions are occurring simultaneously. An authority figure who believes in the child or adolescent, and who is, in turn, viewed positively by him, can often begin the healing process by helping the child understand what has happened and why, and by assuring him that he is not an inadequate or *bad* person. New ways of viewing problems and positive plans for future situations are usually also addressed. With someone the child or adolescent trusts, secret fears, anger, disappointments and hurts can be examined and put in their proper perspective. The therapist is often the one who conveys hope and sees positive possibilities which neither parent nor child may envision in their present moments of despondency.

For those psychologically damaged by years of failure, rejection, frustration, and negative feedback, the process of psychotherapy may not be one of choice, but of necessity for those children and adolescents whose potential is to be realized to the fullest.

◆ SUMMARY ◆

It is hoped that this chapter has acquainted parents with the psychological treatments for attention deficit disorders most widely utilized in the field today. Many of these interventions will be addressed in greater depth in Part III, *Your Goal As a Parent.* We believe that interventions—multiple interventions simultaneously—are critical for the long-term success of children and adolescents with attention disorders. You are encouraged to understand the psychological treatments that are available and to seek out those you believe will be of benefit to your child and to your family.

Overwhelmed by conflicting advice, most Americans have thrown in the napkin on healthy eating.
                                        —*Newsweek*, May 27, 1991

Nutrition, Food Intolerances, Allergies and Chemical Sensitivities

This feature headline of a weekly newsmagazine captures the feelings and behaviors of those in today's health-conscious climate who try to get a grip on food. Besieged by conflicting opinions from expert after expert and expected to change habits ingrained from birth, many are opting to ignore all the advice and simply eat as they always have. The role of diet, nutrition and food intolerances in attention deficit disorders is even more controversial.

In 1975 Dr. Ben Feingold wrote that certain food additives and salicylates caused hyperactivity. A year later, Dr. Lendon Smith named sugar as the culprit. Parents, distraught by their children's behavior, eagerly embraced these diets despite lack of scientific support, and Feingold Associations flourished throughout the country. Some children responded very positively to the rigorous diets imposed, and were, indeed, more manageable and enjoyable, while others experienced little benefit.

For fifteen years, behavioral research has attempted to determine the role of diet and nutrition in behavior. Current research suggests that diet is, indeed, important. Investigators examining the effect of food intolerances, for example, have found that while eliminating offending foods one at a time may not produce differences in behavior, eliminating multiple food offenders may be effective in treating some children and adolescents with attention disorders (Egger, et al., 1985; Kaplan et al., 1989). Dr. Keith Connors has also found a link between when certain foods are eaten and their effect on behavior. Sugar and carbohydrates, for example, do not appear to cause behavioral or attentional problems if eaten with protein but may when eaten alone (Conners, 1990). The role of nutrition, diet and food intolerances in behavior and attention is more complicated than at first believed and will require extensive investigation before definitive answers are available. There is, however, much information which has achieved consensus among professionals working in the field.

◆ DIET AND NUTRITION ◆

Americans have long utilized the four basic food groups as the organizing principles of their daily diets, with special emphasis on meat and dairy products. Research in cancer and heart disease, especially, have shown how faulty this configuration can be and clearly show how our eating habits are killing us. The American diet is often compared with that of the Japanese who eat mostly rice, vegetables and some fish, and who have longer lives than anyone else in the world.

There is change in the air as nutritionists, nutritional scientists, and even the U.S. Department of Agriculture, insist on restructuring the diet to emphasize the importance of fruits, vegetables and grains, and to de-emphasize meat, dairy products and animal fats. The Physician's Committee for Responsible Medicine would like to include only fruits, vegetables, grains and legumes, but others appeal for greater moderation and less drastic modifications.

Fruits and vegetables containing Vitamins C, A and E are considered essential to defend the body against attackers. Weakened immune systems are a national problem as evidenced by the alarming increase in allergies; food intolerances; ear, throat and sinus infections; and infectious diseases.

Increased insults to our children's immune systems (and our own) from both their diets and the toxins and chemicals in their environments are resulting in increased numbers of children at risk for many kinds of problems including attentional, behavioral, learning, emotional, and physical ones.

All agree that we cannot continue to abuse our bodies and those of our children without paying a painful price in the future. Parents of children with attention disorders have an even greater responsibility not to add dietary insult to ADD injury. Instead, they must give their children the best possible health advantage to overcome the disorders.

◆ FOOD INTOLERANCE/SENSITIVITY ◆

There is little question that many people are intolerant of or sensitive to certain foods, food additives and chemicals.[8] According to the New England Journal of Medicine, approximately 7.5% of all

---

[8]Reactions of the body to foods and chemicals which show no evidence of involvement with the immune system are not considered allergies by allergists and immunologists. More suitable names for those reactions which cause physical or behavioral changes, but do not affect the immune system, and ones generally accepted by the medical community, are food/chemical "sensitivity" or "intolerance."

children have adverse reactions to cow's milk (Gern, 1991). Some are intolerant because they lack the digestive enzyme for lactose, the sugar in milk, while others are allergic to the milk protein. While most food reactions are mild, some children are so sensitive that even small amounts can cause serious reactions.   Many nutritionists believe cow's milk should be ingested only by cows, and they urge people to obtain the nutrients found in milk from other sources.

Two other common food intolerances are corn and wheat. Milk, corn (usually corn syrup) and wheat are found in almost all processed food and beverages. Prolonged colic, respiratory disorders, formula changes and ear infections are more characteristic of ADHD/ADD children than not.   The infant who is intolerant of lactose or allergic to milk protein is much better when switched to a soy formula.   However, if the problem is corn, the change may not be helpful since soy formulas are usually sweetened with corn syrup.   Children who have corn intolerance often find relief only after cow's milk is introduced or milk is eliminated altogether.

Wheat intolerance frequently causes both lethargy and hyperactivity, while chronic wheat problems can result in potentially life-threatening Celiac Disease.

Another area of frequent concern is that of *inactive* ingredients in medicines, especially antibiotics.   Dr. Kumar and his associates identified sweeteners, flavorings and dyes in 91 antimicrobial preparations commonly used in children, and the adverse effects they can cause (Kumar, et al., 1991).   Many children thought to be allergic to the drugs, for example, penicillin, were actually allergic to, or intolerant of, the inactive ingredient in the medicinal preparations.   Many parents frequently report a dramatic increase in hyperactivity or behavioral problems following the administration of medicine containing dyes, sweeteners or flavorings. While *strawberry good-good*, a three-year-old's name for his antibiotic, may taste good, the after-effects for an intolerant child are rarely positive.

Part of the secret of success in life is to eat what you like and let the food fight it out inside.——Mark Twain

Many drug companies and physicians are conscious of the problems inactive ingredients can cause in some children and medicines without such additives are increasingly available.

The most common food allergies and intolerances of Americans include:

- Milk, especially cow's milk
- Grains, particularly wheat
- Corn and corn syrup
- Eggs
- Nuts
- Peanuts, which are legumes
- Fish, especially shellfish
- Meat protein, particularly beef and pork
- Yeast
- Citrus fruits
- Strawberries
- Additives including MSG, sulfites, tartrazine and flavorings, among others
- Food dyes, especially red and yellow
- Caffeine
- Chocolate (tyramine)

When food intolerances are suspected in a child, or oneself, the best plan of action is often self-testing, utilizing an elimination and challenge diet. A very simplified one for children is offered in

Tracking Down Hidden Food Allergy, by William Crook.

A comprehensive but easily understood overview of allergies, sensitivity and immunology is offered by J. Joneja, Ph.D., immunologist with the University of Victoria, British Columbia, and L. Bielory, M.D., Director of the Division of Allergy and Immunology at UMDNJ-New Jersey School of Medicine, in *Understanding Allergy, Sensitivity & Immunity: A Comprehensive Guide.*[9] They offer a 3-step plan for self-testing for food sensitivities:

Step 1: Selection of Suspects

a) List symptoms
b) Keep an exposure diary
c) Analyze the exposure diary
d) List suspects

Step 2: Elimination of Suspects

a) Through fasting, or
b) Eating the essential amino acids and minerals in pure form, or
c) Eliminating the suspects only, or
d) Eating an elimination diet that consists of only lamb, carrots, parsnips, squash, lettuce, pears, pear juice, canola oil, purified water, sea salt, agar-agar and tapioca for one to two weeks.

Step 3: Challenge

The challenge procedure involves reintroducing foods which are suspect one at a time and observing the response. Several hours between the introduction of each food is required. Many people introduce only one each day. Initially, small amounts are eaten but increased amounts are eaten if no reaction occurs.

---

[9]Copyright © 1990, by Rutgers, The State University.

This step in the plan may require direct medical supervision by your physician if severe allergies or intolerances are suspected. A severe sensitivity, intolerance or allergy to a food or food additive restored to the diet can potentially cause an extreme reaction requiring emergency care. Allergic symptoms can be worse during the challenge phase than normally. Therefore, close monitoring is necessary to avoid potential problems.

Parents who suspect allergies or food intolerances in their children should consult a physician knowledgeable and interested in this area. Since ADHD and ADD are life-long disorders for many, it is important to eliminate as many root causes as possible.

♦ ALLERGIES ♦

It has long been observed that children with attention disorders and hyperactivity seem to have more allergies than non-attention disordered children. Symptoms suggestive of allergies include:

- Dark circles under the eyes
- Chronic ear, sinus, and respiratory infections
- Constant running nose recognized by *the allergic salute,* or a crease at the end of the child's nose, or a stuffy nose
- Fatigue/lack of energy
- Congestion
- Pallor
- Hyperactivity
- Mood swings
- Irritability
- Bedwetting past age six
- Stomachaches
- Headaches

Dr. William Crook, in *Help for the Hyperactive Child,* suggests that nutritional, biologic, allergic, environmental and toxic factors play important roles in causing attention disorders, hyperactivity and associated learning and behavioral problems. These factors include:

1) Improper nutrition
2) Food allergies and sensitivities
3) Environmental toxins, and
4) Repeated antibiotics leading to yeast overgrowth

♦ CHEMICAL SENSITIVITIES ♦

When one begins to recognize the many potential hazards of daily living, it can feel overwhelming. It is, in fact, next to impossible to eliminate all sources of potential harm.

While the source of toxins in food may be minute organisms (for example, toxins produced by algae and fungi), or an indirect residue of poisonous plant materials (for example, cows eating toxic plants), chemical toxins are among the most frightening. The industrial pollution of the rivers and lakes, especially with compounds containing heavy metals such as lead, cadmium, cobalt, mercury, arsenic and iron, among others, may poison both our drinking water and the fish we eat. Acidic foods and beverages stored in containers made of copper or tin or sealed with lead solder are another source of heavy metal poisoning.

While the great majority of those with ADHD/ADD will require medical, behavioral, educational and psychological intervention, it is important that we not overlook the environment in which we live and the food we eat as equally important in our search for solutions. Drs. Joneja and Bielory present a medically sound, compelling case for examining the role of allergies, food intolerances and chemicals and inhalant sensitivities in the illnesses and behavioral disorders of children, adolescents and adults. They state:

> Further research may one day vindicate the allergy sufferers who know that the neurological, emotional and behavioral changes that accompany many allergic reactions are very real, even though they are now

considered by many medical practitioners to be merely anecdotal and subjective. (p. 269)

♦ SUMMARY ♦

Many times, simple, healthy prevention and intervention are far more effective than the more costly and time-intensive treatments required when the basics are ignored. As Americans become ever more mindful of the relationship between food and behavior, there is promise that the attention disorder symptoms resulting from dietary and environmental causes can be eliminated. *We are what we eat* has never been more true than today. The perils of our climate, i.e., the chemicals we eat, breathe and drink, have, likewise, never been as great. If we are truly concerned about our children, we must expend some of our energy ensuring that their world is a healthy place, and that what their bodies ingest and absorb promotes wholeness, not psychological and physical damage. Children's developing brains and bodies are far more vulnerable to the hazards of our world than are those of adults. Parents have an obligation to protect them by making their world—whether your kitchen or the environment at large—a healthier place.

YOUR GOAL
AS A PARENT

Life is a one way street and you never have a chance to travel back over it. To be what we are, and to become what we are capable of becoming, is the only end of life.

—Robert Louis Stevenson

Building Your Child's Self Esteem

Raising a child with a healthy sense of self-esteem is never easy. Nevertheless, this goal is one of our most important as parents. It is self-esteem that ultimately determines whether a child does indeed fulfill his true potential.

Raising an ADHD or ADD child with a strong sense of self-worth is even more challenging. Although unintentionally, the world is rarely kind to the child with an attention disorder. Rather, it will constantly be reacting negatively to either his antics or his lack of performance, leaving him feeling worthless, inadequate and unlovable, unless you intervene. The greatest gift that any child can receive is to be loved unconditionally, not only for all his genuinely admirable qualities, but for his faults and short-comings as well. Only with this sense of genuine acceptance at home will he be able to face the world with a positive, confident attitude.

The first step in this process is the most difficult. It requires acceptance, complete acceptance, of the ADHD/ADD child as he is.

While unconditional acceptance may sound simple, it is not. Instead, it is probably the most challenging of all the demands placed upon parents of ADHD and ADD children.

Most of us secretly wish that our child could be different, perhaps even perfect. Isn't that truly what we envisioned when we planned our *bundle of joy*? We at least wish our ADHD or ADD child could be somewhat different. We know that life would be much easier for him, and for us, if he could change just a little. While we may know intellectually that he cannot, and we understand all the physiological reasons why, it is not always easy to come to terms with this reality. The gap between our intellectual and emotional acceptance causes many troublesome negative feelings which include guilt, anger, helplessness, denial and despair. The following is a list of adjectives compiled by a group of ADHD and ADD mothers describing how they felt about their situations:

Depressed	Hopeless	Angry
Frustrated	Trapped	Overwhelmed
Overprotective	Discouraged	Embarrassed
Tired	Intimidated	Ashamed
Judged	Controlled	Powerless

Unfortunately, without assistance, these feelings often prevail and are communicated to children as disapproval of them. The children, in turn, internalize and act out the negative feelings of their parents, actions which only serve to reinforce the children's emotional difficulties. If not interrupted, this vicious cycle continues and grows in intensity.

No matter how much we may wish to change our child's nature, even for his own benefit, we simply cannot. We can only help him realize his full potential by creating an environment which nurtures his strengths and accepts his weaknesses. Instilling a sense of worth in a child begins with our own appreciation of him. He cannot perceive himself as worthy until his parents do. As Zig Ziglar, author of *Raising Positive Kids in a Negative World*, states, "Until and unless we recognize the ability and worth of our children, we're not going to be as excited about helping them develop and realize their potential."

But, how is this accomplished? What can parents do to help their ADHD/ADD children feel good about themselves?

◆ WAYS TO PROMOTE SELF-ESTEEM ◆

◆ *Encouragement is the Key*

The key to developing self-esteem in children is encouragement. When we encourage children to do their best in all situations, it demonstrates to them that we believe they are capable of succeeding. ADHD/ADD children tend to be very aware of their shortcomings and are frequently quite hard on themselves. Most parents become distressed when their child says, "I'm no good at this," or "I guess nobody likes me." A gentle, "I know you can do it," or, "We have confidence in you, son," or, "Remember who you are, not what you are *not*," can go a long way toward encouraging a child to persevere.

Any child lucky enough to have even one person who believes in him can generally make it. Einstein, for example, had a very difficult time in school, but he succeeded due largely to his parents' unwavering confidence, even when he wasn't talking at four or

I can live for two months on a good compliment.——Mark Twain

reading at seven. If the ADHD or ADD child's parents believe in him, he is more likely to believe in himself. It is, in fact, his internalized image of what he believes his parents think of him that becomes what he thinks of himself. What parents say to him is crucial to his developing self-concept. They have the power to make or break their child.

Encouragement does not always mean praise. When it is deserved and genuine, praise is extremely important. Children know instinctively when they have not done well, and unearned compliments do not enhance their sense of self-worth. Expecting the best from children, however, motivates them to expect the best from themselves.

The principles of reinforcement which will be discussed in Chapter 11, clearly illustrate the benefits of encouragement and incentive and the negative impact of criticism and punishment. Parents must be ever mindful that their actions are accomplishing what they truly desire.

Encouraging a child in the early years may have special benefit when he becomes a teenager. Psychological studies suggest that when children reach adolescence the only enduring power parents have is their ability to influence.   If teenagers have continually seen their parents as supportive and encouraging, they are much more likely to listen to them during these critical years. Parents can then use their influence to love their children into becoming the positive, healthy adults that they want them to be.

◆ *Set Realistic Goals*

Often it is necessary to lower our own expectations for our child to help him in setting realistic goals for himself. Steve may not become captain of the football team, but he may be the most enthusiastic and devoted team manager they ever had. Erica may not be the star of the school play, but her ability to run the technical crew may be superb. If a child sets goals which fit his abilities and interests and are attainable, he will have a sense of accomplishment and success.

Such constraint may be especially necessary for short-term goals. A parent's hopes for the child as an adult, however, are often realistic and worth retaining. It is important not to decide too early what your child will be like later in life. Values and priorities shift. Those things which contributed to success in childhood may not be the same as those needed in adulthood. Many an ADHD or ADD child with support, guidance and structure has gone on to become a highly successful, competent and happy adult.

Constantly watching for those things that a child can do well and encouraging him is one of the most important roles a parent can play in his child's life. There is talent in almost every child. Researchers have identified six areas of talent or special ability: general intellectual ability; specific academic aptitude; creative or productive thinking; leadership ability; visual and performing arts including art, music, sculpture, etc.; and psychomotor ability such as sports (Gardner, 1983). If encouraged to pursue a special gift in one of these areas, a child may develop a lifetime focus. Success in later life is often determined more by the development of a child's talent than by his grades in school (Bloom, 1985). Ultimate success is usually the result of someone having believed in you, hard work and pursuing a dream. It is often not apparent in childhood which children are going to be successful. Frequently it is not the ones who seemed so blessed in elementary, middle or high school.

For example, Dr. Robert Jarvik, the inventor of the artificial heart, was never good in language. However, he was a whiz in

---

Remember, no one can make you feel inferior without your consent.——Eleanor Roosevelt

spatial ability. To this day he can invent extraordinary medical devices but relies upon his more verbal associates to write the technical explanations. Einstein, who had a reading disability, was a genius in math and logic. An intelligent father of a preadolescent with whom we worked described how he never performed exceptionally well in school. However, he was always *people savvy.* He understood what makes people tick and used that understanding to meet their needs and gain their confidence. Despite his *B* and *C* grades throughout school, he is currently second in command at a large brokerage firm and is making over a million dollars a year. His mother constantly remarked: "People like you and trust you. You could probably sell ice to an Eskimo."

In a five-year study of one hundred and twenty of the most talented people in their fields, Dr. Benjamin Bloom learned that *superstars,* the name he coined for them, are not born. The Olympic swimmers, world-class mathematicians, concert pianists, sculptors, tennis players and neurologists he studied all had in common parents who were alert for signs of potential in their children and encouraged them. The influence of home, especially encouragement and the work ethic, was unexpectedly found to be the strongest influence in the development of each superstar's unique talents and abilities (Bloom, 1985).

It is important to remember, however, that while encouraging a child to strive toward excellence is often desirable, if goals are set unrealistically high he may feel the need to perform perfectly. As Dr. David Stoop cautions in *Living With A Perfectionist,*

> Throughout American history, children have been thought of as seeds to be cultivated by parents, all for the purpose of some larger goal or purpose. When this goal is to fulfill some perfectionistic needs within the parents, however, the child is in trouble. Parental worship of success deprives the child of personal needs, especially the need for self-direction. The child takes on the goals of the parents, which are usually impossibly perfectionistic. In addition, the child's goals are derived from the parents' own frustrations and have nothing to do with the child's interests or abilities. But the child, as we have seen, often internalizes the goals of the parents and becomes a taskmaster. (Stoop, 1987)

The parents of true superstars, by contrast, rarely had a master plan. Instead, they instinctively provided at each stage what the child needed. They offered far more support and encouragement than direction.

♦ *Plan Extracurricular Activities*

Exposing your child to a variety of extra-curricular activities at an early age is a good way to observe those in which he is likely to experience success or failure. It is often apparent quite early which sports or activities should be encouraged and which may need to be discouraged. If your child starts noticing that she is "not dancing as gracefully as everyone else," or says, "they laugh at me every time I miss the ball," perhaps it is time to begin exploring other activities.

Once an area of strength and interest surfaces, it is important to help the child focus in on it and seek mastery in that endeavor. ADHD and ADD children tend to be easily side-tracked and may want to do it all. Constant encouragement may be necessary to help them persevere in only one or two activities so they can reach a sufficiently high level of achievement to feel successful. Otherwise, they may move quickly from one interest to another and never feel the satisfaction of developing competence in one or two areas of endeavor.

Athletics—Experience has shown that many attention-disordered children are excellent athletes. If so, they should be encouraged to gain as much mastery as possible in a sport to enhance their self-esteem. For other children who are not athletically inclined, karate is often an excellent sport. It emphasizes all the traits an ADHD or ADD child needs: discipline, self-control, thought before action, and a sense of mastery over one's body. Self-confidence can be greatly increased when a child knows he has the ability to defend himself. While parents may worry that karate will give their impulsive child a weapon, those who work with ADHD and ADD children report that this does not happen.

If an ADHD/ADD child does not experience success in his early years with team sports, it is often wise to encourage individual sports when he reaches adolescence. Many ADHD teenagers excel in running, biking or swimming, for example, where they are competing primarily against themselves. With his high energy level and desire to do things quickly, an overactive teen may enjoy practicing at his own pace to increase his skill in one of these outdoor sports. With encouragement and incentive, he may develop the discipline necessary for success. Without pressure to conform to team rules and anxiety about letting team members down, he may become more relaxed and positive about mastering an individual sport.

Scouting—Scouting is an activity that many ADHD and ADD children find especially rewarding. While sitting still at the meetings may sometimes be difficult, the goal setting, working on projects, and ability to achieve specific objectives appear to help ADHD/ADD children immensely. ADHD and ADD boys respond especially well to the structured program offered by the Boy Scouts.

Art—Many children have artistic ability which may be seen at an early age. Lessons in drawing and painting may be very relaxing for them and develop their fine-motor skills as well. If a child is not talented in art, he may still find sculpting, working in clay, or tie-dying to be creative and mind-expanding.

Those who are gifted in this area will probably be recognized early and should be encouraged to continue. One mother frames two or three of her daughter's pictures each year and places them in positions of honor around the house. While it is encouraging for the child to have his framed pictures on the walls of his own room, placing them in other rooms of your home demonstrates your pride even more. When a seven-year old's picture hangs in the living room, he truly believes that his parents value his creative endeavors.

Music—Music is an area that appeals to many ADHD and ADD children. They may be great appreciators of sounds and rhythm, even if they do not possess great ability to master an instrument. If they show interest in studying an instrument such as the piano, the discipline involved, as well as the development of hand-eye coordination, can be very helpful. Even if their progress is slow, they often take great pride in logging their own accomplishment. It is important to find music and art teachers who understand the impulsive temperament of the ADHD child, or the more methodical temperament of the ADD child, and can appreciate his unique approach to these art forms. Sergei Rachmaninoff, a world-famous composer, conductor and concert pianist, showed many characteristics of the ADHD child during his early years.

Computers—Use of the computer is another area in which many ADHD/ADD children tend to excel. They respond well to the quick pace, immediate feedback and visual stimulation of computers. Many children with attention disorders learn to type quite

---

When I was a child, my mother said to me, "If you become a soldier you'll be a general. If you become a monk you'll end up as the Pope." Instead I became a painter and wound up as Picasso.——Pablo Picasso

proficiently, making them even faster on the keyboard, both in playing games as well as working. Visual ADHD/ADD children often intuitively understand the workings of the computer and demonstrate ability to fix all manner of complicated problems with VCR's, computers, telephones and many other electronic devices. As teenagers, they may be interested in mechanics and engineering.

♦ *Accentuate the Positive*

Every child has *something* he does well. Simple statements, such as "Eric sets the table better than anyone in the family," or "Marsha has a terrific sense of humor," have a tremendous impact on children. The more they are reminded of their good qualities, the more they will tend to focus on them. One children's gift shop sells a booklet containing *Catch'em Being Good* coupons. Various coupons such as *World's sweetest brother, Best mannered child* or *Terrific worker* can be traded in for rewards. The idea is to reward the child for positive behavior when he does not even realize he is doing something desirable.

As frustrating as ADHD/ADD children may be on a day-to-day basis, it is often not easy to stop and remind ourselves that they

---

Men take only their needs into consideration—never their abilities.——Napoleon Bonaparte

possess admirable qualities such as tender-heartedness, compassion or determination. One mother has a special corner of her refrigerator where she places a list for each of her children. It says, "We are thankful for Matthew because..." and new qualities are listed every week. Another family has a nightly routine at the dinner table of each saying something positive about another family member before they begin eating. While some days it may be more difficult than others to recall your child's endearing traits, most of us can usually think of them when we put our minds to it.

◆ *Develop Pride in the Family*

Having a strong conviction that he is part of a unit greater than himself gives a child a sense of security, continuity and purpose nothing else can. When a child feels pride in his family, he feels increased pride in himself. Knowing that his family has always been there, and always will be, enables him to face the unknown with a greater sense of security. Family jokes, photographs, vacations or reunions are excellent ways to reinforce that sense of intimate togetherness.

Discipline, too, can be an opportunity to reinforce family values. Parents can emphasize that "In our family we do.....or don't do...." The child is often heard repeating such family rules to friends or to dolls when playing. These rules provide security and structure. It is important for parents to be clear and strong with their values. One five-year-old, for example, had internalized her family's emphasis on keeping one's word, as she told a friend, " I've got to 'cause in my family if we say we're gonna' do it, then we do it."

Closeness with siblings, cousins, aunts, uncles and grand-parents helps a child to know who he is and how he fits into the greater whole. Knowing that there are certain standards set by those who preceeded him may well help a child set acceptable goals for himself. This can be especially important during the teen years, when there will be temptations to try new and different roles that may be unacceptable within his family. Knowing this can often be enough to prevent a teenager from pursuing the wrong path.

ADHD/ADD children often find they have an uncle, cousin or grandparent who is of a similar temperament and perhaps also has ADHD or ADD. If that relative spends time with the child and demonstrates his understanding and caring, it can be extremely beneficial in helping the child to better understand himself. When grandparents develop a close relationship with the child, there is often the added benefit that they will volunteer to keep him while the parents have some well-needed vacation time. Family members may have trouble understanding and dealing with his attention disorder, however, unless you educate them.

In families where there is only one parent due to divorce, death, or other reasons, the bond can be equally strong. It is not necessary to have a large number of relatives to feel that one is part of a family. Even if grandparents are deceased or live a great distance away, stories and experiences of relatives can be related to give the child a sense of who he is. Children of all ages love stories, especially those about themselves or their family.

Spending time together is important not only to establish a bond as a family, but also to communicate to your child that you value him. When you show a child that you enjoy his company, he knows that you love him. Finding appropriate activities for the entire family may be difficult with an ADHD or ADD child, but the search is well worth the effort. Sports, camping, attending church or going to the movies are some of the conventional ways that many families spend time together. One family that loves music has created a family band. While mom, dad and fourteen-year-old Stacey sing, Danny, who is twelve, plays the guitar and five-year-old Jason plays the cymbals.

ADHD and ADD children especially enjoy family outings that are spontaneous and purely for fun. Children are aware when parents put the other stresses in their lives aside and devote their energies entirely to the family. Flying kites, for example, or building a snowman are ways that some families have found to relax and enjoy their children's company. Working together can also be great fun when approached positively.

◆ *Help Friendships Grow*

Many ADHD and ADD children have trouble creating and sustaining friendships. In fact, studies have shown that children who are viewed negatively by their friends are more likely to have difficulty adjusting in adulthood (Cowen et al, 1973).   It is important for children with attention disorders to realize as early as possible how their behavior affects other people. Those with high energy levels may interrupt frequently, unwittingly tear up friends' toys or generally exhibit *nuisance behavior.* Those who are more passive need to recognize that they may appear unresponsive to, or disinterested in, a family member's needs or those of a friend. Recognizing this behavior, and the consequences of it, is the first step in changing it.

Observe your child at play—Observing a child at play with neighbors or friends who come home after school is an excellent way to evaluate his social skills. If he is monopolizing, not sharing, or playing unfairly, this behavior can be discussed with him when the friend leaves. If the friend becomes angry with him, your child may be disappointed and welcome the opportunity to discuss it with you. Most ADHD and ADD children are sociable and eager to have many friends. They are frequently surprised   at their friends' reactions, however, and do not understand what they have done to upset them. In spite of painful rejection by friends, ADHD and ADD children are often not aware that their impulsive, inappropriate, and sometimes negative actions have caused the rejection. If a parent is able to help a child understand how his unpleasant behavior has caused others to feel hurt or angry, the child may begin to realize the importance of controlling his actions.

Suggesting that your child have only one friend over at a time can help prevent the overstimulation of the ADHD child which is so common in group situations. Both ADHD and ADD children often relate best in a one-to-one situation, whereas two or more playmates may increase the likelihood of competition or over-excitement for the ADHD child and withdrawal by the ADD child.

Occasional monitoring of your child and his friend can help you to spot trouble before it erupts. If you sense that they are becoming restless, suggest a change of activity or offer a snack to help alleviate the problem.

Accepting a leadership role in some of your child's social activities can sometimes help him to be accepted and to participate. If time permits, volunteer to be the Scout leader, soccer coach or room mother at school. Not only will your child feel more involved, but you will have an excellent opportunity to observe his inter-actions with others. If, on the other hand, your involvement interferes, try to gain insight and to be of assistance in other ways.

Be alert for positive friendships—Some children seem to bring out the best in each other. As in a good marriage where partners complement each other, certain friendships can provide checks and balances to the child's personality. Some friendships are not as positive. Two ADHD children attracted to each other, for example, can sometimes mean *double trouble.*

If a child is highly impulsive, it may help him to overcome this difficulty sooner if he has a good friend who reacts more slowly and thinks things through. A very withdrawn child, on the other hand, may benefit greatly from associating with an enthusiastic, vivacious child who encourages him to try new activities. Unfortunately, children with attention disorders seem to have an instinctive attraction to each other, especially those who are hyperactive. Parents can provide an important role in gently encouraging those relationships which have a positive effect on their child and avoiding the more explosive combinations.

As ADHD and ADD children enter adolescence, it may be necessary to encourage them in taking the first step in promoting friendships. Most teenagers experience some insecurity about the way they are perceived by their peers. ADHD and ADD teens are often unusually sensitive, especially if they had difficulty sustaining friendships in earlier years. Suggesting that they call a friend to play tennis, go jogging, get a pizza, or watch a video may help them to have the confidence they need to initiate and develop relationships with peers. Inviting a friend to join the family for a week-end trip or vacation provides an opportunity for your child to spend some uninterrupted time with a potential friend, without the distractions of daily routine chores or activities. When the friends of ADHD and ADD children see how interesting and fun they can be in situations other than school, or other very structured activities, it often helps them to like and feel closer to them. Being placed in environments of spontaneity and creativity often brings out the best in children with attention disorders.

It is especially important with teenagers that your preference for one friend over another not be made obvious. At this age, most children will stand firm on their ability to choose their own friends. If they realize their parents do not approve of a certain friend, they may deliberately foster the relationship. It may be helpful, however, to comment on positive qualities you observe in their friends. Telling a teenager that you like his friends means to him that you trust his judgment and have confidence in him. In this way, you may still be able to encourage those friendships that you see as constructive, while keeping open the lines of communication between you.

◆ *Encourage Love of Pets*

Pets always accept a child. No matter what the child has done, or not done, the pet is still there, eagerly awaiting his arrival home. The most delicious secrets, devious wrong-doings, or earth-shattering disappointments may be shared with a pet who listens without judging and always seems to understand. The security, companionship and affection offered by a pet teaches a child how to care for others.

Living with a cherished pet is also an excellent opportunity to teach responsibility. Most daily chores such as feeding, walking, grooming and cleaning can be handled by even young children. When something he loves depends on him for his care, a child may be more motivated to remember and follow through on assigned tasks.

As the pet becomes older, the child may even enjoy training him or entering him in shows. Some children have greatly enjoyed the unique accomplishments of their pets and have taken pride in relating these experiences to friends. Training a puppy, keeping and showing a pony, teaching a parakeet to talk, breeding Persian cats, caring for tropical fish, and raising rabbits have been unique sources of self-esteem for many a child.

♦ *Get Physical*

ADHD and ADD children, more than most, respond positively to physical contact with adults. One preschool teacher found that holding a hyperactive four-year-old in her lap during the school day was the only way to keep him calm and in control. Her closeness and reassurance enabled him to control his restless, active nature. In early years especially, ADHD and ADD children may try to show how much they like a teacher or parent by holding their hands or hugging them. One of the charming qualities of these children is that they do not learn to inhibit the desire for touching as early as others. This can endear them to the hearts of many a would-be intolerant or annoyed teacher.

The desire to be touched is a basic human need. From the newborn infant to the great-grandparent, we all respond to a gentle, loving touch from one who cares. In some instances, a literal pat on the back does more to communicate love and support than words could ever hope to accomplish. Children never outgrow

---

Every child is an artist. The problem is how to remain an artist once he grows up.——Pablo Picasso

their need to be loved physically. During their teen years, they may act distant, removed or uninterested in physical contact. It is important, however, especially at this time to continue demonstrating your affection for them. While a teen will probably not acknowledge your caring, he will appreciate it and feel better about himself because of it.

The bedtime ritual of a good-night kiss may be a good one to encourage even as the child becomes older. It not only communicates caring, but establishes a routine which gives an internal sense of security to ADHD/ADD children. As one parent said, "I always kiss Tom good-night, even though many days I have to grit my teeth as I do it. I know it makes him feel secure and I always feel glad afterwards." This positive expression of love may be the most helpful on those days when a child has been especially difficult. As Jill's mother confesses, "Yesterday, as I was secretly considering running away to Tahiti, I hugged Jill goodnight and suddenly things didn't seem so bad."

It may be more difficult for fathers to find opportunities to express their affection physically. Since the mother usually spends more time with the child during the day, it is likely that she will have more occasions to offer a hug, a touch on the arm, or to hold hands. Our culture does not seem to encourage this paternal contact as much as other countries. French and Italian fathers, for instance, are portrayed much more frequently in the media hugging or embracing their sons. Nevertheless, physical signs of acceptance are especially important from dad, since ADHD/ADD boys often feel a special closeness and identification with their fathers.

◆ *Provide Opportunities for Power*

As a parent, your goal is to help your child succeed. You want to create situations which will be *win-win* for both you and your child. If your child feels like a winner, he will have an increased sense of self-esteem and will, therefore, be a more pleasant person to be around.

Every child is born with the desire to master his world. As he matures, he is constantly learning what areas he can control, or have power over, and what areas he cannot. When he controls his bladder, takes his first step, drives a car, or receives a paycheck, he has obtained power over another part of his world. If he is guided toward exercising this power in positive ways, he will be less likely to search for negative ways to be in control.

It has been suggested that there are three basic motivators that influence personality: the need for achievement, the need for affiliation and the need for power. To some degree everyone is motivated by all three, but one is usually more dominant in each person. Having good friends may be more important to Mary than winning the spelling bee, while Kevin may have to be the top student in the class, even if the other children do not like him. The child who is influenced most by power wants to be influential. He wants to exercise his authority to make things happen. If this is the primary motivator for your child, establishing appropriate vehicles for expressing power may be especially important.

Making his own decisions helps a child feel in control. Deciding what clothes to wear, when to do his homework, or how to spend his money makes a child feel important and competent. As age permits, it is advisable to allow him to make those decisions which he is capable of making. Martha, at age four, may enjoy deciding on her afternoon snack. When she is seven she may help prepare her lunch to take to school. By fifth grade, she might like to suggest certain meals for the family's dinner and help prepare them. In high school she is very capable of doing the grocery shopping as well.

There is something that is much more scarce, something rarer than ability. It is the ability to recognize ability.——Robert Half

As a child demonstrates an area of competence it is often possible for the family to defer to his judgment in that area. This ability to be influential in the family makes a child feel valued and powerful. Cynthia, at age fourteen, is a whiz in math while her mother dislikes intensely anything to do with numbers. To the delight of everyone, Cynthia has taken over balancing the checkbook, which she enjoys tremendously. Obviously her mother is in control of the finances, but the mechanics of making monthly statements and the checkbook match is Cynthia's domain. Scott is only eleven, but has a keen knowledge and interest in cars. He has helped research the purchase of the next family car and has offered many valuable suggestions. Carrie, who is twelve, has an excellent eye for color and design and enjoys helping her mother buy and coordinate outfits for both work and fun. She is far better at it, in fact, than her more left-brain mother, and each enjoys the special feelings this activity has fostered.

◆ *Keep Humor Alive*

Humor is a survival technique that many parents have found essential over the years, especially parents of ADHD/ADD children. The intensity of daily life can be softened by the presence of humor. It often helps a parent to keep minor events in perspective and to realize that their child's antics will not have earth-shattering consequences. When Derek turns suddenly in the middle of the school play to yell gleefully from center stage, "Hi, Mom," it may help to alleviate the tension by chuckling at his spontaneity instead of being mortified. Even though he may have spoiled the most dramatic moment of the scene, he may have brought joy to the hearts of other sympathetic parents in the audience.

The low frustration tolerance level that many ADHD children possess causes them to have frequent outbursts of temper. Calmness and the presence of humor in the parent will frequently soften the moment. John, an irate five-year-old, was trying very hard to appear furious as he related a story to his father. The more he attempted to maneuver his facial muscles to portray anger, the more his father smiled and imitated his expressions. Finally ending up in gales of laughter, they had a delightful time trying hysterically to see who could appear the most angry. When the laughter had subsided, John was then ready to discuss calmly the upsetting event of his day.

Encouraging outside activities that promote humor may be an excellent way to assure continued laughter in the house. When children study magic, for example, they may constantly delight their families with fascinating new tricks they have learned. Even their mistakes are humorous to watch, as they struggle to master new techniques. One boy with whom we worked was born with a terrific sense of humor and his parents swear that he entered the world laughing. Over the years his parents have encouraged him to perfect the art of joke-telling and a local comedian has become his teacher. Another naturally talented comedian, sixteen-year-old Danny spent one summer in *Circus School* learning to be a clown. Not only did his unique skill increase his self-esteem, but his family enjoyed being his practice audience as well. He now earns extra money performing at children's birthday parties.

◆ *Be Kind to Yourself*

To accept and encourage children successfully, parents must begin by modeling acceptance, encouragement and forgiveness of themselves as parents and people. With the constant minor issues which must be dealt with on a daily basis, it is all too easy to begin to see oneself as a failure. In fact, many parents of ADHD/ADD children believe their children's symptoms would disappear if they were better parents. While parents may intellectually know this is not the case, they often nonetheless interpret their children's misbehavior as a sign of their own inadequacy. The resulting feelings of helplessness and frustration cause them to become angry with themselves. Unfortunately, however, the child often becomes the recipient of this anger, which only creates increased guilt and anger within the parents, as well as within the child.

In an attempt to alleviate this guilt, parents often overreact and/or overindulge the child. Such behavior is confusing to him because of its inconsistency. If a parent is frustrated one minute and indulgent the next, the child quickly learns which behaviors push the guilt button and he will employ them frequently, both to his own detriment and that of his parents.

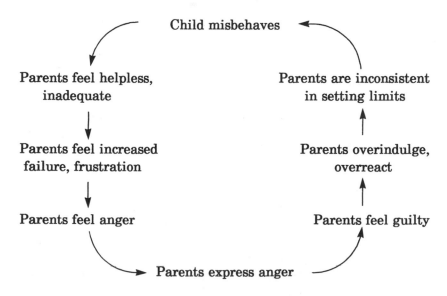

In some cases the feelings of failure a parent experiences may lead to depression and withdrawal which, in turn, can result in an even greater lack of structure and limit-setting in the home. This inevitably creates more problem behavior on the part of the child, thus repeating the cycle. It is often helpful to discuss these feelings with a professional or to seek the support of other parents. Parents of ADHD/ADD children desperately need opportunities to share openly their frustrations, as well as their successes, and to know they are not alone. Hearing what parenting methods have worked for others can be helpful as well as comforting. Observing the antics of another ADHD/ADD child and his family often gives parents a new perspective on their own situation and reduces the emotional intensity that is so often created.

Even though parents make mistakes, and we all do, it is important to decide what your strategy of child-rearing will be and then implement it with confidence as best you can. The ability to remain consistent and firm with your decisions will be accurately interpreted by your child as strength. This strength makes him feel secure and cared-for. Often the value of counseling is simply to have someone in authority affirm what you know to be best.

Everything's OK. It's only a phase my folks are going through.

When mothers and fathers can support and praise each other, both privately and in front of the child, it provides an added sense of unity and security. The most difficult task seems bearable when it is faced with a friend. This is true of parenting as well. On those days that try our patience the most, an encouraging word or compliment from a spouse can provide the needed incentive to help us remain motivated. As an added benefit, when our child sees us graciously accept a compliment, "Yes, I did handle that well. Thanks for noticing," he learns that it is acceptable to feel proud of oneself and what one has accomplished.

All parents of ADHD/ADD children need time away to replenish their energy and renew their commitment. Sometimes the best thing you can do for your child is to leave him with a competent sitter you trust and give yourself time to focus on you. One mother related her experience, as follows:

> *When John was three, I started to wonder if parent-hood had been a mistake. The terrible two's had been more than terrible, and I felt ready to escape. Mac and I planned a few days away on a vacation and I could hardly wait. As I hurriedly made all the arrangements, I secretly hoped we would be shipwrecked on a deserted island somewhere and be away for months. Poor sitter . . . if only she knew what might lay ahead for her. The day finally arrived for our departure and we boarded the ship with great anticipation. For twenty-four hours I did nothing but eat, sleep and lounge lazily in the sun. The second day I pulled a few pictures of John out of my suitcase and put them on the wall in our cabin. By day five, the walls of our room were plastered with pictures of John, and our fellow shipmates were tired of hearing about my wonderful child. By the time we arrived home I was so eager to see him that I didn't even stop to eat dinner. Being away from John made me realize how intensely I loved him and put many of my feelings and beliefs back in perspective.*

A long walk through the neighborhood, a cup of coffee with a friend, or an afternoon away from home to run errands can all do wonders to renew the body, mind and spirit. Sometimes only ten minutes away from the child in another part of the house may be all that is needed to rejuvenate your energies. One mother retreats to her bedroom frequently during the day for five minutes of quiet time. It is her time out. The children know not to disturb her when she closes the door, and they always mind willingly. They have even come to look forward to her time away, since she usually returns in a better mood.

◆ *Provide Education on ADHD/ADD*

The earlier a child understands who and what he is, the sooner he can begin the process of self-acceptance. For ADHD/ADD children this means that it is vitally important for them to have an understanding of their attentional difficulties. Our current knowledge suggests that the child will probably have to deal with this problem for many years. It is far more desirable for him to understand his difficulties than to spend years wondering why he is angering his teachers and friends or disappointing his parents.

If a child has a broken leg, we think nothing of explaining the doctor's diagnosis to him and what the treatment will be. We assure him that we will provide assistance until he is able to walk alone, and we offer understanding, encouragement and support. When a doctor, psychologist, or other professional diagnoses ADHD or ADD, it is frequently more difficult for parents to communicate these facts to a child. Obviously, the child should not be given more information than he can handle at his age, but even young children can start to recognize, in a positive and constructive way, that certain activities may be difficult for them, while others may be easier.

Kevin, a hyperactive eight-year-old, was waiting in the lobby of his dentist's office for what seemed an eternity. He had managed to bounce around in his chair, circle the waiting room several times, pace repeatedly from one end of the room to the other, and remove every magazine from the shelf. By the time the hygenist arrived, she was quite irritated. Her patience had obviously been stretched to the limit. With vexation she asked, "Why in the world don't you sit still?" He responded quite honestly, "I'm sorry. Sittin' still is hard for me. I'll try to be better next time. I really didn't mean to bother you." While his explanation hardly solved the problem, it did enable her to begin understanding. Even at young ages, children with attention disorders can help others understand their temperaments, resulting in less friction and negative comments from adults.

Against the assault of laughter nothing can stand.——Mark Twain

An older child can verbalize his frustrations more easily. He can also frequently offer rational solutions to difficult situations. When teachers complain about hard-to-read papers, Susie may ask permission to type them. When a coach is repeatedly annoyed by John's inability to remember to bring his soccer shoes each day, John may suggest that he bring an extra pair and leave them in his locker. If a child accepts those things which are difficult for him, instead of fighting them, he can begin to think constructively about solutions and alternatives. The ultimate goal is that the child be responsible for his own behavior. The sooner he understands his strengths and weaknesses, the sooner he will begin to assume that responsibility for his life.

◆ *Listen*

Nothing communicates love as profoundly as listening. When we give our undivided attention to a child, it tells him that he is the most important person in the world to us at that moment. With the constant demands that are placed upon parents, both at work and at home, it is not always easy to find the time to stop everything and sit down and truly listen to their child.

A simple response of "un-hmm," or "I see," will usually encourage a child to continue talking and expressing his thoughts. He will be much more agreeable to suggestions offered by parents if he feels that he has genuinely been heard first. In fact, often a child will end a long, involved story with, "What do you think I should do?" When a child has been allowed to relate an incident uninterrupted, he feels understood and valued.

True listening involves making eye contact with your child and not asking questions or offering suggestions. Dr. Ross Campbell in his book, *How to Really Love Your Child*, says,

> Eye contact is crucial not only in making good communi-
> cational contact with a child, but in filling his emotional
> needs. A child uses eye contact with his parents (and
> with others) to feed emotionally. The more parents make
> eye contact with their child as a means of expressing
> their love, the more a child is nourished with love and
> the fuller is his emotional tank. (Campbell, 1977)

Studies of children of working mothers have shown that the internalized image the child has of his mother's perception of him, influences him all day long (Sanger, 1988). If a child is to know that his mother believes in him, it is important for that image to be positive. Listening, more than any other single factor, may demonstrate her care, positive regard and acceptance of him.

If you lose your temper, it is a sign that you have wrong on your side.——Chinese Proverb

◆ SUMMARY ◆

Raising an ADHD or ADD child in a way that ensures a healthy sense of self-esteem may not be easy, but it is certainly possible. Graduation, his first date, observing a confident handshake upon meeting a new person and successfully navigating his first job are peak experiences in the lives of the ADHD/ADD child's parents. Each signals growth in their child's developing sense of self-worth and demonstrates the positive impact their years of support and encouragement have had on their child. Like the nursery magic described in *The Velveteen Rabbit*, parental encouragement over the years has magic of its own.[10]

> *"What is real?" asked the Rabbit one day, when they were lying side by side near the nursery fender, before Nana came to tidy the room. "Does it mean having things that buzz inside you and a stick-out handle?"*
>
> *"Real isn't how you are made," said the Skin Horse. "It's a thing that happens to you. When a child loves you for a long, long time, not just to play with, but REALLY loves you, then you become Real."*
>
> *"Does it hurt?" asked the Rabbit.*
>
> *"Sometimes," said the Skin Horse, for he was always truthful. "When you are Real you don't mind being hurt."*
>
> *"Does it happen all at once, like being wound up," he asked, "or bit by bit?"*
>
> *"It doesn't happen all at once," said the Skin Horse. "You become. It takes a long time. That's why it doesn't often happen to people who break easily, or have sharp edges, or who have to be carefully kept. Generally, by the time you are Real, most of your hair has been loved off, and your eyes drop out and you get loose in the joints and very shabby. But these things don't matter at all, because once you are Real you can't be ugly, except to people who don't understand."*

---

[10]From <u>The Velveteen Rabbit</u>, by Margery Williams, Avon Books, 1975.

It is better to be both right and consistent. But if you have to choose — you must choose to be right.

—Winston Churchill

Using Discipline Effectively

Enhancing a child's self-esteem is often one of the most rewarding of parenting experiences. Discipline, by contrast, is perhaps the most frustrating and exhausting part of parenting. When a child's behavior is negative, inappropriate, or not conducive to his long-term best interests, most parents feel a need to change it for both the child's welfare and that of others. For most, the process of intervening and modifying their child's behavior is a manageable, if not the most fulfilling, part of their parental responsibility.

ADHD and ADD symptoms, unfortunately, do not respond to the normal and customary methods used to modify children's behavior. "No discipline works!" is the constant refrain of parents who have tried. Their child's chronic lack of compliance, inappropriate behavior or poor performance eventually lead to parental feelings of frustration, helplessness, failure, and, subsequently, anger and rage. Explosive emotions are often the rule, not the exception, in ADHD/ADD homes. While many parents vowed they would never scream at their children, and they truly believe that physical punishment is harmful, they, nevertheless, find themselves doing all the things they said they would not: spanking, saying hurtful things to their children and punishing them constantly. When parents' emotions erupt, so do their children's. Often guilt, resentment and intense feelings of inadequacy on the part of both parent and child are experienced afterward. The inability to make their children mind and their loss of confidence as parents are the primary reasons parents seek professional assistance.

Given their impulsivity, low frustration tolerance, strong wills and activity-level problems, children with attention disorders are going to misbehave. What, then, is a parent to do, since nothing seems to work? What discipline is effective?

To discipline an ADHD or ADD child happily and successfully requires much energy and unflagging patience and determination on the part of his parents. It also requires an understanding of the goals of discipline and a guiding philosophy of human behavior.

Discipline, while often viewed negatively, is really quite positive. Discipline comes from the Latin root *disciplina,* which means *instruction.* The goal of discipline is to teach . . . to instruct a child in such a way that he will be able to interact in the larger world independently and responsibly without the intervention of authorities. To teach a child effectively requires that one motivate him in a positive way which respects his dignity, self-worth and desire for self-determination, while coming to terms with limits and expectations. Good teaching enables the child to realize his potential to the fullest.

In our practice, we encourage parents to think of themselves as teachers, not parents, for there is a psychological license one often gives oneself as a parent. Parents are, likewise, encouraged to think of their children as students with a blank slate. To accomplish the long-term objective of raising their ADHD/ADD children to become responsible, independent, fully functioning adults is not necessarily easy, but it can be accomplished.

In this chapter we will discuss principles of behavior we have found effective with ADHD/ADD children and adolescents, as well as practical behavior management programs you may choose to use as models for your own interventions. We stress that behavioral programs merely mirror one's own philosophy of human behavior and social interaction. They are only as sound as the principles which guide them.

◆ PRINCIPLES OF HUMAN BEHAVIOR ◆

◆ *Principle One—The need for attention is the driving force behind children's behavior, and children will fulfill their attentional needs regardless of whether the consequences of their behaviors are positive or negative.*

This principle is perhaps the most important one to understand and accept in raising children. It is especially critical to working with children with attention disorders, for their needs for attention often appear so profound. It is the ability to meet the ADHD/ADD child's needs for attention in positive ways that often determines the fate of his self-esteem.

For example, a situation encountered frequently with the ADHD child especially is that of teasing or *bugging* his siblings. The goal: your attention. Parents often respond to the child's behavior without realizing the underlying goal of attention and do indeed give him attention—negative attention. While it meets his attentional needs, your frustration and/or punishment do little for his self-esteem. He often becomes angry and negative when you reprimand him, feeling misunderstood, and he will continue his disruptive behavior at the earliest possible moment. Not only is attention a motive now, but a desire for revenge may well become one.

An alternative to this typical scenario is to approach the child who is teasing his sibling, being aware of his need for attention, and to divert him into helping or interacting with you. You can then discuss his desire for attention and give him positive ways to meet this need. A child taught to express this need for emotional contact feels free to approach his parents and say "Hey, I need some attention." Both he and you have a clear fix on his need and can meet it appropriately. Good gas is put into the proverbial *emotional tank* rather than bad gas and will go far in fostering his esteem.

Adults, too, need this positive attention. One mother with whom we worked cued her husband of this need with one word— *Roses*. It was his cognitive cue that she was not receiving the attention she needed to feel fulfilled. With children, too, cognitive cues can be developed so that a word or sign communicates a wealth of emotional and cognitive information.

If acknowledging and meeting the child's attentional needs is not sufficient to break a bad habit or a negative behavior, an incentive program, to be discussed in the next section, can be implemented to assist him in overcoming an ingrained response.

Acting out in the classroom to get the attention of the teacher is another frequent complaint, especially for ADHD students. Withdrawing in anger and rejection of school values are others. One teacher solved this problem by meeting her most difficult, hard-to-manage student at the door each day with a smile, a touch on the arm, and a welcoming comment—all of which took fifteen seconds. While the student initially thought that she had lost her mind, he soon began waiting for her at the door if she were not there, and in a few weeks they had established a very positive rapport. At the end of the school year he hugged her and said, "You're the only teacher I've ever liked." A few seconds of positive interaction and the regard it communicated did more for this *behavior-disordered* student than five years of time out, suspensions and explusions had achieved.

For those children and adolescents who are impulsively going to do something wrong within thirty seconds of entering the class or coming home, both parents and teachers may have to *meet them at the door*—before they are frustrated by the often unintentional, but nevertheless inappropriate behavior of the child. Only then can one be genuinely positive toward the child and effectively communicate these feelings. Children will meet their attentional needs one way or another. Adults, however, decide whether these needs are fulfilled positively or negatively.

♦ *Principle Two—Learning is a trial-and-error process shaped by both positive and negative reinforcers which occur simultaneously in our daily lives. Positive attention meets children's attentional needs best and reinforces behavior the most; negative attention, while not good, is next best; while no attention is least effective in producing desired results.*

Children, like all of us, learn by trial-and-error. As they experiment with various behaviors and attitudes, they retain those that get positive results, and they abandon those that achieve undesired results. For example, if a child is misbehaving and you reprimand him, he is likely to continue misbehaving, despite momentary compliance. He has received your attention, even though it was negative attention, and he will continue his undesirable behavior because it was reinforced. If a child, on the other hand, is quiet and hardworking, he is likely to continue his *good* behavior if you let him know how much you like and appreciate his efforts.

Studies of accomplished artists and athletes show how powerful your attention is. What you selectively attend to frequently shapes their behavior in very dramatic ways. The principles of reinforcement apply to behavior—i.e., you increase the behavior on which you choose to focus. It also applies to activities you enjoy and praise. For example, Dr. Benjamin Bloom, in his studies of giftedness and talent, found that many of the world's great pianists had mothers who were pleased and responsive as their youngsters banged mercilessly away at the keyboard. Other pianists, equally talented, quit piano because no one was interested. Many great artists' mothers kept all their children's paintings, but did not reinforce writing by keeping even one English composition. Other parents paid attention to sports and ignored music and art; their children became great athletes.

Another example of how we all tend to repeat behaviors and actions that are reinforced and to abandon those that are not is revealed in many of the responses of children raised by deaf parents. Within three months many babies raised by parents who cannot hear cease to make noise when they cry. Instead, they squirm, turn red, and shed tears because their parents cannot, and thus do not, respond to their cries. Since they do not get the attention they need through crying, they develop other behaviors that are successful in achieving their goal.

Parents powerfully influence their children's lives through their selective positive and negative reinforcement of both their activities and their behaviors. It is, therefore, critical to carefully evaluate precisely what it is you are reinforcing and to determine if that, indeed, is what you want.

Are you, as a parent, reinforcing the wrong things—behavior in your children you do not desire—through negative attention? Are you ignoring the things you do want, such as politeness, good grades, neat rooms, responsible behavior, and sensitivity to others' needs, thereby not helping your children achieve these goals?

Adult behavior is molded in much the same way as that of children, through positive and negative reinforcement. Like children, we tend to repeat actions and behaviors that reward us and avoid those that are negative. We are often unaware that we are responding to this positive reinforcement. We may receive praise, recognition, raises or new opportunities; or the reward may be more intangible, such as fulfillment as a parent or personal growth. When our jobs or relationships are negative, we tend to avoid them or to be negative in return.

The principles of reinforcement are identical for both children and adults. However, in most cases a child's greatest reward is the attention he receives from his parents. Almost every child wants to be loved and accepted by both his mother and his father more than anything in the world beyond his physical needs. Your child can thus be expected to repeat acts that win your attention, whether positive or negative, and to eliminate those that do not. It is important to make certain you are reinforcing the right things in your children.

◆ *Principle Three—Negative reinforcement and punishment may change behavior. They do not change attitudes except to make them worse. Positive attitudes are the critical factor for caring, sensitivity and responsible behavior long term.*

This principle is especially true for impulsive children, who more frequently than not, do not intentionally do things wrong. An

ADHD adult described saying to his father repeatedly as a child, "I don't intend to make you mad, Dad. I don't know why I do these things; they just happen." He also described his father's punishment as merely *fueling the fire* between them. The punishments never changed his impulsive behavior. They did, however, devastate his self-esteem. Appropriate medication and ten years of psychotherapy were necessary to partially heal what he described as his *inner wounded child.*

While one can, perhaps, punish a non-ADHD child into compliance and change his behavior short-term, the necessary understanding of why certain behaviors are desirable is not achieved. To help the child incorporate these beliefs into his own philosophy of life and into the principles of human behavior which will guide him requires the respect and dignity conveyed in discussing these issues with him. He must also be helped to learn positive ways of achieving change. Strategies that help a child understand what he has done and why, and how to change, will produce the most significant improvement in the inappropriate behaviors of impulsive children.

♦ *Principle Four—Final compliance with an adult request must always be positively reinforced, no matter how long it takes to obtain the behavior.*

One of the most difficult attitudes we deal with in parents is the concept that their children are *supposed* to do what they want them to do, believe what they believe, value what they value, and become what they want them to become. It is as though their children are an extension of themselves without their own individual needs, desires and goals. This is one reason it is helpful for parents to think of themselves, not as parents with rights and privileges already granted, but rather as teachers who achieve in their children only those goals they conscientiously set out to impart to them as students.

Parents are often frustrated because their children do not obey requests or do as they are told. For example, a father may ask his son to take out the garbage—once, twice . . . or five times. By the

---

The art of being wise is the art of knowing what to overlook.——William James

fifth time he has made this request, he is often frustrated and his voice has risen two decibels . . . or ten. When finally the task is completed, he responds to his son angrily, "It's about time!" The child is equally angry, feeling misunderstood and even verbally abused. He is unlikely to respond positively to his father's next request. The cycle of command-avoidance-frustration-forcing of compliance and subsequent resentment drives a deeper and deeper wedge between parent and child.

By contrast, the father who has insisted that the job be done, but who responds positively to the final compliance, "Thanks, son, I really appreciate your doing that," leaves his son feeling grudgingly grateful. With continued positive reinforcement the son's behavior will become increasingly cooperative and the goal of shared responsibility will more likely be achieved.

Most of us have been trained to take the positive behaviors and actions of those around us for granted, and to take action on noncompliance and negative behaviors. One of our exercises for parents is to have them go for two days not uttering a negative word. If they feel negative or angry, they are to write down what is bothering them. These concerns become the behaviors for which positive goals are established, and positive means of achieving them are determined. The interesting part of this assignment is that parents often find themselves very quiet.

When we ask kids what they want from parents, they frequently say, "I want my parents to stop nagging and fussing at me." Discipline is a concrete way of deciding upon objectives and utilizing positive reinforcement and incentives to accomplish them.

♦ *Principle Five—Rules are a necessary part of any organized group, whether a family or a nation. They should, however, not be imposed for the sake of control, but rather as a means to positive cohabitation.*

When one works with families where there are no concrete expectations, or with teachers whose behaviors are based more on whim than carefully designed requirements which are reasonable, logical and predictable, it is very easy to see why rules are a necessary part of responsible parenting and teaching.

The world is a complex place, often even a dangerous one. Externally imposed rules are a means of ensuring that guidance is there until the child is mature enough to develop his own standards of behavior. Rules can be communicated in ways which are ego-enhancing rather than demeaning: "In our family, we do . . . ." When children receive positive attention for following the rules, they usually incorporate them into their set of values. Unlike parents' fears, children adopt the majority of their family's values by their mid-twenties if their family experience has been a positive one.

For rules to be effective there must be positive consequences for following them and logical, predictable, nonemotional negative consequences for breaking them preceded by discussion and an understanding of why the child broke the rule. Compromise may be necessary if the rule is excessively arbitrary or incomprehensible to the child. It is helpful to let children know, at the beginning of a discussion, which differences are negotiable and which are not. Changing the rule about bedtime may be negotiable, whereas changing the rule about respecting others may not be. Even when the rule is not subject to change, it is important to hear the child out and to communicate your understanding of his point of view and his feelings with your attention. It is then equally important to share the reasons and philosophy behind your rule and your obligation as a parent to have your judgment as a parent prevail over some of his judgments as a child. Always communicate that the rule is designed to serve *his* long-term best interests.

When children are not treated with dignity, fairness and respect as you uphold your rule, they will break it regardless of what you do. Many times they even feel justified and vindicated: "It serves you right because you're so unreasonable." We understand that ADHD children and adolescents often have to learn everything the hard way and may be determined to do things their way regardless of your rules. Nevertheless, with patience and continued follow-through of pre-established consequences for both compliance and noncompliance, our experience is that these children and adolescents do eventually come around. It takes longer, but the additional effort is very worthwhile when one assesses the negative consequences of not persisting with this child.

Having no rules in the home is the worst thing that can happen for an ADHD/ADD child. Arbitrary rules which make no real sense can be equally negative. Reasonable, sensible rules that thoughtful people can adopt are those which truly influence behavior in positive ways. It is these guides to behavior that assist children in maturing to the point that they can develop their own rules—rules which will serve them better than yours within the fabric of their own lives and their time in history.

◆ *Principle Six—Encouragement and incentive are the most powerful tools for change.*

An incentive program is an external method of rewarding your children for changing their behavior. It is based on the belief that a child, like most of us, will work harder when he feels appreciated and noticed, or when he can see and understand the positive results of his efforts.

Negative feedback often serves only to meet the frustrated needs of a parent. Be very careful with your *constructive criticism*. It may not be as constructive as showing or telling the child, not what you don't want, but what you *do* want.

When a program of incentive and encouragement is begun, most children respond positively and enthusiastically. However, many parents are uneasy with this approach and feel it may be bribery. It is important to understand the difference. Bribery is telling your child he can have his reward *if* he will do something. Incentives tell your child he can have his reward *when* he has done what is expected. In bribery, the child is in control. You, the parent, have control when incentives and encouragement are utilized.

Many parents make the mistake of expecting a child to have good behavior because it makes them feel good, or, at the very least, because they *should* . . . because they are *self-disciplined*. We, likewise, expect children to be responsible and helpful for the same reasons. It would be nice if children could reward themselves for a job well done with feelings of satisfaction and accomplishment. Parents, however, often fail to realize that the development of an internalized sense of well-being and the desire for accomplishment are learned. Most children are too young to have developed a strong sense of internal reward to motivate them. Instead, these are qualities which develop gradually as a result of many positive and successful experiences which you have both facilitated and reinforced with your attention and pleasure.

Until an internal reward system is developed, it is your job as a parent to motivate your child with external incentives, encouragement and positive interaction. It is a job that can be far more fun, creative and fulfilling for both you and your children than nagging, harassing and criticizing. As your child becomes more responsible, more competent and more caring, he can be expected to develop his own sense of pride and satisfaction in his accomplishments and in who he is.

♦ *Principle Seven—Human reinforcement is far more powerful than physical activities or reinforcers.*

Behavior modification as a method of changing behavior has exerted a very strong influence on psychology, as well as parenting, since the days of Dr. B. F. Skinner and his early conditioning of rats and pigeons with food and water reinforcers. With children we have graduated from pellets to M&M's, stickers, stars and checks, and in the process we have sometimes forgotten that a word of encouragement or a *thumbs up* for a job well done are far more powerful in motivating our children than checks or chips. While behavior management programs have been very successful in delineating the principles of reinforcement which determine behavior, they have also inadvertently suggested that children are more motivated by things and activities than by the positive attention and regard they receive from their parents.

The power of human reinforcement has not, however, been replaced. Positive touch, affirming eye contact, intense attention, and the pleasure the child experiences from your company continue to be far more effective as true motivators of behavior than all the stickers in the world. It is important for parents to become aware of their power in children's lives and focus again on those human elements which communicate one's true affection for another.

♦ *Principle Eight—To effectively manage a child's behavior you must effectively manage your own, for the behavior of the child is often nothing more than a mirror of the parent's own.*

One of the greatest benefits of any disciplinary strategy or behavior management program, in our opinion, is the confidence it gives parents in establishing effective strategies with their children, thus enabling them to approach the child's behavior in a reasonable, understandable and predictable way for the child. Even when children do not especially like consequences, they are usually willing to follow guidelines which are presented in an organized, nonemotional way and are implemented in a context of respect and concern.   The power of example is ultimately the strongest influence any parent has, and it is the parent's relationship with the child which will determine the degree of that influence. If you, as a role model, exhibit uncontrolled emotions . . . anger, rejection, criticism . . . or use manipulation and coercion to obtain control, your children will do the same. Children do, indeed, learn what they live.

A classic example of children copying parents' behavior is observed in situations of conflict. As parents become frustrated, they often raise their voices in an attempt to gain control over their child.   Each increase in volume by the parent is usually accompanied by a reciprocal increase in volume by the child, often to the point that both are screaming at each other. The child's screaming was precipitated by the adult's, but the child may then be reprimanded further for being disrespectful. In reality, he is simply following the example set by his parent. At the point that his parent overpowers him, he may stop talking, but he often continues to scream back inside. Thus, little is accomplished except further alienation and denigration.

Effective conflict resolution relies upon this same principle, that children model their parents' behavior. To resolve a conflict with your child, you are, therefore, encouraged to get quieter and closer. The child will respond in kind.

♦ PRACTICAL BEHAVIOR MANAGEMENT PROGRAMS ♦

Two behavior methods utilized successfully in our practice are the *Thinking Room* for negative or inappropriate behavior, and the *Chip* or Point Incentive Program for positive accomplishment and behaviors.

♦ *Thinking Room Concept*

The *Thinking Room* is a variation of the *time-out* concept. It emphasizes not only teaching appropriate behavior, but developing cognitive understanding and appropriate social skills as well. Talking about behavior and planning future appropriate responses is critical to positive change.

To use the thinking room concept, it is suggested that you have a family meeting and explain to your child or children that your job as parents is to help them grow up to be capable, responsible, independent and, hopefully, happy adults. To help them, you will be using a new plan. Certain responsibilities and behaviors will be expected of them. When they do what is expected, they will earn chips or points which they can use for activities and special things they want. When they do things which are not acceptable to the family, they will go to the thinking room to think about what they have done, why they have done it, and to problem-solve for future situations.

The thinking room is the powder room, laundry room, or other small and relatively uninteresting room for the child. We do not recommend the child's room, which is, hopefully, a haven for him.

The joy of the young is to disobey—but the trouble is, there are no longer any orders.——Jean Cocteau

When your child does something he shouldn't have done, or doesn't do something he should have, he goes to the thinking room. If there is room, it is helpful to have a *thinking chair* in the room. The child sits in this chair. A timer is set and placed outside the door. The time period is roughly one minute for each year of age. The purpose of the thinking room is not punitive. Rather, it is a method by which the parent instructs the child that a behavior is not acceptable, and that consequences occur when the child engages in unacceptable behavior. The thinking room is also a place where new and appropriate behaviors can be decided upon. When the child enters the thinking room, the door is closed and the timer is set. If the child screams, kicks, or cries (which he may in a fit of anger, and that's okay), he is quietly told that he cannot think and cry at the same time, and the timer will be set only when he is thinking. If the child continually comes out, he is told that if he cannot control himself, the door will be locked. Children intensely dislike locked doors and rarely is it necessary to lock it more than once or twice. If you do not like locked doors, it is crucial that you have a way of being in control without verbally or physically controlling or hurting the child.

When the timer goes off, the parent goes to the thinking room and talks with the child about what happened and why that behavior is not acceptable in their family. We encourage families to use "in our family" often as they discuss what they will and will not accept. It gives the child a sense of rootedness and easily explains that what his parents expect may be very different from what other parents expect.

At this time, parent and child also talk about the feelings that might have led to the behavior and how those feelings might be expressed in more appropriate ways. For example,

> "I know you're frustrated with your sister, but in our family we don't hit people. Everytime you hit someone, you'll have to go to the thinking room and think about it. Since you can't hit people, what can you do when you get angry with your sister?"

Three-and-a-half year old sent to the Thinking Room for the first time. When the kitchen timer rang, a quiet little voice said, "Me through cooking, Mommie!"

The child is encouraged to come up with *cognitive alternatives* such as,

> "I could hit a punching bag, or I could come tell you, or
> I could just ignore her."

If the child does not come up with cognitive alternatives, the parent supplies two or three. While it may take two or three visits to the thinking room, or even twenty, eventually the child will choose an alternative and more appropriate behavior.

When the child is old enough to write, sentences are added. For example, "I will be respectful of my mother," for the child who has been rude. We usually start with ten sentences for a younger child and increase by ten's. Rarely do we have a child who doesn't change his behavior before he reaches 150 sentences. Older children are started with 25 sentences and they are increased by 25 until the behavior is no longer worth the consequences. Rarely does the child exceed 300. While some parents and teachers worry that writing sentences may interfere with their child's desire to write, it is a method of discipline used, historically, quite effectively as early as John Locke, and it continues to be used in the finest, most disciplined boarding schools in England today. We have found over the years that writing sentences exerts a more positive effect on behavior than a negative effect on writing.

If the child refuses to go to the thinking room, force should not be used. Instead, the parent merely tells the child that he cannot do anything fun until he does go. The parent then goes on about her activities, and each time the child asks to do something, the parent states, "Of course, that's great, as soon as you have been to the thinking room."

At the end of each thinking room session, talking is critical. Feelings and future behavior strategies must be discussed for maximum effectiveness of this approach. It is also helpful to develop a cognitive cue with the child to alert him that he is about to behave inappropriately. If the child responds to the cue, he is immediately positively reinforced with eye contact and a special sign expressing your pleasure at compliance. It is important not to leave the thinking room without a hug and "I love you." While punishment *per se* accomplishes little with ADHD/ADD children, the thinking room accomplishes wonders. Parents are usually amazed at both its simplicity and its effectiveness.

♦ *Positive Incentive Program for Behavior Change*

The thinking room is ideal for negative behaviors. However, we know that honey is always better than vinegar for accomplishing goals. Therefore, a positive incentive program is also established to obtain those behaviors you want in your child. Anytime a child exhibits a negative or inappropriate behavior, parents should decide on the positive behavior they want instead and target that behavior with an incentive program to help the child understand what is expected.

When establishing a positive incentive program, appropriate behaviors are decided upon and placed on a chart. The behaviors might include getting along with siblings, being respectful of parents, minding the first time asked, coming home on time, and not persisting, among others. Examples of behavior charts for use at home and at school are included on pages 246-248.

The Behavior Chart may initially have to be established for short time intervals, such as fifteen minutes. The time is gradually extended until it includes an entire morning, afternoon, or evening. Rarely can a child go longer than a third of a day without reinforcement. For appropriate behavior, the child earns chips or points and your positive feedback and attention. For inappropriate behavior the thinking room is utilized.

The points or chips earned in this program are utilized for activities and things the child wants. It is critical that the child work toward a goal important to him—not one you decide upon for him. For example, we have had some children far more motivated by a camping trip with their father than by a new video game. Activities are encouraged over *things*, but the child's motivation must provide guidance for the appropriate choice of incentives.

Most children, even impulsive ADHD children, are quite willing to change negative behaviors to achieve *their* goals. Not only does the child earn chips or points, but he also earns your approval and praise.

The great majority of children want to please their parents. ADHD and ADD children likewise do, often even more than others. They develop a sense of internally motivated self-discipline, however, only after many successful experiences with external limits and rewards. Until that is developed, it is your job as a parent to motivate your ADHD/ADD child through the use of positive and negative consequences for his behavior. The Thinking Room, the Chip or Point Reinforcement System, incentives, positive emotional feedback and encouragement, are far more fulfilling to both you and your child than nagging, spanking, and coercion. Your ADHD/ADD child will need your ongoing structure, guidance and encouragement to develop the internal controls he lacks. Children and adolescents with attention disorders need parents who will take the time and learn the methods to teach them to behave in ways conducive to their own development and happiness.

◆ SUMMARY ◆

Discipline is one of the most difficult tasks for most parents of children with attention disorders. It can also be the challenge which offers some of the greatest fulfillment when approached constructively. The skills and values your child can learn as he experiences your disciplinary program are often the ones which determine his success in the later endeavors he will undertake. Perhaps more importantly, however, these experiences determine in great measure the kind of person he becomes.

(Example of Home Behavior Chart)

DAILY PROGRESS REPORT

Name: _____

Week: _____

		Morning	Afternoon	Evening
1.	I got along with _____. (sibling)	☐	☐	☐
2.	I was respectful of my parents.	☐	☐	☐
3.	I minded the first time asked (or at least the second!).	☐	☐	☐
4.	I waited patiently when Mom was on the phone (I did not interrupt).	☐	☐	☐
5.	_____	☐	☐	☐
6.	_____	☐	☐	☐

_____

TOTAL

Code:

GOOD
1

OK
2

POOR
3

Positive Consequences: For 1's ("Great"): 2 chips toward an activity or purchase of something desired. For 2's ("OK"): 1 chip.

Negative Consequences: Thinking Room or Thinking Room plus sentences. No chips.

Goal: _____chips for _____

(Example for Younger Children - School)

DAILY PROGRESS REPORT

Name: _____

Week: _____

CODE:

GOOD   OK   POOR
1   2   3

1. I was a good listener.

2. I completed my work on time.

3. I worked without disturbing others.

4. I controlled my talking.

5. I walked in line without pushing
    and shoving.

I need help in:_____

_____

_____

_____

_____

_____

Parent's Signature

(Example for Older Children - School)

DAILY PROGRESS REPORT

Name: _____

Week: _____

Rating Scale:

1 - Excellent   2 - Satisfactory   3 - Unsatisfactory

	Mon	Tues	Wed	Thur	Fri
A. Behavior					
1. I was cooperative with the teacher and did *not* argue.	—	—	—	—	—
2. I used very good language—no cursing.	—	—	—	—	—
3. I was nice to other children—*even* if they were not sometimes.	—	—	—	—	—
4. I did what the teacher asked the first time asked.	—	—	—	—	—
B. Completed Class Assignments					
1. On time.	—	—	—	—	—
2. Neatly.	—	—	—	—	—

Positive Consequences:
For 1's ("Excellent"):   2 chips toward an activity or purchase of something special.
For 2's ("Satisfactory"): 1 chip.

Negative Consequences:
1) If sheet not brought home, in room rest of day with books, toys, radio only.
2) "3"—Write 10 times (ex.) "I will try very hard to be cooperative and not argue." Second time for same problem write 20 times; third time—write 30 times, etc.

I hear and I forget. I see and I remember. I do and I understand.

—Chinese Proverb

Teaching Responsibility

It has been said that parenting is the most frustrating of all professions for if it is done well, parents work themselves out of a job. How true. The ultimate goal of parenting is to let go and to create a child capable of handling his own life with little or no assistance from parents. This is not an easy accomplishment for any parent, and it may be especially difficult for the parents of a child with an attention disorder.

To facilitate this independence, a parent must teach the child how to be responsible for himself. The many daily issues of home and school, however, require so much parental energy that it is often easy to lose sight of this basic objective. Nonetheless, teaching a child the value of work and responsibility is critical; in fact, it may determine his success in adulthood far more than the grades he makes or the school he attends. Studies show that those children who have learned the skills and problem-solving abilities necessary to accomplish tasks at home fare better in elementary school through college. Those who have struggled with the problems inherent in fulfilling responsibilities as children and adolescents are not easily overwhelmed when faced with the tasks of young adulthood (Vaillant, 1977). They are comfortable both with responsibility and interacting with the adult world in a mature and reciprocal way. Drugs and alcohol, the great escapes, are less likely to be used by those who have developed skills, effective interpersonal communication, self-esteem, strong work values and positive goals.

In recent years it has become apparent that many American children have not learned the value of work. Rather, they have grown up with a sense of entitlement. They feel that necessities, as well as many of the luxuries of life, are their parents' or others' obligations. When they do not receive those things to which they feel entitled, they become angry and demanding. They are not motivated to obtain these things for themselves.

While widespread indulgence of children is a phenomenon that has always existed, excessive indulgence has been rampant in America since the mid-1950's. With the advent of technology after World War II, children were no longer needed to fulfill their traditional economic and labor roles in the family. Instead people began having children to meet their own emotional needs. They wanted their children to be happy so they might be fulfilled as parents.

The thing that impresses me most about America is the way parents obey their children.——Duke of Windsor

To achieve this goal, parents have given with abandon to their children. They have provided every opportunity they could afford, as well as many they could not. At some level parents have believed that if they provided every possible advantage for their children, they would assure their children's success and happiness as adults.

♦ *Success in Adulthood Correlates*
With Work in Childhood

The remarkable results of a forty-year research project undertaken by Harvard University highlight the problem (Vaillant, 1977). This investigation revealed that responsibility, not indulgence, accomplishes parents' real goals. Researchers found that happiness and success in adulthood were not associated with how much parents did for or gave to their children. Rather, these outcomes were correlated with the amount of meaningful work done as a child and adolescent.

The study followed the lives of over four hundred boys for approximately forty years. The investigators found that those who had assisted with household chores, had part-time jobs, engaged in extracurricular activities, made good grades relative to their ability, and learned to cope with problems were much happier and far more successful than those who had not. As adults, they were healthier and lived longer; they were twice as likely to have warm relationships with a wide variety of people; and they were five times more likely to be well paid. They also had greater job satisfaction, and they were sixteen times less likely to be unemployed. They had better marriages and closer relationships with their children.

By contrast, those who had worked least in childhood were far more likely to have been arrested and ten times more likely to have emotional problems, while six times as many had died. Intelligence, amount of education and socio-economic status made no real difference in how the boys turned out. Rather, the development of a responsible work ethic seemed to be the key to later happiness and success.

♦ Hazards of Child-Centered Philosophy

We are now realizing some of the pitfalls of our child-oriented philosophies of the sixties, seventies and eighties. Teachers are distressed by their students' lack of responsibility, organization skills and commitment to excellence. Many employers today are also complaining about the declining work ethic among their younger employees. They report a lack of loyalty, disregard for company rules, absenteeism and little personal dedication to the job. In fact, some have speculated that American buyers are choosing to purchase foreign goods because of their reputation for quality. It is said, for example, that *the American work ethic is alive and well in Japan.* It is not surprising that Japanese parents begin teaching children at a very young age about the importance of responsibility.

Many American parents have begun to feel frustrated and trapped by their children's sense of entitlement. They wonder why their grown children are not able to be independent and self-supporting. Many fathers and mothers are baffled as increasing numbers of adult children move back home to live. Today twenty-two million U. S. children over the age of eighteen live at home with their parents (Okimoto and Stegall, 1987). In fact, the book entitled *Boomerang Kids* offers parents suggestions for structuring parent-child relationships with adult children who return home to live.

◆ *Indulgence of ADHD/ADD Children and Adolescents*

Parents of children and adolescents with attention disorders are more vulnerable than parents of non-ADHD/ADD children to giving too much and requiring too little. They often feel sorry for their youngsters who seem destined to create ill-will and provoke rejection at every turn. They feel guilty, too, because they have become impatient and have said or done things they wish, as they lie awake at night, they had not. Out of both pity and guilt, they give excessively. Surely, they think, reciprocity operates with children: "If I give to them, they will in turn be cooperative and appreciative."

Unfortunately, reciprocity does not work this way with children. Instead, they learn what they live. If they have only received and never given, that is all they know how to do. If they have only played and never worked, work will be foreign to them and they will continue to play.

Children with attention disorders need more organization, structure, planning and routine than their non-ADHD/ADD counterparts. They desperately need the satisfaction and sense of competence which comes from a job well done at home, especially when they may be having difficulty at school. They need activities of which they can be proud. They must become self-disciplined, cooperative and contributing family members if they are to become fully-functioning adults. Consider the experience of the "*Butterfly*" family in the following story:

Once upon a time there were two butterflies who were delighted when their own baby caterpillar came into the world. As most parents do, they looked forward to seeing their young one turn into a beautiful butterfly just like they were. Even when he was tiny, they knew he was a little different from the other caterpillars —more active, less organized, more demanding. They felt sorry for him. They even felt sorry for themselves. But they kept trying because they cared so much. They gave him everything a young caterpillar could want. They even helped him build the protective cocoon in which his long-awaited metamorphosis would take place. Then they waited with eager anticipation for a beautiful young butterfly to make a grand entrance into the adult world.

At last they saw the cocoon breaking away. To their shock and dismay, their young caterpillar emerged without having changed at all. The small caterpillar greeted them with an explanation, "It's too tough to be a butterfly these days. You have to fly on your own and find your own food. There's no one around to take care of you or to remind you to do things. So, I've decided to stay just the way I am and to keep you company." To the parent's distress, that is just what the apprehensive young caterpillar did. (Original source unknown)

Most parents want to do what is best for their children. Parents of ADHD and ADD children often want to do even more. As they shower them with gifts, educational experiences, material possessions and good times, they may well be teaching them to be receivers in life and not givers. Children with attention disorders, especially ADHD children, quickly pick up on these dynamics and by the age of five can become, quite unintentionally, master manipulators and professional malingerers. Unless parents are careful and alert, children can learn how to avoid even the simplest of household tasks. By adolescence, it may be next to impossible to change this pattern so ingrained in them.

It must be stressed, however, that this is not a choice the children have made. Rather, it is what parents have conditioned them to expect from life. Unfortunately, however, the children will later pay the consequences of such indulgence, while parents sit on the sidelines, distraught spectators, with little real power to influence their children's adult life.

The paradox appears to be that the more we give to our children, the more we are actually taking from them. By not expecting responsibility, competence and the earning of privileges, we are actually keeping them from experiencing many of the successes and joys of life.

Few things help an individual more than to place responsibility on him, and to let him know you trust him.——Booker T. Washington

◆ EXPERIENCES MISSED BY ◆
OVERINDULGED CHILDREN

Rarely do parents intentionally cause problems for their children. Indulgence, nonetheless, robs them of many attributes which will be sorely missed in later life.

◆ *Motivation*

Without needs or desires there is little motivation. We deprive children of the motivation to be productive if they receive everything they want or need for the asking. When motivation is strong, however, even children with attention disorders can focus their energies and be quite productive. In evaluating adults who have been tremendously successful, one always finds a person with strong motivation, often originating from many, not few, needs.

◆ *Independence*

When a child is given things by his parents instead of earning them, he quickly learns that what he receives is dependent upon his parents. Such dependence robs the child of the personal power he could experience by controlling his own destiny, determining what he receives and when he receives it. Instead of responding yes or no to a child's frequent requests, parents can begin saying, "Sure, great. You may when...." This response will liberate both parent and child. Giving the child the responsibility for earning what he wants also eliminates a frequent family conflict, i.e., one parent in the position of being the good guy (the one who says "Yes"), while the other parent is the bad guy (the one who says "No"). Instead, both parents can usually agree that the child can have what he wants after he earns it.

◆ *Accomplishment*

There is tremendous satisfaction in accomplishing a task successfully and basking in the joy of a job well done. The child or adult who works for what he wants is almost always happier and takes greater pleasure and satisfaction in his possessions and activities than one who has not earned them. A special book bag that is earned over several weeks will be treasured far more than one that is bought immediately upon request. A bicycle that is purchased by a child after months of working and saving will bring far more pleasure than one that is casually given to him by his parents. Work, like love, is one of the major pleasures of life when the goal is strong. Dr. William C. Menniger of The Menninger Foundation has said, "One who learns to accept responsibility also finds reward in the opportunity to express individual initiative so that work becomes a means to an end rather than an end" (Menninger, 1964).

Children really enjoy work. The urge to help and to belong comes almost as soon as the child can walk. Every preschool teacher knows the favorite learning center is housekeeping where the children sweep, wash windows and dust enthusiastically. There is no one prouder than the three-year-old who has sorted the socks, the six-year-old who has helped with the dishes, nor the twelve-year-old who has cooked dinner for the family. Children *want* to be included. With encouragement, work becomes a source of both pride and joy for a child.

Dr. Benjamin Spock, in his comments on raising children in the twenty-first century, has stated,

> Parents can make a profound difference by teaching spiritual values—helpfulness, cooperation, generosity, love—throughout childhood. Two-year-olds can be

encouraged to help set the table, then thanked and praised. Teenagers can be expected to work in hospitals and to tutor younger children. Such jobs don't need to be presented as distasteful—shouldn't be. Children love to take on adult jobs when these are presented as opportunities and are appreciated." [11]

♦ PROBLEMS EXPERIENCED BY ♦ OVERINDULGED CHILDREN

Not only are overindulged children deprived in several ways, they also experience many problems as a result of their constant overgratification.

♦ *Spoiling*

Giving too much and saying *yes* too often can create a child who is spoiled—one who is unable to interact with others with give and take but instead must have his own way.

Why is it that parents say yes so often to their children?

Some parents say *yes* from a sincere desire to please. Those parents who grew up learning to please and to take care of others are especially vulnerable to saying *yes* for this reason. Others say yes to avoid a tantrum or a hassle. Still others say *yes* because they want childhood to be a time of fun and pleasure for their child.

---

[11]Copyright © 1989 by Dr. Benjamin Spock.

Regardless of the reason, saying *yes* too often may create a problem far more serious than the child's temporary disappointment, anger, or even a full-fledged toddler or teenage temper tantrum.

◆ *Insecurity*

Indulged children can be quite demanding at home. However, they are often insecure outside the home because they have not developed the confidence and the strength which come from dealing with setbacks and disappointments. Nor have they developed the sense of competence and fulfillment that comes from ultimate accomplishment of objectives through hard work and perseverance.

◆ *Lack of Self-Discipline*

Self-discipline, which all of us seem to want in our children, is rooted in the discipline and limits received from parents. When bargaining with parents who have said *No*, a child learns interpersonal negotiating skills. He also acquires the character that develops from coming to terms with limits. The indulged child, on the other hand, becomes a child who must either be in control or who is controlled by others, depending on the child's level of comfort and security. These are children who are sometimes referred to as *Dr. Jekyll and Mr. Hyde*. They are usually compliant away from home because of their insecurity, but can be quite overbearing with their parents whom they are certain will tolerate their insufferable behavior. Indulgence is a friend neither to parent nor child.

◆ *Rejection*

Children who grow up accustomed to having their own way can be selfish and demanding in their relationships as teenagers and adults. They often become disappointed and resentful when life is not true to the picture given them by their parents, that is, that *they will be given what they want.* They quickly learn that peers and teachers will not accommodate them in the same way their parents do, and they are often rejected for immature or unreasonable behavior.

Those children, on the other hand, who have had so much responsibility that others feel sorry for them fare much better. They are, in fact, most likely to succeed. Work and responsibility do not weigh these children down. On the contrary, it appears to give them a sense of confidence and competence that nothing else can. After twenty years of working with ADHD and ADD children, we have seen clearly the difference in success between those children and adolescents who had responsibility and developed self-discipline and those who did not.

A note of caution for parents who are trying too hard to do it all for their children. *Supermoms* and *Superdads* do not produce *Superkids, i.e.,* really great, caring, responsible children, unless they share the responsibilities of running a family with them. With family size decreasing, more moms working, more dads traveling, and very complex work and extracurricular schedules, there is much to be done and too little time in which to do it. Instead of sitting bored on the sidelines and watching parents frantically trying to do everything, children can be involved. By offering incentives and making chores a family affair, parents can develop in their children a sense of belonging and purpose—a meaningful place within the family—and in the process allow them to experience the true joy of a job well done.

◆ GUIDELINES FOR A SUCCESSFUL ◆
RESPONSIBILITY PROGRAM

Now that you have decided to help your child become more responsible and independent, you will want to design a responsibility program that will work for your family. It will require the cooperation of every member of the family and should be fun. Our experience has shown that responsibility will not happen by accident. Rather, it must be carefully nurtured and developed. When deciding how to implement this program in your household, it is important to keep in mind the following guidelines.

◆ *Include Children in the Planning*

Give children as much choice as possible in what, when and how tasks are to be done. A Sunday night *Family Meeting* is a wonderful time to choose responsibilities, draw undesirable ones from a hat, and organize and plan for the week. It is an ideal time for feedback from the week before - positive, of course.

Research has shown that to achieve greatest improvement, one should positively respond to what was done correctly. While negative feedback is better than none at all, it has been found to be of limited usefulness in encouraging children to be more responsible. When privileges are dependent upon successful completion of responsibilities, parents can be supportive and kind, but also firm: "I am so glad you can go out Friday night," or "I am so sorry you can't....but I know you'll do better next week." Consequences, not words, bring changes in behavior. The *Family Meeting* also provides the ADHD or ADD child with the sense of structure, security and belonging that he especially needs.

Another advantage of the *Family Meeting* is that it gives the child an opportunity to plan his week. Children often respond better to completing jobs when they have plenty of warning and can schedule times that are most convenient for them. This is especially important with teenagers, who often have very busy schedules of their own. They frequently need advance notice, especially for major jobs that will require more time.

Every calling is great when greatly pursued.——Oliver Wendell Holmes, Jr.

♦ *Remember the Real Goal of Responsibility*

The object of household responsibility is not to have the children do all the chores.   Rather, it is to assist them in developing age-appropriate skills, competence and values. Well-kept bedrooms or perfect toy boxes are less important than developing confidence and capabilities.   Establish goals with your children and then utilize encouragement and praise to accomplish them.   Avoid criticism, nagging, coercion or punishment, which will only sabotage the enthusiasm and willing participation you desire.

♦ *Include Very Young Children*

Be alert to when your children are developmentally ready to help with particular tasks.   Two-year-olds are very willing and able to set the table, with plastic dishes of course, or to sort laundry. Seven-year-olds can vacuum, help with dinner and do the dishes. Children are capable of far more responsibility than most parents might expect.   For example, in one study families were asked whether their four-year-old children would be able to set the table, vacuum, sort clothes, save energy, clean the bathroom after a bath, and wake up to an alarm clock.   Only 9 percent of the parents agreed that their children could successfully complete these responsibilities.   However, it was demonstrated that 99 percent could complete them when they were introduced one at a time with appropriate training and encouragement (Wallinga and Sweaney, 1985).

Children are a great comfort in your old age—and they help you to reach it faster, too.——Lionel M. Kaufman

◆ *Teach Your Children the Skills*

Children do not know how to do most jobs. You must teach a new skill until it is mastered. After that, stand back and offer guidance only as requested. Encouragement and appreciation are helpful all the time.

◆ *Set Realistic Standards*

After you teach your child how to do the job, then encourage and support the child's efforts. Parents can obviously do most jobs better and more efficiently than children. It is important, however, to resist the temptation to do it over or to do it yourself. This undercuts the child's sense of accomplishment and esteem. A bed with lumps made by a proud 4-year-old is better than a perfect one made by his mom. In struggling through the problems encountered in these tasks, children will learn problem-solving skills they will use for a lifetime. Figuring out what to do if the vacuum cleaner gets clogged with a toy or if the fitted sheet will not pull over the mattress corner provide critical problem-solving experiences for the situations they will face later as adults. Little victories early in life lead to big successes later.

As Zig Ziglar states in the book *Raising Positive Kids In A Negative World*,

> You raise positive kids by teaching and requiring them early on to do the little things around the house. Step by step they naturally progress into accepting more and more responsibility until the happy day arrives when they will be able to do many things better than either parent.

♦ *Divide the Tasks into Manageable Portions*

Children are sometimes initially overwhelmed when faced with new tasks. ADHD and ADD children find it especially difficult to break a large job down into several small steps. If parents do this for them, it may enable them to stick with the job until it is completed. Requests should be very specific. For example, "Put the toothpaste away *with the top on it*." It also helps organize the ADHD or ADD child if parents indicate when the tasks will be done. Scheduling *morning, after school, evening* and *weekend* tasks will help the child begin to learn the planning skills necessary for later success at school and work.

♦ *Do Not Bribe Your Child*

"If you will,....then I will...." are words which spell disaster for the ADHD/ADD children and their parents. Bribery leaves both adult and child feeling manipulated, used, or, at the very least, somehow less of a person. It is absolutely essential for the ADHD/ADD child to perceive his parents as the ones in charge and that he understand that obtaining what he wants follows from doing what is expected of him. It is best for parents to maintain the motto at all times, "When you have...., then you may...." This statement is very different from "If you...then I..." When a child understands that obtaining what he wants is dependent on his efforts, he has come a long way toward developing a mature sense of responsibility, cause and effect, and the way the real world operates. Throughout this process it is important to use encouragement, reward and incentive generously.

◆ *Remain Firm but Kind*

After stating your demands, it is important not to weaken or feel sorry for your child. One of the seven deadly sins of parenting is feeling sorry for your child. If a parent feels sorry for a child, the child will feel sorry for himself. Remember, in the future his teacher will assign a paper and expect him to complete it. Likewise, his employer will expect him to do his job well. Childhood is the time to learn that life will encompass a world of work, where expectations are set and must be met. If a child is to experience success, a parent must not bail him out. It is important for parents to remain firm in their expectations and to be encouraging of their child's ability to complete a task: "Of course, you can do it. You're a great kid."

◆ *Don't Overdo It*

Occasionally a child has too many duties which may then interfere with other aspects of his life and become a drudgery. Fifteen to thirty minutes of work daily for a younger child and one to two hours on the weekend can provide valuable skills, confidence and independence without interfering. Even very busy children need this much time devoted to household responsibilities. A note of caution: Many parents emphasize only academic accomplishment stating, "His work is school. I expect him to make good grades." It is important, however, to give your child a more realistic and well-founded sense of responsibility. School work can become a very narcissistic goal and may do little to teach the cooperative responsibility so necessary for group endeavors later on.

◆ *Keep it Fun and Positive*

Above all, remember to keep the atmosphere in your home positive and fun. Emphasize the sense of satisfaction from accomplishing a task and the fun of working together as a family. If your attitude becomes one of drudgery, the child will soon follow. One family with whom we worked turned the evening chore of washing dishes into the best part of the day. No one could leave the kitchen until everything was clean and put away. They chose teams and raced against a timer each night to see if they could improve their time with different strategies. With everyone helping, this previously onerous job was fun and took less than seven minutes most evenings. Then no one was left in the kitchen feeling isolated and resentful.

◆ *Encourage Work Outside the Home*

As the child becomes older opportunities abound for demonstrating responsibility outside of the home. Babysitting, mowing lawns, sacking groceries, selling ice cream, assisting at the local hospital, nursing home or day care center, and other jobs will help a child learn to work with other adults and to cope with different peoples' standards. These outside experiences increase their independence and responsibility. To adolescents, positive feedback from an outside adult is often more meaningful than the same words from a biased parent. The income that a child will receive from these jobs provides an excellent opportunity for a parent to begin teaching him how to manage money. This is often a difficult area for ADHD/ADD children and most need much guidance to help them become fiscally responsible adults. As soon as you feel your child is ready, it is wise to open a savings and checking account for him. As he earns money, he can then decide how much he will spend and what amount he will save. Initially, you will need to spend time showing him how to balance a checkbook and record his expenses. We have found that even very young children understand money. They enjoy the sense of personal power they derive from deciding how to spend the money they have earned. Some children enjoy, as we all do, just knowing it's in the bank.

◆ ESTABLISHING A ◆
RESPONSIBILITY PROGRAM

Now that you have decided it is important to teach your child to be responsible and you have enlisted the cooperation of your family in assisting with household chores, you must decide how to keep a record of the jobs that have been assigned and completed and how to reward your child for his efforts. Many well-intentioned families often falter at this point, since, without an organized plan, follow-through may be impossible. The following responsibility program has been used with great success by many families with whom we have worked.

◆ *Design a Job Chart*

Discuss responsibilities with your child and establish what the expectations are. Draw up a job chart that lists the responsibilities and when each one is to be completed. Examples of responsibility charts for boys, girls and teenagers are included in the Appendix. You may wish, however, to have the child create his own.

◆ *Check Off Jobs as They are Completed*

After completing a task, the child should check it off on his chart. Checking the list is the child's responsibility. Parents may remind him to look over the chart, but they are encouraged not to remind him of specific tasks. Nagging and constant reminding are to be avoided. One of the beauties of a responsibility chart is that if things are not done, it is the child's problem, not yours. You do not need to fuss, nag or become frustrated. The chart becomes the reminder. At the end of the morning and evening, parents of young children should review the chart with them. Parents of older children will find that once a day, usually in the evening, is sufficient. Older teens may even suggest that once a week is adequate. Two strongly held rules are: (1) if the chart is not checked, the reinforcement is not given; and (2) if something is checked which was not indeed done, grave consequences follow. While children and teens can be expected to test these guidelines, they usually follow the rules once negative consequences are enforced.

◆ *Give Your Child His Reward Immediately*

Daily checking of the chart and rewarding of the child is recommended. It only takes a few minutes to check his efforts. Doing so provides the child with the incentive to remain motivated. ADHD/ADD children, especially, respond best to immediate reward. They may not even associate the reward with the appropriate task if it is delayed. As the child becomes older, you may want to use the system to begin teaching him how to delay gratification.

We have found chips to be an effective and immediate reward and utilize *Chipper Chips®* in our practice. These are colorful chips with Chipper Bear® on one side and a positive statement such as "good job" on the other. Three checks on the chart are usually equal to one chip. Poker chips work well too, with a different color chip for each child in the family. Each day a child can earn from three to ten chips, depending upon his age and how much he does. Children enjoy saving the chips, counting them and playing with them. They like knowing exactly how they can earn what they want. They begin to realize they can have anything in life, of which their parents approve, for which they are willing to work. This gives children a satisfying sense of power and control over their lives.

As chips are given to the child for jobs completed, it is important for you to praise what he has done, offer encouragement for things not done, and assurance that you know the child will do well tomorrow. Hugs and smiles, verbal and written praise are all powerful motivators for children. Praise will lead to increased acceptance of responsibility, while criticism usually leads to discouragement and fewer jobs done.

When using this program parents are encouraged not to lecture or scold their child. Merely enforcing the consequences will teach the child all he needs to know. The positive consequence is acquiring chips toward activities and purchases he desires. The negative consequence is not earning privileges the child may currently take for granted.

◆ Assign Values to the Ultimate Rewards

Activities, special privileges, toys desired, among other things, should be assigned values. Being driven to a friend's house may require one chip, while having a friend spend the night may cost six chips or more if a movie and pizza are part of the evening. The message should always be, "I'm very happy to do my part if you do yours." The way the child shows he has done his part is through chips earned.

Older children and teenagers are usually on a point system. Use of the car for an evening might be one hundred points, while going to a movie might be fifty. For the chip or point system to be effective, the child or adolescent must spend his chips and points for some (not all) of the things he currently takes for granted, such as extra T.V. time, going to the park, having a friend over, going to get an ice cream, driving the car or receiving an allowance.

In addition to receiving chips or points, it is helpful to insist that 80 to 90 percent of the daily responsibilities be completed in order to have afternoon and evening privileges. If they are not, the child completes the responsibilities and then spends the rest of the afternoon in his room without television, games and special toys. This strategy was devised when we discovered that if no chips or points were needed for a specific goal, children sometimes decided they did not have to do anything. If this seems a little harsh, think of the response your child will receive from his high school English teacher when he fails to do a term paper or from his boss when he forgets an important appointment. To have a confident, capable, cooperative adolescent and adult, a parent must be willing to endure hurt feelings and frustrating moments in the early years. A preschooler who loses T.V. privileges, for example, is usually very willing to do his jobs the next day. Likewise, a second grader who misses soccer or riding his bike with his friends will remember to do his responsibilities. A social butterfly, who must cancel a friend's visit, will be more cooperative in the future; likewise will the teenager who can't use the phone or must cancel a date. The consequence, you must constantly remind him, is his choice, not yours. You are simply the mediator between his choices and his consequences.

◆ *Give Your Child the Ultimate Reward*

It is important to keep your commitment when the child has earned enough chips to reach his goal. The sooner you allow him to cash in his chips for the desired incentive, the more motivated he will be to work for additional goals. Be cautious, however, about committing to certain rewards simply to placate your child. Children are quite willing to work for what they want, and to save for it, if told the cost.

One six-year-old, for example, with whom we worked wanted a dog desperately. His mother was equally adamant about not having a dog. The price: one thousand chips. While his mother did not want a dog, she was willing to have one if he could show her that he could be responsible for taking care of a pet. Six months and two weeks later, he obtained his goal. While this is an unusual example, we have found children very capable of delaying gratification for long periods to obtain what they really want. If a child is not willing to work for a goal, the desire is usually a passing fancy that he would soon have discarded anyway.

Of course, the ultimate reward for both parent and child will be his developing a sense of self-discipline and the ability to internalize the necessary tasks of living to make them routine in his life.   As children become older, parents begin to see this happening.   Children will handle many tasks automatically, such as brushing their teeth, making their beds or cleaning their rooms, and will not expect to be rewarded for their completion. Neuronal pathways in the brain will have been established much as those automatic patterns associated with driving a car.

As children become more proficient at helping with household tasks, you may even find that they will become very aware of what other family members are doing. Some families have found this can become quite embarrassing if either mom or dad is not doing his or her fair share to help.   One research study found that kindergarten children who had received responsibility training became quite distressed with parents whom they perceived as not contributing.   Many even began shaming their parents into fulfilling their responsibilities. Most parents were delighted. Even those who were somewhat frustrated by their child's new sense of industriousness for the whole family begrudgingly pitched in (Wallinga and Sweaney, 1985).

♦ RESPONSIBILITY IS A FAMILY AFFAIR ♦

To alleviate the problem of unequal participation in household responsibilities and to maintain a sense of fairness, some families have found it helpful to design responsibility charts for mom and dad as well as the children. This helps promote a team spirit and shows everyone how the tasks involved in maintaining their home are being divided and managed.

A Family Organization Calendar is also helpful with the ADHD/ADD child and adolescent. At the weekly *Family Meeting* everyone's activities for the next two to four weeks are discussed and recorded on the calendar. Each person's appointments and activities are scheduled, as well as birthdays of relatives, holidays, etc. The family then looks at everything posted, organizes it and decides what must be done to accomplish successfully the activities and goals for each week.   Duties are then assigned and are, likewise, posted. Each person has a different colored highlighter to emphasize those things pertinent to him. He can then easily spot his activities and responsibilities daily and plan ahead. He can also see what other members of the family are doing and how they are contributing to the overall well-being of the household. Children are often amazed at parents' responsibilities.

C'MON DAD- THE GRASS SURE NEEDS MOWING

This calendar not only facilitates grouping, organizing and delegating, but it makes it apparent which family member may be having an especially difficult week. Others can then redistribute responsibilities to help equalize the tasks that must be accomplished.   Children and adolescents have a much better understanding of the overall organization of the family and of how they fit into its activities and needs. Seeing the total picture in this way is helpful to the ADHD/ADD child or adolescent who inherently struggles with organization. Each family may wish to design it's own simple or elaborate calendar, or use the Family Organization Calendar included in the Appendix.

Teaching an ADHD or ADD child to be responsible and to enjoy working is a progressive task that requires considerable effort on the part of parents for many years. As the child becomes older, discussions can begin to focus on what parents and others do at their jobs. Children enjoy visiting the workplace and learning about the occupations of their parents and relatives. Preparing a child or adolescent for the world of work is one of a parent's most important and vital tasks. Having a vision of what life may be like after he completes school can be highly motivating and encouraging to the child or adolescent with an attention disorder. The years of early and higher education are difficult for most and are filled with disappointments and obstacles to overcome. Ultimately, it is in their work that most ADHD and ADD people find their real sense of self-esteem and begin to feel the best about themselves. When the person with an attention disorder enters the workplace, his true talents and abilities are often rewarded for the first time. Unlike the academic environment, success stories abound among adults who have ADHD and ADD. Our clinical experience has shown that those with attention disorders, especially ADHD, are very likely to own their own businesses and to be successful entrepreneurs. The high energy, independence, persistence and unwillingness to accept *No*, often considered negative characteristics in childhood and adolescence, become assets in adulthood, especially in work situations which capitalize on these very positive traits. The following story, related by a successful ADHD adult, demonstrates this point.

> *As I sit in the comfortable surroundings of my office and look at my stationery which says, "PRESIDENT, Jones Advertising Agency," it is hard to believe where my life was ten years ago. It is a miracle that I am here.*
>
> *As a young boy I was the apple of my parents' eye. I was energetic and alert . . . a verbal child who was everywhere and took in everything. I forever followed my parents around asking, "Why?", "Can we do this?" and assuring them "You'll be proud of me when I grow up." From an early age I seemed destined for success.*
>
> *My parents were like most who had survived the Depression. They were conscientious and hardworking; people of moderate means but a wealth of dreams, especially for their children. My mother frequently voiced her objective for us: "To make us independent and stand on our own two feet." My parents persuaded themselves and also me that education and hard work could guarantee a happy life. They scrimped to send me to a private military school to harness my energy and to help me succeed.*
>
> *Despite many raps on my knuckles for talking out of turn and incessant laps around the bull ring for mischievious behavior, school went reasonably well; that*

is, until third grade. My inability to focus and concentrate, my bossiness with my classmates, and my disorganization and forgetfulness were increasing problems. My father thought discipline would solve the problem, and he used lots of it. However, it was like throwing gasoline on a fire. Our relationship became increasingly confrontational and I lost all of my self-esteem. I remember saying to my father, "Dad, I don't intentionally get in trouble or try to upset you. I don't know what's wrong with me."

I could feel my grades slipping—and myself as well. Despite many conferences between my family and the school, things did not improve. In fact, every year was worse. By the end of high school I was barely passing. I graduated second from the bottom of my class. I hated school. The despair I felt was intolerable enough, but the sadness I saw in my parents' eyes was unbearable. The day I graduated I joined the Merchant Marines. I felt my family would be better off without me.

The discipline and structure of a ship at sea helped some. It could not, however, alleviate the pain I felt so intensely. "How could a child of such promise have become such a failure as an adult?" I found myself drinking to drown my consciousness and soon drugs, too, entered the picture. I was a complete mess.

I was discharged from the Merchant Marines honorably, but barely so. I was determined to go to college and prove to my disillusioned parents that I could be the son they had so hoped me to be. During this time I fell in love with a wonderful girl. We married when I was a freshman in college.

Despite my intense desire to be successful, I had no control over my mind, which was determined to wander, and my impulses, which were forever getting me in trouble. My wife, who I know loved me, could finally take it no longer. The angry outbursts, the impulsive buying, the incessant activity were more than she could endure. Tearfully, but determinedly, she departed.

I hit bottom. I knew I could not go on. I sought refuge in solitude and drugs. I returned to college and managed to earn a degree. I grew increasingly uneasy about my drug usage and knew professional help was essential.

I saw a psychiatrist, a wonderful man, who for eight years was my therapist, my medicine man, my mentor and my best friend. He diagnosed my attention disorder and prescribed Ritalin - 10 mg. four times daily. He insisted on psychotherapy as well. Together we sorted out the emotional baggage I had collected for thirty-five years.

During the interim I opened an advertising agency, settled down in the community in which I grew up, and am now an active participant. I have even become a local politician. My income has reached levels not dreamed of before. The high energy and inquisitiveness that plagued me in my early years are now assets that have caused me to succeed beyond my wildest expectations. Finally my parents have reason to be quite proud. That has been perhaps the greatest satisfaction of all.

◆ SUMMARY ◆

Children and adolescents with attention disorders desperately need a sense of the future and its bright possibilities. This is especially true for those bogged down by the requirements of school. Early introduction to the world of work can help facilitate that vision. Many a struggling ADHD/ADD student has been told, "If you can hang on until adulthood, the odds shift dramatically in your favor." This is true, of course, if their self-esteem has remained intact.

Work and responsibility are essential to the development of the ADHD/ADD child and adolescent's potential. While not often stressed, it should, perhaps, be treated as an intervention equal in importance to behavior management, cognitive therapy and social skills training. In adulthood, self-discipline and the love of work frequently become the factors which separate those who succeed from those who do not.

For the things we have to learn before we can do them, we learn by doing them.

—Aristotle

Handling the Homework Hurdle

Of all the educational issues handled by parents of ADHD and ADD children, perhaps none is more demanding and difficult to deal with than homework. In fact, homework time is often a more dreaded event for the ADHD/ADD child's parent than for the child himself. Most children with attention problems do not come home from school and after a brief pleasant visit with their parents gleefully announce their eagerness to begin homework. Rather, they will use every device possible to avoid this task. They may tell you there is no homework, that it was completed at school or that the substitute teacher did not give any assignments. They can be extremely creative in finding ways to avoid homework.

In actuality, homework may not ever be the child's favorite activity. Neither, however, does it have to be a nightmare. As difficult as it may seem to believe, it can even be a vehicle for bringing you and your child closer together if structured properly. It can also be an opportunity for you to reinforce your child's good qualities and provide some positive balance to the other demands of his day. Once they realize it is a task they cannot avoid, most ADHD/ADD children, who really want desperately to do well in school, are eager for help from caring and interested parents. Evidence suggests that supervising homework is the most important thing parents can do to make certain their children succeed in school. Further, children who are given appropriate guidance with homework do better in school even if their parents have not had a formal education, according to a recent survey of professionals (Feldman, 1987). It is a parent's structure and interest that are critical.

Homework is a way for the teacher to evaluate what a child has learned and what still needs further explanation. When used correctly homework can also teach a child many of the life skills which will be so critical to his future success. Managing one's time, following directions, completing difficult tasks, taking initiative, being resourceful, accepting responsibility and relying on oneself are all experienced daily as the child completes his assignments. Since most ADHD/ADD children learn by repetition, nightly homework can provide an opportunity for these skills to be practiced repeatedly until they become internalized and part of the child's natural way of approaching life.

The following strategies have been used with success by many parents of children with attention disorders. While implementing all of them consistently would be extremely difficult and some suggestions may be more appropriate for certain children than others, we hope they will provide a framework to assist you with this major aspect of life with your ADHD or ADD child. Helping your child establish good homework habits will result not only in his increased success but in a more harmonious household for all.

◆ BASIC HOMEWORK GUIDELINES ◆

◆ *Keep the Responsibility Focused on the Child*

Working together on homework has the best possibility of succeeding if it is continually emphasized that homework is the responsibility of the child and not that of the parents. Parents must emphasize to their child that they are always willing to assist him in reaching *his* homework goals, but that they will not do things for him that he is capable of doing himself. If assignments are difficult and he complains that he *can't* do the homework, parents may need to help him understand the directions or go over with him again the material that was covered in class. If the amount of homework being required is truly excessive, and it often is for ADHD/ADD children, parents may need to discuss with the teacher the difficulties and problems being experienced as a result of such a heavy homework load. Accommodations may well be in order. Parents should not, however, complete a child's homework for him. To do so only serves to undermine his sense of self and make him feel inadequate.

A child should be involved as much as possible in all decisions such as where and when to study and for how long. The more he feels in control of these decisions, the more willling he will be to carry them through. Ideally a child should feel capable of handling most tasks on his own but know that his parents are there when he really needs them.

♦ *Determine an Appropriate After-School Medication Regimen*

Anyone who has studied with an ADHD or ADD child or adolescent knows that they can turn a 20-minute assignment into an all-afternoon and evening endeavor. While some of the dawdling, distractibility, slow work rate and inattention may be avoidance, for most students these are the typical symptoms which require medication at school. If a child has more than 30 to 45 minutes of homework and especially when he is studying for tests, a third dose of stimulant medication is more often required than not for those taking Ritalin and Dexedrine. Determine the usual homework expectations with your child's teacher, and consult with your physician regarding appropriately medicating your child for this portion of the day. Giving a child or adolescent medication for school only suggests that after school assignments are not important. This approach is rarely successful by third or fourth grade. The family conflict created by the homework issue can be far more detrimental, in our opinion, than any negative medication effects.

♦ *Organize the Child for Learning*

Your basic task is to help your child learn how to learn. The first step in this process will be teaching your child how to become organized. Helping him establish a homework routine in the early grades will hopefully enable him to internalize a sense of structure and time management for himself as he matures. Designating a certain time and place each day for homework is essential for the ADHD/ADD child and will help eliminate the most common argument about homework—when it will be done. Design a *Weekly Homework Schedule* to show when homework assignments will be completed each day. It is important to indicate outside activities, practice schedules, appointments and meetings, as well as study times on the schedule. This will help a child begin to understand planning ahead in order to accomplish a number of things in one day. Helping to design and fill in the *Weekly Homework Schedule* gives a child a sense of control over his time and is more likely to

---

The mother's heart is the child's schoolroom.——Henry Ward Beecher

increase his motivation to follow through with completing the schedule.

It may also be helpful to have your child complete a monthly calendar in addition to the one completed by the family. Use it to show the due dates of long range assignments, projects or papers, research trips to the library, a time to gather supplies for projects, etc. Such a schedule will demonstrate to him visually that in organizing you must begin with the big picture and then break tasks down into more finite parts and schedule time more specifically. Many children and adolescents require a visual to understand the total picture.

Scheduling and organizing do not come naturally to the ADHD or ADD child. You will initially meet much resistance. Hold firm to these expectations stating both verbally and in your actions, "This is important even if it's hard; you'll learn how to do it easily with a little practice." Remember your goal is not to make your child happy but rather to prepare him for success.

Help your child establish the habit of recording assignments each day into a separate assignment notebook or on a homework assignment sheet for younger children. Have the teacher initial the notebook daily to make certain the assignments are correctly recorded. She may also wish to make comments in the notebook about your child's daily progress. These comments should, however, be positive ones in order to motivate and encourage your child. For younger children, you may even wish to ask the teacher to make certain the assignment sheet is placed in the bookbag. Frequently this is necessary at the start of the year until it is established as a routine and becomes a habit for your child. You are also encouraged to use a notebook which the child must take to school and bring home every day. We call it *The Notebook* and dire consequences ensue when it is forgotten. This notebook has the Weekly Assignment Sheet scotch taped to the inside cover and three color-coded folders for *Work to Be Done, Completed Work* and *Papers to Save*. Teaching the child to utilize this notebook and to take it with him to every class and bring it home each day can save many a parent or teacher from becoming frustrated over lost or forgotten homework, homework to be done, or completed work to be turned in.

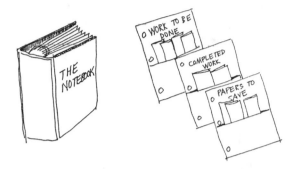

Making color-coded book covers and then color coding and coordinating your child's books will also help to ensure that he remembers to bring home the correct notebook for each subject. For example, the math textbook cover and notebook may be green, while the science textbook cover and notebook are red. Once decided, the colors often continue throughout school.

◆ *Become a Phantom Partner in Homework*

Your goal is to supervise your child's completion of his daily homework without making him feel coerced. An awareness of your presence is sometimes enough to give an ADHD/ADD child the sense of security and control he needs to settle down and begin working. It also reinforces the message that homework is a priority in your household. Gentle suggestions that he take a brief break, encouragement that he is doing well, or a quick answer to a question may eliminate frustration before it builds to an explosive level. As your child increases in his ability to handle most assignments on his own, convey to him that you are there to assist as needed, but you are not there to police him.

Many children with attention disorders need the calming presence of a positive person for many years. While it may not seem fair that other parents of even much younger children do not need to supervise homework at all, this will be an important task for you as the parent of an ADHD/ADD child well into his high school years. If you are not able to be home in the afternoons it is important that you establish the homework time for the evenings when you are home or that you arrange for someone to be with your child in the afternoons. Often an older high school or college student that lives in the neighborhood can be found to sit with your child while he completes his assignments.

◆ *Be Prepared to Answer Questions*

It is helpful to review the chapters that your child is studying before he comes to you with problems. This will enable you to answer his questions quickly. ADHD children especially are extremely impatient and become frustrated if you must spend several minutes reading the material before answering their questions. Hopefully you will not be responsible for teaching the material to your child and ideally it is not desirable for you to do so. Using teaching methods that differ significantly from the teacher's may confuse your child. However, children with attention disorders often miss significant concepts and explanations that are given in class and you may be able to provide an important missing link that will enhance their understanding.

If the teacher's style differs significantly from your child's learning style, much more actual teaching will be required. For example, a dysphonetic child, i.e. one who cannot learn phonics, might have to be taught a sight or whole-word approach to reading at home if his school utilizes a primarily phonetic reading series. Kinesthetic learners may require reteaching using more motor and hands-on methods. Before attempting to assist your child or adolescent, you should understand both the teaching style utilized in the classroom and your child's learning characteristics. If significant discrepancies exist, intervention or classroom modifications will be required. Homework assistance alone will not be adequate.

◆ *State Your Expectations Clearly*

Before your child begins an assignment have him explain the directions to you. Confusion arises when a child is not certain exactly what is expected of him. For example, if written answers to questions must be in complete sentences specify this from the beginning. Many ADHD/ADD children think three word answers will suffice. For younger children, ask the teacher to assist you in making certain your child has recorded assignments correctly on his assignment sheet. Inattentive children often miss important parts of assigments and directions that are given in class. You may need to check your child's assignment sheet or pad for several years until he is able to remember consistently to write down assignments completely and accurately.

Since every teacher's homework expectations are different, you should consult with the teacher to determine her requirements. If your child is taking more than 1 1/2 times the amount of time she says is appropriate, you should consult with her and modifications should be implemented. Spending three, four, five hours and longer is very disruptive of family life and can create problems more severe than lack of homework. Both spouses and siblings resent a parent's spending hours each day supervising the homework task.

We have also found it helpful to refer to this time as *study time*—not homework time. This avoids the arguments that arise when a child insists that no homework was assigned. If a child states that he finished all his homework at school or that no homework was given, it is generally wise to avoid the temptation of breaking the homework habit. Encourage him to spend the allocated study time for additional reading or review of previous assignments. Consistency is important with ADHD and ADD children.

If your child is having trouble finding enough time to do homework, his day may be overscheduled. While it is usually helpful to keep the ADHD/ADD child structured and involved with interesting afterschool activities, it is important not to overprogram him so that he does not have time to complete his homework in a relaxed manner. Carefully completing the *Weekly Homework Schedule* should assist in minimizing this problem.

It is important to determine the amount of homework time your child can utilize effectively and your family can incorporate into its existing structure without being unduly disruptive. The following homework time guidelines have been found to be appropriate and workable for many families:

•	First-Third Grades	½ - 1 hour
•	Fourth-Sixth Grades	1 - 1½ hours
•	Middle School	1½ - 2½ hours
•	High School	2 - 4 hours

♦ *Determine the Optimal Time for Homework*

Most ADHD/ADD children are fatigued after a day of concentration and need time to unwind and relax before tackling homework. Others, however, have a need for total closure of the day's requirements and are eager to complete their homework and then enjoy the rest of the day. Talk with your child and determine what time of day best suits his needs. Then enter the chosen time on the Weekly Homework Schedule for each day. Of course, if your child is taking medication, it is important to schedule homework during the time his medication is effective.

♦ *Minimize Distractions in the Study Environment*

Children with attention disorders need a well-organized work space more than most. While almost all children benefit from a study environment that is quiet and has a minimum of distractions, for most ADHD/ADD children this is essential. Ideally they should work in a designated study area with few visual or auditory distractors. Exciting pictures on the wall, mobiles overhead and flashing lights can be very distracting for a visual child. Radios,

To teach is to learn.——Japanese Proverb

tape decks and compact disc players should be utilized only to facilitate the studying process. What is helpful may be surprising, however. Many children and adolescents study better with background noise, even loud music. To determine the best environment for learning requires input from the child. Television, however, is rarely helpful. Rather, it is usually the worst of all distractors, being both visually and auditorally stimulating.

If there are several children in your household you will probably want to discourage your ADHD or ADD child from studying in the same room with your other children. This is usually too distracting for an attention-disordered child unless there is a studious older sibling whose presence is calming and motivating.

The telephone often causes frequent interruptions and can be the source of much anxiety for ADHD or ADD children who are very socially involved. Establish a policy that no phone calls will be accepted during the designated study time and then either screen them yourself or use an answering machine. Some parents even unplug phones their child or adolescent can hear, for as soon as it rings the child wonders who called. Taking it off the hook is another option. Just advise your family and friends. Your children's friends will quickly learn to respect your rules and begin calling after his study time.

◆ *Determine What Your Child Does Not Like About Homework*

When parents question their ADHD and ADD children about homework they are often surprised to learn that what bothers them is not what the parents expected. Some children dread the loneliness of sitting in a quiet room to do homework. For these children, working at the kitchen table while mom prepares dinner may be the most effective place for them to study. The noise of the kitchen can serve as background noise for these children and may actually enable them to concentrate more efficiently. Insisting that a child work in a totally isolated part of the house may be counterproductive. If a parent is not home when the child is studying, the presence of a pet can sometimes serve to make a child feel connected and not alone.

When a child avoids or refuses to do homework, problem-solving is in order. Listen to your child and try to determine the cause of the problem. Perhaps he does not understand the assignments or he is not using his time wisely. Is he having trouble with organizing or does he dread the written work? Listen carefully to your child's complaints and decide together on appropriate remedies.

♦ *Prioritize Homework Assignments*

Begin the homework session each day by reviewing with your child the assignments on his homework sheet. Help him estimate how long each assignment will take and how much total time he will need to spend on homework that day. Explain to him the benefit of doing the most important or difficult assignments first, while he is the most rested. If he needs the reinforcement, have him complete the easier ones first. Make sure he schedules some breaks during his study time to allow for physical movement. Most children with attention disorders, especially those with ADHD, cannot sit still for long periods of time. A break to bring you a completed assignment can enhance their concentration during the study time that follows. Other brief breaks every 15 minutes can also be helpful. Teach your child to spend some time each day working on long-range assignments.

By perseverance the snail reached the ark.——Charles Haddon Spurgeon

♦ *Break Each Assignment into Workable Intervals*

Most ADHD/ADD children need to be shown how to divide an assignment into several smaller steps that can be completed one at a time. This inability to take the whole and break it down into manageable parts is the source of much of the ADHD/ADD child's frustration with homework. This skill requires much neurological integration and may be delayed for several years. Unfortunately, it does not come naturally for most ADHD/ADD children. We have worked with many college students who continue to struggle with this task. The earlier you begin helping your child understand this approach to learning, the sooner he will be able to internalize it. Initially, it may be helpful to set time limits and give rewards for each section of an assignment the child completes. For example, if he has twenty pages to read in history, he might break it into two ten-page intervals with a five-minute break after each interval. A younger child may need to break the assignment into four five-page intervals. You know your child's attention span and tolerance for concentration better than anyone and can help him to establish workable and realistic guidelines for himself.

Long reading assignments are a source of difficulty for many ADHD/ADD students, especially those with weak reading comprehension skills. Reading and understanding information require numerous skills and may be extremely difficult for children with attention disorders. Dividing material into manageable portions, reading it out loud together and discussing it, reading it into a tape recorder and allowing frequent breaks may help your child complete this task with a minimum of frustration. For visual children, rent a video of the material they are studying for an exciting overview. Learning about the brain can be thrilling on video, but may be overwhelming in a textbook. *Hamlet* and *Jane Eyre* are, likewise, more enjoyable and comprehensible in a visual format. One student commented on how much he enjoyed *hearing* Shakespearean verse and how much he disliked reading it.

♦ *Provide Adequate Materials and Supplies*

It is essential to have a designated area in your home where your child can always find the paper, pencils, notecards, ruler, paper clips, folders, scotch tape or glue needed for completing assignments. Many parents have also found it helpful to purchase additional copies of their child's textbooks to keep at home for those occasions when he may lose a book or forget to bring it home. It is also beneficial for some children to underline major ideas, highlight important information, or write notes in the margins. If possible, you should have a dictionary, atlas, thesaurus and encyclopedias or other reference materials available. For brief reports, especially in earlier grades, this can save frantic, last minute trips to the library.

The most important item you can provide for your child is a home computer. Much frustration over written assignments can be eliminated if the teacher will allow your child to type his assignments on the computer. Most children with attention disorders respond naturally to the computer and enjoy the fast pace and immediate feedback they receive from the keyboard. In addition, there are many excellent computer programs available that can help your child review what was learned at school and complete his homework more efficiently. It would be helpful if typing and keyboarding were required by second grade for those with attention disorders.

◆ Teach Your Child Library Skills

A good understanding of the organization of a library becomes more and more essential the older a child becomes. Even in elementary school, however, it is critical that the child understands the location of the card catalog and how the Dewey Decimal System works. While this is typically taught at school, the ADHD/ADD child often benefits from additional explanations by parents. It is even helpful to begin familiarizing your preschool child with the library. Get him a library card as soon as he is old enough to understand and let him choose books to check out. Most libraries have story times and reading clubs that children can join. Becoming comfortable with the library and knowledgeable about its resources can be of great benefit to ADHD/ADD children throughout their school years, especially during the high school years.

God could not be everywhere and therefore he made mothers.——Jewish Proverb

◆ *Give Special Assistance with Papers*

Even though most teachers explain in class what is expected in a written paper, many ADHD/ADD children struggle with these assignments and need additional help. The several steps involved in successfully completing a paper are difficult for many ADHD/ADD children to master and often take several years to become automatic. Selecting a topic, researching, taking notes, writing an outline, writing a final draft and proofreading all require great attention to detail and concentration, which are not the ADHD/ADD child's forté. It is usually necessary to show students the basic parts of a paper and help them think through the structure and organization of their essays. Write a schedule for them showing how to break the work into small tasks that can be completed over several days.

If your child becomes discouraged with writing, suggest that he work on another section for a while, such as the bibliography, title page or a visual. Some children will need to dictate their information into a tape recorder since the writing component of the task is so defeating. For older children it is helpful to remind them to answer the basic literary questions of who? what? when? where? why? and how? This helps not only with composing ideas for a paper, but with the understanding and comprehension of lengthy reading assignments as well.

♦ *Minimize the Frustration of Math Homework*

Many children with attention disorders find it extremely difficult at the end of a tiring school day to pay attention to the many details involved in math homework. Fatigue and lack of sustained attention combine to cause many careless errors. To help minimize these you may wish to suggest that your child work on math homework first. Have him circle the sign in each problem to make certain that he pays attention to it. He is less likely to multiply if he has just circled the sign for division. Many ADHD and ADD children find that doing their homework on graph paper, with blocks fitted to their normal writing size, helps them keep figures aligned.

Cindy   February 21

1) 2,948
   (+) 7,382
   10,330

2) 7,429
   (-) 5,873
   1,556

3) 86
   (÷) 43
   172
   344
   3,612

4) 35.95
   (+) 87.44
   123.39

5) 3,896
   (×) 53
   11,688
   194800
   206,488

6) 3,261
   (-) 1,896
   1,365

It is also helpful to have a child read and discuss math word problems with you out loud. Thinking out loud often helps the ADHD or ADD child to process information more clearly and become more organized.

♦ *Reinforce Your Child Generously for Completing His Assignments*

Homework is an excellent opportunity to teach ADHD/ADD children the importance of sticking with a task until it is completed. The more you enable a child to feel the satisfaction that comes from completing his work, the more able he will be to finish future assignments. Rewarding and encouraging your child will increase his confidence and feeling of competence. Rewards should be offered immediately after the task is completed. Often a pat on the back and verbal praise are sufficient to keep the child motivated. You may wish to also have rewards for homework completed as part of the chip or point reinforcement program described in Chapter 12.

♦ *Make Certain the Completed Homework is Returned*

It is critical to help both children and adolescents develop the habit of placing completed homework to be returned to school the next day, in their notebook. You may have to watch the younger child put his notebook in his bookbag as soon as his work is finished and then put his bookbag and books in their designated place—by the door, in a chair, etc. Have your child put everything he needs for school in this place before he goes to bed. Doing so avoids frantic searching in the morning and lost or forgotten papers for school.

♦ *Consider the Help of Tutors*

As the ADHD or ADD child gets older, it is both natural and desirable for him to begin wanting to handle his work with no assistance from others, especially mom. Mom is usually equally ready for a reprieve. For many ADHD/ ADD children, however, this is not yet a task they are developmentally ready to handle alone. If structure and reinforcement are all that is needed, often a tutor, especially an older student whom the child admires, can be of great help to the child and simultaneously reinforce his own understanding of the subject matter. If more is needed, a trained tutor may be required. When it becomes apparent that your parent and teacher roles are beginning to conflict, wisdom dictates that it is time for a change.

In teaching it is the method and not the content that is the message . . . the drawing out, not the pumping in.——Ashley Montague

◆ *Model Working at Home to Your Child*

Many children, especially ADHD children, view homework as a punishment and do not realize that the true value and purpose of homework is to reinforce what has been learned during the day. It is helpful for parents to bring work home to review in the evening so that children come to realize that working, reading and studying are as much a part of life as eating and watching television.

All parents have *home work* they need to do. While your child is completing his assignments, tackle the jobs you have to do. It can be a great time to pay bills, write letters and organize your schedule. Model the behaviors you want your child to adopt. Read assigned books along with your child and discuss them afterwards. As time permits, study and prepare with your child. Take practice tests with him and discuss your right and wrong answers together. It is important to be aware of what your child is studying and participate as much as possible. Generally, the more involved you are as a partner in learning, the better he will do.

◆ *Be Alert to Signs of Frustration*

Homework is often a time when ADHD/ADD children freely express their frustration. After struggling to control his behavior at school all day, a child may *lose it* in the comfort of familiar surroundings. In fact, the more stressful school is, the more likely this is to occur. Home behavior is an excellent barometer of what is happening in school. Perhaps, that is why many ADHD/ADD children and adolescents are so much easier to live with in the summer.

When a child becomes frustrated, find out what the problem is. Is there a particular subject or teacher that is giving him difficulty? Is he consistently becoming frustrated over the same thing, such as handwriting or assignments involving auditory or visual memory? Encourage him to express his thoughts and problems with you and then attempt to address them as straightforwardly as possible. It is important, however, that you respond only to genuine frustration. Don't let him manipulate you with his frustration into relaxing your requirement that homework be completed.

♦ *Ask the Teacher for Assistance*

If the homework load seems to be more than your child can handle, discuss it with his teacher. In our experience most teachers are willing to be flexible when they know an ADHD/ADD child and his family are trying. For example, if your child writes slowly, especially in the afternoon after a long day of school, perhaps the teacher will permit him to complete every other math problem assigned. Many teachers are sensitive to a child's needs once they understand the tremendous frustration the ADHD/ADD child experiences. After all, the goal of homework is to reinforce learning—not to discourage the learner!

♦ *Help Your Child Maintain a Positive Attitude About Homework and School*

And finally, if all else fails write a note to his teacher explaining why he has not finished. On occasion, schools may unwittingly assign more homework in an evening than is reasonable for your child. This especially becomes a problem in higher grades when teachers may not realize the other assignments that have been given.   If a child is extremely frustrated and the school does not understand, action is required. After all, the tail should not wag the dog. Homework is intended to reinforce what is learned in school, not to so defeat and baffle a child that he has no interest in future learning. Hopefully you will not reach this point with your child. If, however, you do, help him survive a temporary bad time and don't let him doubt that you are on his team. You can do so without making negative comments about the school or the teacher. For his school experience to be the most effective, your child needs to see you and his teacher working together as a strong team. Let him know you will schedule a conference where the three of you can meet to devise a more successful strategy.

♦ ADVANCED HOMEWORK GUIDELINES ♦

Now that you have mastered the basics of guiding your child in the completion of his homework, you will want to begin experimenting with creative ways to enhance your child's learning and maximize the effectiveness of his homework time.

♦ *Use the Power of Humor*

Enthusiasm on your part is essential to help the ADHD or ADD child maintain interest in homework. It is important, of course, that your child realize the seriousness you place upon academics and learning. However, beginning each day's assignments with enthusiasm and eagerness will motivate him more than a stern, serious approach. In your role as *homework coach* you are part cheerleader, part teacher, part policeman and part counselor with a heavy emphasis on the cheerleader role. Share jokes occasionally, make each other laugh and share stories about your own foibles with homework. Your positive approach and encouragement can help make homework more bearable for your child and for you.

Display your continued excitement about learning and growing. At age thirty-five begin playing a new instrument, learn to sky-dive, take up jogging, or learn how to be a gardener. Let your child see that learning is a natural and exciting part of life.

♦ *Be Creative with the Homework Location*

While most homework should be completed in the place and under the condition found most conducive to your child's learning, we have found that having fun with homework can certainly help reinforce learning. To vary the routine on occasion may be just the change your child needs to refresh him for further studying. Take your child outside on a beautiful day to study under the trees, or join him for a walk around the block while you review math facts.

♦ *Experiment with Sounds*

For many children, music in the background while trying to study is a distraction. For others, however, the steady beat of classical or baroque music may help reduce distractions. The proponents of Superlearning have found that music with four-four timing and sixty beats per minute increases concentration and memory (Ostrander, 1989).

Rhythm can also be used very effectively to help a child read, learn multiplication tables or history facts. Some children have been able to master long memory assignments by repeating them with a melody or with the rhythm of a favorite song. Most of us learned our ABC's easily by singing the *ABC Song*.

♦ *Be Open to New Techniques*

Children, especially ADHD/ADD children, can be very insightful and intuitive. They often know which conditions and situations help them learn best. Ask your child what is most effective for him. As you listen to his responses you will begin to have a better sense of his learning style. You can then help him build on his strengths and learn to compensate for his weaknesses. Knowing whether your child is an auditory, visual or kinesthetic learner can assist you greatly in creating effective methods of presenting material to him. Your child also needs to understand his learning style. Children love learning about themselves. Guiding a child toward an understanding of who he is should, in fact, be one of the greatest goals of education.

If your child is a visual or kinesthetic learner you may especially need to find additional ways to review the material that has been covered in class. Auditory, left-brain children tend to be the most responsive to traditional classroom teaching. Mind-mapping, for example, is a technique many parents have found to be effective with right-brain, visual learners. The student draws a picture of the material to be learned and labels it with important facts and key ideas. The following Mindmap was created by a fourteen-year-old in his American History class.

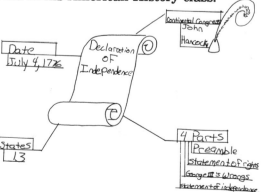

The use of highlighters, color-coded books and notebooks, multi-colored pens and either colored notecards for important facts or white notecards with colored ink are also essential tools for the visual learner. With the teacher's permission, you may also wish to rent videos of the novels your child reads in school. There are also many excellent travel videos on foreign countries that can help to bring alive what he is reading in social studies.

If your child is a kinesthetic learner, have him make the letters of the alphabet on a velvet- or felt-covered board or surface. The same can be done for math facts and spelling words. If practicing in the car, one's clothing provides an excellent tactile surface. For a visual learner, tape the material to be learned on his mirror or on the ceiling above his bed. Auditory learners learn most effectively by constant repetition, especially by repeating material out loud or by subvocalizing it. As he becomes older, he may find a tape recorder helpful to tape the lectures. Being able to play back the material later in small segments can be helpful to many ADHD/ADD children who are auditory learners.

Talking oneself through a problem is another very important component of the learning process for most children, especially auditory learners. An ADHD/ADD child must learn how to progress through a problem sequentially without being distracted internally by other messages. Teaching positive *Self-Talk* is also important. Many children with attention disorders have learned over the years to give themselves negative messages while working, such as, "I cannot do this;" "I'm no good at math;" "This is going to be too hard." These children need to be taught how to turn down these negative messages and turn up the volume on positive messages to themselves.

Kinesthetic learners, especially ADHD children who have diffi-culty with handwriting, have found the computer to be an effective tool for reinforcing classroom instruction. There are many excellent programs that help teach math, spelling, history, reading and study skills. Learning to use the computer at an early age and obtaining permission from the school for the child to type papers has been a lifesaver for many an ADHD/ADD child and his family.

Kinesthetic learners also need ample time in the afternoons for physical activity. Creative ways can be found, however, to combine some of this time with studying. While learning new concepts have your child move. Walking around the room or jumping on a trampoline while concentrating on new material are ways some students have found to help the brain be more receptive. Juggling is also an excellent activity for a kinesthetic learner to master. It seems to stimulate the body and brain simultaneously.

We have found that most children, however, benefit greatly from a combination of all three approaches. For example, have a child say 3 times 5 equals 15 as he writes it with his finger on a rough surface and then with his whole arm in the air. Then, have him write it with a colored pencil on a piece of paper and drill him orally. The more the whole brain can be involved, the more effective and long-lasting the learning will be.

◆ *Investigate Your Child's Ideal Body Position for Studying*

Observations by professionals in the field of learning have sug-gested that all brains may not operate at their peak level when the body is sitting upright. Researchers have speculated that the children who prefer to study while laying on the floor, or in a chair with one leg draped over the arm, may actually be doing so because their brains function the most efficiently in this position. One very spacey ADD girl with whom we worked is convinced that she is the most efficient when she sits on the floor with her back against the foot of her bed. Another student studies lying stomach down on the bed with his book on the floor.

Our children are delivered to schools in automobiles. But whether that adds to their grades is doubtful.——Will Rogers

◆ *Give Special Assistance with Studying for Tests*

A major source of difficulty for many attention-disordered children is preparing adequately for tests. They are frequently overwhelmed by the amount of material assigned and feel it is impossible to review it all. If this is a problem for your child, help him divide the information into daily sections for studying and reward him at the end of each day for completing his review. It may also be helpful to reward him as he finishes each section.

As appropriate, help him prepare notecards with important facts, dates, vocabulary words, etc. Have the child look at the card and read it out loud, give you the answer, and then turn it over and read the correct answer. Those answered correctly go in one pile and the incorrect answers go into another. Children enjoy holding the correct responses and seeing the stack grow as they continue drilling. Many children, especially visual learners, find this method of studying the most effective.

If your child is a strong auditory learner, it is effective to review the same information by oral drilling. Call out a vocabulary word to him and ask him to give the correct meaning verbally. Another effective method is to have him repeat the word and its meaning into a tape recorder and play the tape back. Hearing one's own voice is an effective way to learn. All these methods of studying are easily portable and can be employed effectively while driving to afterschool activities, waiting in traffic or even while doing the dishes together. Drill and practice should finally be completed in the same format in which the test will be given. Before a test have your child write his spelling words when you call them out if that is what his teacher will do.

In those subjects where it is feasible, prepare a sample test for your child to take a day or two before the actual test. In subjects such as spelling, the child can actually prepare his own test either in writing or with the tape recorder. Calling his words into the recorder and then playing them back to be spelled can actually be an enjoyable activity for many children.

When a lot of reading material is covered on a test, it may be helpful to discuss the ideas and concepts with your child to help him understand the way the material is related. This is especially important in subjects such as history or English. Often an ADHD/ADD child will read the material well enough to comprehend the main idea but not be aware of the subtleties of cause-and-effect and relationships.

To help your child remember significant amounts of reading material, group the content into sections with separate titles for each, such as the following list created by a high school sophomore for his biology class:

Confidence...thrives only on honesty, on honor, on the sacredness of obligations, on faithful protection and on unselfish performance. Without them it cannot live.——Franklin Delano Roosevelt

The Ten Systems of The Human Body

Nervous System
Endocrine System.
Circulatory System
Digestive System
Skeletal System
Respiratory System
Urinary System
Muscular System
Skin System
Reproductive System

Then have your child take the first letter from each section and create a new word that forms a sentence he thinks he can remember. For example:

Never Eat Cereal Daily Since

Raisins Upset My Skin Rash

Sometimes the more nonsensical the sentence is, the more memorable it is to him. This is especially helpful for long lists of material that must be remembered in a definite order. Your child will also be more likely to remember the sentence if it is his original creation.

A brief review the morning of the test is helpful for some children, although others may become extremely anxious when such a review is attempted. Determine which techniques are most effective and help your child approach the test feeling as prepared and relaxed as possible.

◆ SUMMARY ◆

To be the most effective in helping your child with homework, it is important to remain positive and let him know you have confidence in his ability to succeed. Your continued support and encouragement are as important to him as the study skills and techniques you teach. ADHD/ADD children often feel defeated and lack belief in themselves. They are keenly aware of their differences in the schoolroom and are frequently given negative messages by their peers. These messages can be at least partially offset by loving and supportive parents who understand and appreciate the individual differences of their children. Let your child know you prize his uniqueness and view it as a positive strength. Perhaps the following story by Robert Fulghum offers a refreshing perspective that you will find inspiring.

Giants, wizards, and dwarfs was the game to play. Being left in charge of about eighty children seven to ten years old, while their parents were off doing parenty things, I mustered my troops in the church social hall and explained the game. It's a large-scale version of Rock, Paper, and Scissors, and involves some intellectual decision making. But the real purpose of the game is to make a lot of noise and run around chasing people until nobody knows which side you are on or who won.

Organizing a roomful of wired-up gradeschoolers into two teams, explaining the rudiments of the game, achieving consensus on group identity - all this is no mean accomplishment, but we did it with a right good will and were ready to go.

The excitement of the chase had reached a critical mass. I yelled out: "You have to decide now which you are - a GIANT, a WIZARD, or a DWARF!"

While the groups huddled in frenzied, whispered consultation, a tug came at my pants leg. A small child stands there looking up, and asks in a small, concerned voice, "Where do the Mermaids stand?"

Where do the mermaids stand? A long pause. A very long pause. "Where do the Mermaids stand?" says I.

"Yes. You see, I am a Mermaid."

"There are no such things as Mermaids."

"Oh, yes, I am one!"

She did not relate to being a Giant, A Wizard, or a Dwarf. She knew her category. Mermaid. And was not about to leave the game and go over and stand against the

*wall where a loser would stand.   She intended to
participate, wherever Mermaids fit into the scheme of
things. Without giving up dignity or identity. She took it
for granted that there was a place for Mermaids and that
I would know just where.*

*Well, where DO the Mermaids stand?   All the
"Mermaids" - all those who are different, who do not fit
the norm and who do not accept the available boxes and
pigeonholes?*

*Answer that question and you can build a school, a
nation, or a world on it.*

*What was my answer at the moment? Every once in a
while I say the right thing. "The Mermaid stands right
here by the King of the Sea." says I. (Yes, right here by
the King's Fool, I thought to myself.)*

*So we stood there hand in hand, reviewing the troops of
Wizards and Giants and Dwarfs as they rolled by in wild
disarray.*

*It is not true, by the way, that mermaids do not exist.
I know at least one personally. I have held her hand.*[12]

[12]From <u>All I Ever Need to Know I Learned in Kindergarten</u>, by Robert Fulghum,
pp. 81-83. Copyright © 1986, 1988 by Robert Fulghum. Reprinted by permission of
Villard Books, a Division of Random House, Inc.

Epilogue

Often it is hard to see the forest for the trees. With the hundreds of minor crises which must be handled on a daily basis, it is difficult to realize that someday this child will be grown. So much energy is consumed handling the child's antics, and your guilt about them, that sometimes not enough is left for constructive purposes. Parents often forget that it is not their fault that their child has ADHD or ADD.

The problems experienced in the family of an attention-disordered child are intense and unrelenting. It is our hope, however, that you will not blame yourself, nor be disappointed in your child. Rather, we hope that you can find contentment in the knowledge that your child has the greatest possibility of succeeding in adulthood because of your recognition of his attention disorder and your pursuit of appropriate interventions.

We now know that many children with attention disorders will continue to experience some of the symptoms in adulthood. Many of you have probably recognized yourselves in these pages and know that you, too, continue to struggle with the effects of your ADHD or ADD. Research is just beginning to recognize that adults suffer from attention disorders. This group of the population is, in fact, growing rapidly. We often hear from adult ADHD/ADD patients how dramatically different they believe their lives would have been had their attention disorders been recognized and treated earlier in their lives. Attention disorders in adulthood are addressed in Appendix I, where many adults' stories have been shared.

Your attempts to understand every aspect of attention disorders will have increased both your knowledge and that of your child. His understanding, we believe, is your final goal. As an adult, it is *he* who must ultimately assume the role of managing and coping with his difficulties in the context of the life he chooses to live. Your years of nurturing and support will have given him the strength and confidence he needs to accept this responsibility for himself.

In concluding this book, we would like to remind you of our beginning thoughts. Raising a child with an attention disorder can be a challenge. However, we believe it will be a little easier if you can see your child, not as one with problems, but rather as one who hears a different drummer, as Thoreau suggested. Your child's drum may beat a little faster or slower than most, and his notes may not always be in sync with the group, but in the end these differences may have the unexpected benefit of increasing his sensitivity, creativity and concern for others. He may ultimately be the one who creates the most beautiful music of all, and you will experience the joy of knowing you nurtured and raised *A Different Drummer.*

APPENDICES

APPENDIX 1

ADHD/ADD in Adulthood

Once considered a disorder of childhood, attention deficit disorders, both ADHD and ADD, are now recognized as life-long disorders that may continue to be problematic in an estimated 30-70% of those affected earlier in life (Barkley, 1990). No one really knows how many adults may have ADHD or ADD, but if a conservative estimate that 3-5% of our children have the disorder, it logically follows that 1% to 3 or 4%, or approximately one and one-half to five million adults, based on the 1990 Census, may continue to experience these effects. The toll being exacted on both the people affected and our country is enormous. It is social, emotional, physical and economic. As a nation, we truly cannot afford *not* to treat this disorder as expeditiously and effectively as possible.

We have previously described ADHD/ADD as being the neurological equivalent of visual problems. The combination of relief, hope and excitement of adults who have not fulfilled their potential and who finally identify the cause of their lack of satisfactory performance in many areas of their lives is truly comparable to those who can see clearly for the first time. We have found adults with attention disorders eager for information and intent upon treatment. The severity of the problem usually determines the intensity of their relief.

While individual psychiatrists, such as Dr. Paul Wender, have successfully treated a few adults with attention disorders since the early 1970's, intense interest was not focused on adult ADHD/ADD until the mid-1980's when Drs. Gabrielle Weiss and Lily Hechtman's hallmark fifteen-year follow-up study of ADHD children was published (Weiss and Hechtman, 1986). They reported that 60-70% of the children they studied as young adults, with an average age of twenty-five, continued to report ADHD and ADD symptoms, including poor concentration, restlessness, inattention, impulsivity and low stress tolerance. Interpersonal difficulties, depression, antisocial behavior, anxiety, and low self-esteem also continued in those not treated and often intensified further as occupational, economic and legal problems mounted.

Since the late 1980's, clinicians and researchers have become increasingly concerned and are beginning to address this overlooked group of sufferers. Adults with attention disorders exhibit a much more diverse and complicated profile diagnostically and require more specific expertise for successful treatment. Most pediatricians, child psychiatrists and pediatric neurologists, already overwhelmed by this time-intensive disorder in children, do not have easily available resources to treat adults. Psychiatrists who treat ADHD/ADD adults quickly find their practices filled when their names are announced at local ADD parent support groups.

The recognition and treatment of adults with ADHD/ADD raise possibilities too exciting to be daunted by the current lack of knowledge and available experts. Many of the adults who are successfully treated experience major positive shifts in their lives. Others, already considered successful, find that their work can be done in much less time and with much less frustration and expenditure of energy. There is more opportunity for family and leisure, and the time spent becomes true quality time. Impulsive behavior, volatile tempers, moody dispositions, poor performance and diminished productivity decrease dramatically and are replaced by a sense of calm control over both one's life and one's destiny. Dissatisfaction, desperation and frustration are replaced by optimism and purpose.

Over the years we have identified and treated many parents of our attention-disordered child and adolescent patients. Their stories are poignant and heart-rending, but replete with determination, perseverance and an unwillingness to accept defeat. Each has intuitively known that some inner enigma has kept him from becoming the person he knows, at the deepest level of his being, he really is. The following are some of their stories.

♦ SAM ♦

One of the first adults with whom we worked in the early 1980's was the father of a child we evaluated. His mother, a teacher, identified her child as having an attention disorder and referred him. Sam, the child's father, was in obvious distress during the evaluation, but unresponsive to queries, so further exploration was not pursued. During the interpretive session, when he learned that his son, a failing second-grader and social isolate, had an I.Q. in the gifted range but could not perform because of the ADD, he wept. At that time he shared that he had recently lost yet another job as a stock clerk because of his disorganization, inefficiency and problems interacting with fellow employees. He, too, had been a child of promise but had encountered only incredible defeat.

We evaluated Sam. He also had an I.Q. in the gifted range. The attention deficit was equally profound. He was referred to an adult psychiatrist and successfully treated with a combination of medication and psychotherapy. Both Sam and his son are doing well today. His son is in high school, a gifted student and a talented artist with many friends and the confidence which only success can bring. Sam has completed college and has already launched a promising career in the print advertising industry. His patient and encouraging wife continues to teach. She is the self-appointed ADHD/ADD expert in her school and has accomplished wonders for those children who have had the good fortune to be selected for her class.

♦ EVELYN ♦

Like so many, Evelyn realized she had ADD in the evaluation and treatment process for her daughter. Bright, sophisticated, successful in her world of community volunteer projects, school fairs, administrating programs for the PTA, and raising her family, she was nevertheless aware that high school and college had not been easy. She described becoming depressed and introverted in elementary school after being made to feel she was *bad* because she talked too much.

In college Evelyn found herself with no place to study. In the pandemonium of the dorm, she felt disorganized and overwhelmed. The library was no better for she heard every footstep, the creak of every chair, the episodic gurgle of the water fountain, and the squeaking book cart the library assistant quietly pushed through unending rows of books. Even the air-conditioning and heating noises were a distraction. In desperation she resorted to her car, and there she spent most of her study hours.

Evelyn had returned to graduate school and was struggling. She was determined to do well and was willing to expend three to four times the effort of others to obtain her good grades. Nevertheless, school was grueling and both her personal life and that of her family suffered.

During the evaluation Evelyn described what was occurring internally. Her *stream of consciousness* was as follows—disjointed but revealing:

> "I've got to hurry so I won't forget."
> "I can remember better when words have rhythm."
> "I saw it as you described it and no longer listened to the words."
> "Look . . . Evelyn . . . concentrate on the yellow spot on your dress . . . that will help focus you."
> "I definitely go in and out of concentration."
> "I have to *make* myself listen to clients."

Regarding school:

> "I would have made much better grades if I hadn't had to look at the instructors. I can concentrate better with my eyes closed, but they always thought I wasn't interested if I did."

> "Attending lectures is pointless. I can't remember them."

Evelyn has been on medication for nearly two years. Ritalin was not effective but a low dose of Dexedrine provided the focus she so desperately needed. She has just completed her preliminary exams for her doctorate and is well on her way to a new set of successful endeavors. She stated that the nicest thing about treating the attention disorder was the change in her self-worth.

Evelyn is typical of those adults, and there are many of them, who overcome the potentially disastrous effects of this disorder by sheer determination. Evelyn is doubtful, however, that she could have obtained her Ph.D. degree without medication. Intellect and perseverance do have their limitations.

◆ FRED ◆

Fred, the father of four children, three of whom had either ADHD or ADD, was a surgeon. Interacting with him, it was clearly apparent that he processed slowly. This characteristic gave his responses the appearance of great thoughtfulness and deliberation; thus, it was not considered a problem—at least by others.

After the evaluation of his third child, Fred questioned whether he had undifferentiated attention deficit disorder. He described significant difficulties in high school and college in attending, staying on task and completing assignments. His major problem was the excessive amount of time everything took. Medical school was also difficult until he began his clinical work as a junior. While still slow, the hands-on learning was infinitely easier. Although life seemed laborious, Fred persevered and was an exceptionally successful surgeon. It was, in fact, his intellect and his fine-motor and spatial abilities which carried him through.

Frustration continued for Fred, however. Work which was accomplished easily and efficiently by other physicians took Fred twice the time. He described struggling to interact with patients because he processed their responses slowly and felt it took forever to formulate his own. Dictation required two to three times longer than for most. Thus Fred often spent fourteen to sixteen hours to accomplish what others did in eight to ten.

Fred was seen by a neurologist who confirmed his suspicions. He was placed on Ritalin—10 mgs. three to four times daily. There was instant improvement noted by all who lived and worked with him. While beloved the way he was, his new efficiency, alertness and ability to interact incisively and sensitively were welcomed by all.

Fred is delighted with his improvement. Likewise is his family for whom he now has more time. His only frustration has been the lack of awareness of adult ADHD/ADD in his community and thus a lack of peer support and understanding.

◆ MARY ◆

Mary still struggles. At 35 she has started and stopped college six times. She continues to live with her parents and has become a clerk in a department store to earn a living. While she is an excellent salesperson and her job has some outlets for her creativity, Mary feels like a failure because she has not completed college. Her successful parents and an accomplished sister are painful reminders of her inability to get her life on track. Her father has thrown up his hands in disgust, while her mother has surreptitiously helped her at the risk of great displeasure from her husband.

Mary's struggle began in elementary school and has continued since. Though bright, her behavior problems, academic mediocrity, and lack of social skills left her feeling dumb and depressed most of the time. Family conflicts worsened despite many changes of schools and aborted attempts at psychological intervention. Mary's mother feels she failed her daughter. In her attempts to protect her, she fostered a dependency which has left her daughter both unable to assume an independent, self-sufficient adult role and angry with her mother because she cannot.

Mary's attention disorder has been diagnosed. Understanding the problem has brought some relief. Mary has tentatively approached treatment and is slowly but steadily making important life changes. Much hurt, many disappointments and a lack of faith in professionals who have, indeed, let her down, make her progress slower and more difficult than for some. Nevertheless, Mary does have the information and has begun to utilize it in her own way and in her own time. As therapists, it is difficult to be patient with Mary's caution and skepticism, and yet her approach to her life and her need to fully control her own destiny must be respected. Mary will succeed, we believe, in achieving that which is important to her. Knowledge of her attention disorder at least gives her a choice.

◆ DIAGNOSIS OF ADULT ADHD/ADD ◆

Attention disorders in adults are such a recent area of interest that there are, at present, few standard diagnostic instruments for assessment. Dr. Paul Wender, from the University of Utah Medical School, and a true pioneer in Adult ADD, has adapted the DSM-III criteria for adult diagnosis. These guidelines, called the "Utah Criteria for the Diagnosis of ADD Residual Type" have been a helpful beginning.

According to Dr. Russell Barkley in a chapter on *Assessment and Treatment of Adults with ADHD* in his comprehensive text on Attention Deficit Hyperactivity Disorder, the new diagnostic and statistical manual (*DSM-IV*) will address adult ADHD and will include symptom descriptions for "inattention" and for "hyperactive/ impulsive behavior" (Barkley, 1990). Hopefully, undifferentiated attention disorders in adults will be given adequate attention in the *DSM-IV*, as well as ADHD. Those who struggle with ADD without hyperactivity urge that it be recognized as a disorder equally as problematic as ADHD (Jaffe, 1991).

Our interest in adults led to the development of the *Copeland Checklist for Adult Attention Deficit Disorders*. This checklist—available on pages 323-324—is comparable to the checklist for children and adolescents found in Chapter 2. It contains the following categories:

    I. Inattention/Distractibility
    II. Impulsivity
    III. Activity Level Problems
        a) Overactivity
        b) Underactivity
    IV. Noncompliance
    V. Underachievement/Disorganization/
        Learning Problems
    VI. Emotional Difficulties

    VII.   Poor Peer Relations
    VIII. Impaired Family Relations

This checklist is routinely administered to the parents of the children and adolescents we evaluate, as well as the ADHD/ADD adults we see in our practice.

    Preliminary standardization is underway. The following results demonstrate how three different groups of adults rated themselves in each category. The groups include: (1) those diagnosed or self-identified as ADHD or ADD, (2) those who identified themselves as non-ADHD/ADD, and (3) a group who attended a seminar and completed the checklist. The third group we think of as being similar to the population at large; thus, they are called a *control group*.

Percentage of Items Checked
(Averaged for Group)

Category	ADHD/[1] ADD N=80 Mean %	Non-ADHD/ ADD[2] N=23 Mean %	Control Group[3] N=109 Mean %
I. Inattention/ Distractibility	57%	20%	26%
II. Impulsivity	57%	20%	27%
III. Activity-Level Problems:			
a) Overactivity	48%	16%	25%
b) Underactivity	45%	15%	20%
IV. Noncompliance	41%	11%	14%
V. Underachievement/ Disorganization/ Learning Problems	47%	14%	17%

---

[1]Self-identified or diagnosed as Adult ADHD/ADD.
[2]Self-identified as Non-ADHD/ADD.
[3]Control Group of Teachers

	VI. Emotional Difficulties	50%	15%	22%
	VII. Poor Peer Relations	39%	14%	16%
	VIII. Impaired Family			
	Relations	46%	8%	19%

Number Checked "Pretty Much" Or "Very Much"
(Averaged for Group)

Category	ADHD/[1] ADD N=80 Mean %	Non-ADHD/[2] ADD N=23 Mean %	Control[3] Group N=109 Mean %
I. Inattention/ Distractibility	59%	10%	14%
II. Impulsivity	56%	9%	16%
III. Activity-Level Problems:			
a) Overactivity	47%	13%	18%
b) Underactivity	45%	3%	8%
IV. Noncompliance	36%	2%	5%
V. Underachievement/ Disorganization/ Learning Problems	45%	9%	10%
VI. Emotional Difficulties	44%	6%	13%
VII. Poor Peer Relations	36%	3%	10%
VIII. Impaired Family Relations	43%	0%	13%

While these results are certainly preliminary, and both increased numbers, more categories and additional research are needed, the data do present compelling trends:

1) There is a distinct and very significant difference between those who are identified by professionals or themselves as ADHD or ADD, and a) those who identify themselves as not having ADHD/ADD, and b) a control group.

2) An interesting statistic is the average number of items, out

of the number possible, which were checked "pretty much," or "very much." The control and non-ADHD/ADD groups obtained average scores of 1 or less per category, while those with ADHD/ADD averaged over half of the items checked as "pretty much" or "very much" in the *Inattention/ Distractibility* and *Impulsivity* categories, and greater than a third for the remaining categories.

3) In the control group of 109 teachers, nine were similar to those identified with ADHD, two were considered border-line by the Examiner, and three clearly had Undifferentiated Attention Deficit Disorder with high scores only in the *Inattention/Distractibility* and *Underactivity* categories. A total of fourteen out of one hundred and nine (13%) is a significant percentage of the general population which may be affected by attention disorders. The group consisted of teachers who volunteered to attend a seminar on attention disorders. Since those with symptoms are more likely to want to attend such a program, the sample does not represent the population at large and may well over-identify attention disorders. On the other hand, the high level of educational accomplishment would under-identify ADHD/ADD. These data suggest that there is a significant group of unidentified adults with attention disorders in the general population.

4) *Inattention/Distractibility* and *Impulsivity* continue to be the areas of greatest difficulty. *Peer Relations* and *Noncompliance*, by contrast, were the least problematic areas for ADHD/ADD adults. The ability to choose one's peers probably accounts for some of the decline in that area of difficulty, while independence is more easily achieved by adults than by peers and thus conformity is less of a concern.

5) Overactivity at 48% and underactivity at 45% appear equally problematic. This finding highlights our need to address undifferentiated ADD as well as ADHD.

These findings also support the belief that checklists can be utilized to identify adults with attention disorders perhaps equally as well as they identify children. Such a checklist can also be of assistance in determining individual areas which need therapeutic intervention and as a reasonably objective assessment of treatment effects.

♦ *Other Diagnostic Instruments*

Adults are diagnosed in much the same way as children.

History—Family, developmental, educational and academic history are critical for the diagnostic process, for the problems have usually been present since childhood. The history also assists in determining the presence of other disorders which may mimic ADHD/ADD, the potential for which are often revealed in past experiences of the individual.

Physical/Psychological Evaluation—Physical and psychological evaluations are equally important for adults as for children. Physical disorders such as hypo- or hyperthyroidism, diabetes, allergies, hormone deficiencies, sleep apnea and narcolepsy, among others, cause symptoms which mimic those of attention disorders. Likewise, depression, bipolar disorders, personality disorders, substance abuse and language/learning disabilities, among others, co-occur or have symptoms in common with ADHD and ADD. A comprehensive evaluation is necessary to assess the full range of difficulties and possible contributing factors.

Psychological/Psychoeducational Tests—Many of the same instruments are utilized in the evaluation of adults as for children. Individually administered tests of intellectual ability, especially those with distinctive ADD patterns of scores; auditory memory measures; and measures of attention, concentration and impulse control are helpful in determining the degree of interference which typically results from ADHD/ADD symptoms. Measures of achievement are often necessary to determine the discrepancy between ability and academic accomplishment.

Understanding of the multiple effects of the attention disorder in a person's life is necessary to achieve significant and positive results from multimodal intervention programs. This knowledge provides a roadmap of strengths upon which to capitalize, weaknesses to be remediated or circumvented, and a pattern of interests which has often not surfaced because of the disorganizing effect of the attention disorder. Thoroughly understanding one's dynamics and realizing one's strengths are often the first rays of hope and provide the incentive so needed to persevere for the person discouraged by many years of failure.

A college student whom we evaluated illustrates the value of psychological/psychoeducational assessment. Sara, the sister of one of our elementary school patients, was referred by her mother. Sara was failing her sophomore year of college. She had scraped by in high school and was determined to do better. Instead, her grades were worse. Her parents were at their wits' end. When Sara was questioned about her major, she stated, "Business . . . because I want to make a lot of money."

Psychological evaluation revealed moderate ADD. She was also found to be a very gifted visual/spatial/creative learner with average language abilities. Her interests were clearly in design and only a little exploring revealed a family legacy of artists. Because she could not draw, however, she had assumed art could not be a pursuit for her. On personality measures and interest inventories she obtained a personality profile typical of artists and designers and very atypical of those successful in business.

Sara's ADD was successfully treated with medication. The next quarter she took a course in sculpture. Sara was a natural! The last time we spoke with her parents, she was excelling in school and was studying Art History in Italy on an exchange scholarship. Because she is now focused and directed, she can pursue activities which coincide with her innate abilities, and she loves what she is doing. Sara is well on her way to becoming the successful adult she so wanted to be.

While adult attention disorders are often treated on the basis of history alone, a multifaceted evaluation is often a necessary prerequisite for a comprehensive intervention program.

◆ TREATMENT ◆

Treatment for adults includes education about the disorder, medical intervention with essentially the same medications used for children, and often psychotherapy. The importance of medical management of adult ADD cannot be overstated, nor can the importance of finding a physician knowledgeable about ADHD/ADD, interested in it, and experienced with the use of the various medications used to treat it. Just as for children and adolescents, medication is usually the cornerstone of adult treatment and enables other approaches to be effective.

Therapy is, likewise, important. The years of failure and frustration take such a heavy psychological toll that effective intervention almost always includes a psychotherapeutic component. Group therapy and support groups composed of others with similar struggles offer unparalleled assistance in understanding the effects of an attention disorder and learning new ways of interacting and coping. A highlight of one of our recent Adult ADD group meetings occurred when two women, one a law-school student, and the other a computer/math scientist, realized that women with ADD aren't like men. Both women had been excellent students and were successful in very structured situations, but both had found the organizational demands of a home and family overwhelming. Each had husbands who were frustrated and angry with their ineptness, the chaos in their homes, and their inability to structure their children. Both had become known and accepted by their friends as *spacey* and disorganized, and each had learned to play the role well. One woman stated, "It's okay on one level to be the ditzy blonde, but on another every part of my being hates the way I am. I have always thought I was bright, but no matter how hard I tried, I couldn't get it together at home. Now I understand."

To share this common bond was an immense relief. Each is currently being treated and both have overcome many of the behaviors so frustrating to themselves and all those around them.

Recognition of adults with ADHD and ADD is in its infancy. Diagnosis and treatment are, likewise, in the early stages of understanding. Nonetheless, an explosion in information, understanding, diagnosis and treatment can be expected in the coming months and years.

Treating children and adolescents with attention disorders has been our professional endeavor for twenty years. Facilitating, in a small way, the dramatic changes which have occurred with them has been indescribably fulfilling. As we now work with adults with attention disorders, we find their pain more intense, their life journeys more poignant, their sensitivity greater, and for those who have survived reasonably intact, their strength of character steeled as only the fire of adversity can accomplish. Many are truly "steel magnolias" . . . fragile perhaps on the exterior, but stubborn and determined on the interior. We ache for those who have succumbed to the despair of untreated ADHD/ADD, many of whom are depressed and hopeless, and we long for the day when this disorder has assumed its rightful place among other medical disorders managed daily with acceptance and efficiency. Treating attention disorders may not be quite as simple as a polio vaccine, but the possibilities for mankind are profound. With the energy, determination and creativity unique to those with ADHD and ADD, this goal can certainly be accomplished.

sPI

COPELAND SYMPTOM CHECKLIST
FOR ADULT ATTENTION DEFICIT DISORDERS

Attention Deficit Hyperactivity Disorder (ADHD)
and Undifferentiated Attention Deficit Disorder (ADD)

This checklist was developed from the experience of many specialists in the field of Attention Disorders and Hyperactivity. It is designed to help determine whether you, or someone you are rating, has ADHD or ADD, to what degree, and if so, in which area(s) difficulties are experienced. Please mark all statements. Thank you for your assistance in completing this information.

Name_____ Date_____

Completed by _____

Directions: Place a checkmark (✓) by each item below, indicating the degree to which the behavior is characteristic of yourself or the adult you are rating.

	Not at all	Just a little	Pretty much	Very much	Score	%
I. INATTENTION/DISTRACTIBILITY, especially						
1. A short attention span, especially for low-interest activities.						
2. Difficulty completing tasks.						
3. Daydreaming.						
4. Easily distracted.						
5. Nicknames such as: "spacey," or "dreamer."						
6. Engages in much activity but accomplishes little.						
7. Enthusiastic beginnings but poor endings.					21 = ___%
II. IMPULSIVITY						
1. Excitability.						
2. Low frustration tolerance.						
3. Acts before thinking.						
4. Disorganization.						
5. Poor planning ability.						
6. Excessively shifts from one activity to another.						
7. Difficulty in group situations which require patience and taking turns.						
8. Interrupts frequently.					24 = ___%
III. ACTIVITY LEVEL PROBLEMS						
A. Overactivity/Hyperactivity						
1. Restlessness — either fidgetiness or being constantly on the go.						
2. Diminished need for sleep.						
3. Excessive talking.						
4. Difficulty listening.						
5. Motor restlessness during sleep. Kicks covers off — moves around constantly.						
6. Dislike of situations which require attention & being still—church, lectures, etc.					18 = ___%
B. Underactivity						
1. Lethargic.						
2. Daydreaming, spaciness.						
3. Failure to complete tasks.						
4. Inattention.						
5. Lacking in leadership.						
6. Difficulty in getting things done.					18 = ___%

Published by **sPI** Southeastern Psychological Institute, P.O. Box 12389, Atlanta, Georgia 30355-2389

COPELAND SYMPTOM CHECKLIST FOR ADULT ATTENTION DEFICIT DISORDERS (Continued)

	Not at all	Just a little	Pretty much	Very much
IV. NONCOMPLIANCE				
1. Does not cooperate. Determined to do things own way.				
2. Argumentative.				
·3. Disregards socially-accepted behavioral expectations.				
4. "Forgets" unintentionally.				
5. "Forgets" as an excuse (intentionally).				

      ___ = ___%
      15

	Not at all	Just a little	Pretty much	Very much
V. UNDERACHIEVEMENT/DISORGANIZATION/LEARNING PROBLEMS				
1. Underachievement in relation to ability.				
2. Frequent job changes.				
3. Loses things — keys, wallet, lists, belongings, etc.				
4. Auditory memory and auditory processing problems.				
5. Learning disabilities or learning problems.				
6. Poor handwriting.				
7. "Messy" or "sloppy" work.				
8. Work assignments are often not completed satisfactorily.				
9. Rushes through work.				
10. Works too slowly.				
11. Procrastinates. Bills, taxes, etc., put off until the last minute.				

      ___ = ___%
      33

	Not at all	Just a little	Pretty much	Very much
VI. EMOTIONAL DIFFICULTIES				
1. Frequent and unpredictable mood swings.				
2. Irritability.				
3. Underreactive to pain/insensitive to danger.				
4. Easily overstimulated. Hard to stop once "revved up."				
5. Low frustration tolerance. Excessive emotional reaction to frustrating situations.				
6. Angry outbursts.				
7. Moodiness/lack of energy.				
8. Low self-esteem.				
9. Immaturity.				

      ___ = ___%
      27

	Not at all	Just a little	Pretty much	Very much
VII. POOR PEER RELATIONS				
1. Difficulty following the rules of social interactions.				
2. Rejected or avoided by peers.				
3. Avoids group activities; a loner.				
4. "Bosses" other people. Wants to be the leader.				
5. Critical of others.				

      ___ = ___%
      15

	Not at all	Just a little	Pretty much	Very much
VIII. IMPAIRED FAMILY RELATIONSHIPS				
1. Easily frustrated with spouse or children. Overreacts. May punish children too severely.				
2. Sees things from own point of view. Does not negotiate differences well.				
3. Underdeveloped sense of responsibility.				
4. Poor manager of money.				
5. Unreasonable; demanding.				
6. Spends excessive amount of time at work because of inefficiency, leaving little time for family.				

      ___ = ___%
      18

TOTAL ___ = ___%
      189

7/90   Published by **SPI** Southeastern Psychological Institute, P.O. Box 12389, Atlanta, Georgia 30355-2389

APPENDIX 2

Suggested Readings and Resources

TEXTS

Barkley, Russell A., Ph.D. (1990). *Attention-Deficit Hyperactivity Disorder: A Handbook for Diagnosis and Treatment.* New York: The Guilford Press.

Goldstein, Sam, Ph.D., and Michael Goldstein, M.D. (1990). *Managing Attention Disorders in Children: A Guide for Practitioners.* New York: John Wiley & Sons, Inc.

GENERAL

Copeland, Edna D., Ph.D. (1989) (Video). *Understanding Attention Disorders: Preschool Through Adulthood.* Atlanta: 3 C's of Childhood, Inc.

Fowler, Mary C. (1990). *Maybe You Know My Kid. A Parent's Guide to Identifying, Understanding, and Helping Your Child with Attention-Deficit Hyperactivity Disorder.* Secaucus, NJ: Birch Lane Press.

Garber, Stephen, Ph.D., Marianne Garber, Ph.D., and Robyn Spizman. (1990). *If Your Child is Hyperactive, Inattentive, Impulsive, Distractible . . . .* New York: Villard Books.

Ingersoll, Barbara, Ph.D. (1988). *Your Hyperactive Child—A Parent's Guide to Coping with Attention Deficit Disorder.* New York: Doubleday.

Stewart, Mark, M.D., and Sally Olds. (1973). *Raising a Hyperactive Child.* New York: Harper & Row.

Taylor, John F., Ph.D. (1990). *Helping Your Hyperactive Child.* Rocklin, CA: Prima Publishing and Communications.

Weisberg, Lynne W., M.D., Ph.D., and Rosalie Greenberg, M.D. (1988). *When Acting Out Isn't Acting.* Washington: PIA Press.

Weiss, Gabrielle, M.D., and Lily Hechtman, M.D. (1986). *Hyperactive Children Grown Up.* New York: The Guilford Press.

EDUCATIONAL INTERVENTION

Anderson, Winifred, Stephen Chitwood, and Deidre Hayden. (1990). *Negotiating the Special Education Maze: A Guide for Parents and Teachers* (2nd ed.). Rockville, MD: Woodbine House.

Clark, Faith, Ph.D., and Cecil Clark, Ph.D. (1989). *Hassle-Free Homework.* New York: Doubleday.

Copeland, Edna D., Ph.D., and Valerie Love, M.Ed. (1989). *Attention Without Tension: A Teacher's Handbook on Attention Disorders (ADHD and ADD).* Atlanta: 3 C's of Childhood, Inc.

Kavanagh, James F. Ph.D., and Tom T. Truss, Ph.D. (Eds.) (1988). *Learning Disabilities: Proceedings of the National Conference on Learning Disabilities.* Parkton, MD: York Press.

Kinsbourne, Marcel, D.M., and Paula J. Caplan, Ph.D.. (1979). *Children's Learning and Attention Problems.* Boston: Little, Brown & Company.

Parker, Harvey C. Ph.D. (1988). *The ADD Hyperactivity Workbook for Parents, Teachers, and Kids.* Plantation, FL: Impact Publications, Inc.

Silver, Larry B., M.D. (1984). *The Misunderstood Child: A Guide for Parents of Learning Disabled Children.* New York: McGraw-Hill.

BEHAVIOR MANAGEMENT/RESPONSIBILITY

Barkley, Russell, Ph.D. (1987). *Defiant Children: A Clinician's Manual for Parent Training.* New York: Guilford Press.

Becker, Wesley C., Ph.D. (1971). *Parents are Teachers: A Child Management Program.* Champaign, IL: Research Press.

Robin, Arthur L. Ph.D., and Sharon L. Foster, Ph.D. (1989). *Negotiating Parent-Adolescent Conflict: A Behavioral-Family Systems Approach.* New York: Guilford Press.

MEDICATION

Copeland, Edna D., Ph.D. (1991). *Medications for Attention Disorders (ADHD/ADD) and Related Medical Problems.* Atlanta: SPI Press.

Kinsbourne, Marcel, D.M., and Paula J. Caplan, Ph.D. (1979). *Children's Learning and Attention Problems.* Boston: Little, Brown & Company.

Silver, Larry B., M.D. (1984). *The Misunderstood Child: A Guide for Parents of Learning Disabled Children.* New York: McGraw-Hill.

Wender, Paul H., M.D. (1987). *The Hyperactive Child, Adolescent and Adult: Attention Deficit Disorder Through the Life Span.* New York: Oxford University Press.

LANGUAGE/COGNITIVE THERAPY

Barkley, Russell A. Ph.D. (1981). *Hyperactive Children: A Handbook for Diagnosis and Treatment.* New York: Guilford Press.

Healy, Jane M., Ph.D. (1987). *Your Child's Growing Mind.* Garden City: Doubleday.

Kendall, Philip C., Ph.D., and Lauren Braswell. (1985). *Cognitive-behavioral Therapy for Impulsive Children.* New York: Guilford.

ALLERGIES, FOOD INTOLERANCES AND NUTRITION

Crook, William, M.D. (1991). *Help for the Hyperactive Child.* Jackson, TN: Professional Books.

Crook, William, M.D. (1989). *Tracking Down Hidden Food Allergy.* Jackson, TN: Professional Books.

Kahan, Barbara. (1990). *Healthier Children: Professional Guidance for Parents in the Areas of Nutrition, Environment and Behavior.* New Canaan, CT: Keats Publishing, Inc.

Joneja, Janice V., Ph.D., and Leonard Bielory, M.D. (1990). *Understanding Allergy, Sensitivity & Immunity: A Comprehensive Guide.* New Brunswick, NJ: Rutgers University Press.

Rapp, Doris J., M.D. (1979). *Allergies and the Hyperactive Child.* New York: Simon & Schuster.

CHILDREN'S AND TEENS' BOOKS

Galvin, Matthew, M.D. (1988). *Otto Learns About His Medicine.* New York: Magination Press. (Preschool and Early Elementary.)

Levine, Mel, M.D. (1990). *Keeping A Head in School: A Student's Book About Learning Abilities and Learning Disorders.* Cambridge, MA: Educators Publishing Service, Inc. (Middle and High School.)

Moss, Deborah M. (1989). *Shelly, The Hyperactive Turtle.* Kensington, MD: Woodbine House. (Preschool and Early Elementary.)

ADULT ADHD/ADD

Barkley, Russell A. Ph.D. (1990). *Attention Deficit Hyperactivity Disorder: A Handbook for Diagnosis and Treatment.* New York: Guilford Press. (Chapter 18)

Wender, Paul H., M.D. (1987). *The Hyperactive Child, Adolescent & Adult: Attention Deficit Disorder Through the Life Span.* New York: Oxford University Press. (Chapter 6)

APPENDIX 3

Parent Support Group Associations

Attention Deficit Disorders Association (ADDA)
P. O. Box 488
West Newbury, MA 01985   (800) 487-2282

Children with Attention Deficit Disorders
(CHADD)
499 N.W. 70th Avenue, Suite 308
Plantation, FL 33317   (305) 587-3700

Learning Disabilities Association of
America (LDA)
4156 Library Road
Pittsburgh, PA 15234   (412) 341-1515

Tourette Syndrome Association (TSA)
42-40 Bell Boulevard
Bayside, NY 11361   (718) 224-2999

APPENDIX 4

Responsibility Charts for Children and Adolescents

_____ (Name)   (Week of)

My Responsibilities

Morning:	Mon.	Tues.	Wed.	Thu.	Fri.	Sat.	Sun.
1. Get up by _____ with alarm clock.							
2. Get dressed and to breakfast by _____.							
3. Grooming							
a. Wash face							
b. Brush teeth							
c. Comb hair							
d. _____							
4. Put pajamas away (dirty clothes in hamper, etc.).							
5. Make bed.							
6. Straighten room. (A = 3✓'s; B = 2✓'s; C = 1✓)							
7. Empty trash can on _____.							
8. Use manners at breakfast.							
9. Remove dishes from table.							
10. _____							
11. _____							
12. _____							

After School:							
1. Put away books.							
2. Hang up coat; put clothes away.							
3. Practice _____ 30 minutes. (3✓'s)							
4. Do homework (in room). (3✓'s)							
5. Pick up den and/or playroom daily by _____ P.M.							
6. Put outside toys away by _____ P.M.							
7. _____							
8. _____							
9. _____							

Dinner and Bedtime:							
1. Set table for dinner.							
2. Manners at dinner.							
3. Remove dishes from table; help clean up kitchen.							
4. Bath. Dirty clothes in hamper. Clean out tub. (3✓'s)							
5. Select clothes for next day.							
6. Get all school papers signed. Put everything together for the next day.							
7. In bed by _____ or earlier to read.							
8. Read 15 minutes in book.							
9. _____							
10. _____							
11. _____							

Behavior and Attitude:							
1. Do what parents request pleasantly.							
2. Be nice to siblings.							
3. Don't argue or talk back.							
4. _____							
5. _____							
6. _____							

Extra Responsibilities/Weekend:							
1. _____							
2. _____							
3. _____							
4. _____							
5. _____							
6. _____							

VALUES: 6✓'s = _____

MY DAILY TOTAL | | | | | | | |

RESPONSIBILITIES HELP YOU BECOME THE BEST YOU CAN BE . . .

Confident, Capable, Cooperative

© COPYRIGHT, 1987, Edna D. Copeland, Ph.D., Child Psychologist

FOR INFORMATION OR REPRODUCTION OF ANY PART OF THIS MATERIAL, CONTACT
3 C's OF CHILDHOOD INC., P.O. BOX 12389, ATLANTA, GEORGIA 30355-2389.

_____   _____
(Name)   (Week of)

Teen Responsibilities

	Mon.	Tues.	Wed.	Thur.	Fri.	Sat.	Sun.

MORNING:

1. Get up early enough to complete jobs.
2. Grooming:
   a. Wash face
   b. Brush teeth
   c. Wash/dry hair
   d. _____
3. Make bed.
4. Straighten room.
5. Straighten bathroom.
6. Get dressed and to breakfast by _____ A.M.
7. Eat healthy breakfast.
8. Remove dishes/clean kitchen.
9. Take vitamins/medicine.
10. _____
11. _____
12. _____

AFTER SCHOOL/DINNER/EVENING

1. Put books away.
2. Hang up coat; put clothes, sports equipment, etc. away.
3. Do homework.
4. Set table by _____ P.M. for dinner.
5. Manners at dinner.
6. Remove dishes from table. Clean or help clean kitchen.
7. Get all papers signed; review next day with parents.
8. Get organized and ready for next day; books in chair; clothes for activities, etc.
9. In bed by _____ P.M.
10. _____
11. _____
12. _____

WEEKLY/WEEKEND

1. Cook dinner on _____.
2. Cook breakfast on _____.
3. Keep weekly budget of income and expenses.
4. Plan calendar and "To Do" list for next two weeks.
5. Participate in meal planning.
6. Thank you calls/notes:
   _____
   _____
   _____
7. Clean own bedroom and bath: change sheets, vacuum, dust, straighten closets and drawers; clean bathroom.
8. Garbage can to street on _____.
9. Garbage can from street on _____.
10. Brush/bathe pet.
11. Collect, sort and wash dirty clothes.
12. Take clothes from dryer, sort, fold and put away.
13. Iron.
14. _____
15. _____
16. _____

BEHAVIOR/ATTITUDE/MANNERS

1. Greet parents with handshake or hug.
2. Do what is requested pleasantly.
3. Be nice to siblings.
4. Music at _____ decibels.
5. Answer telephone appropriately. Be pleasant and courteous to callers.
6. Leave messages.
7. Come in on time (Curfew: _____)
8. _____
9. _____

VALUES: 6 ✓'s = _____

DAILY TOTAL							

SUCCESS IN ADULTHOOD IS DIRECTLY RELATED TO THE AMOUNT OF MEANINGFUL WORK DONE IN CHILDHOOD AND ADOLESCENCE.

—Harvard Report

SUPPLEMENT TO THE AUDIOPROGRAM "THE JOY OF A JOB WELL DONE: TEACHING YOUR CHILD THE
VALUE OF WORK AND RESPONSIBILITY" AND BEHAVIOR INCENTIVE PROGRAM.
FOR INFORMATION OR REPRODUCTION OF ANY PART OF THIS MATERIAL, PLEASE CONTACT 3C's OF CHILDHOOD, INC.,
P.O. BOX 12389, ATLANTA, GA. 30355-2389 (404) 256-0903

©COPYRIGHT, 1988, Edna D. Copeland, Ph.D., Child Psychologist

APPENDIX 5

Family Organization Calendar

GETTING OUR FAMILY ORGANIZED

(MONTH)　　　　　　　　　　　　　　　　　　　　　　　　　　(YEAR)

	MONDAY	TUESDAY	WEDNESDAY	THURSDAY	FRIDAY	SATURDAY	SUNDAY	
TO DO:	ACTIVITIES:	ACTIVITIES:	ACTIVITIES:	ACTIVITIES:	ACTIVITIES:	ACTIVITIES:	ACTIVITIES:	**TO DO:**
WEEK 1:	TO DO:	TO DO:	TO DO:	TO DO:	TO DO:	TO DO:	TO DO:	WEEK 2 (Continued):
	ACTIVITIES:	ACTIVITIES:	ACTIVITIES:	ACTIVITIES:	ACTIVITIES:	ACTIVITIES:		WEEK 4:
	TO DO:	TO DO:	TO DO:	TO DO:	TO DO:	TO DO:	TO DO:	
WEEK 2:	ACTIVITIES:	ACTIVITIES:	ACTIVITIES:	ACTIVITIES:	ACTIVITIES:	ACTIVITIES:	ACTIVITIES:	
	TO DO:	TO DO:	TO DO:	TO DO:	TO DO:	TO DO:	TO DO:	
	ACTIVITIES:	ACTIVITIES:	ACTIVITIES:	ACTIVITIES:	ACTIVITIES:	ACTIVITIES:	ACTIVITIES:	WEEK 5:
	TO DO:	TO DO:	TO DO:	TO DO:	TO DO:	TO DO:	TO DO:	
WEEK 3:	ACTIVITIES:	ACTIVITIES:	ACTIVITIES:	ACTIVITIES:	ACTIVITIES:	ACTIVITIES:	ACTIVITIES:	
	TO DO:	TO DO:	TO DO:	TO DO:	TO DO:	TO DO:	TO DO:	

ORGANIZATION HELPS FAMILIES BECOME . . .

COLOR CODE:
- Yellow ■
- Blue ■
- Pink ■
- Green ■
- Orange ■
- Purple ■

COPYRIGHT 1987 John D. Copland, Ph.D. Child Psychologist

TO GET ORGANIZED:
1. As an activity arises, write it on the calendar.
2. As things occur which need to be done, write them down under "TO DO" on the side. When it is decided when to do them, transfer them to the calendar.
3. Have a "Family Meeting" once a week (Sunday night is best!) to discuss the coming weeks and to get everything scheduled.
4. Choose and/or assign tasks. Color code as assigned.
5. As tasks are completed, cross through with a fine line marker.
6. Group as many tasks as possible to increase efficiency. For example, all gifts and cards for the month can be purchased at the same time. Many errands can be accomplished in one trip.

**CAPABLE
COOPERATIVE
EFFICIENT
And Have More
Time For Fun!**

References

American Psychiatric Association (1980). *Diagnostic and Statistical Manual of Mental Disorders (Third Edition)*. Washington, D.C., American Psychiatric Association.

American Psychiatric Association (1987). *Diagnostic and Statistical Manual of Mental Disorders (Third edition-revised-DSM III-R)*. Washington, D.C., American Psychiatric Association, pp. 52-53, 95.

Anderson, W. (1990). *Negotiating the Special Education Maze*. Rockville, Maryland: Woodbine House.

Attention Deficit Disorder Study Group (appointed by the State of Georgia Department of Education) (August, 1987). Report to Dr. Werner Rogers. Atlanta, State Department of Education, p. 3.

Barkley, R. A. (1981). *Hyperactive Children: A Handbook for Diagnosis and Treatment*. New York: Guilford Press.

Barkley, R. A. (1990). *Attention-Deficit Hyperactivity Disorder: A Handbook for Diagnosis and Treatment*. New York: The

Guilford Press.

Becker, W. C. (1971). *Parents are Teachers: A Child Management Program*. Champion: Research Press.

Bloom, B. S. (1985). *Developing Talent in Young People*. New York: Ballantine Books.

Bombeck, E. (1989). "Heavenly Thoughts." *Their World*, p. 27.

Bredekamp, S., and Shepard, L. (March, 1989). "How to Best Protect Children From Inappropriate School Expectations, Practices and Policies." *Young Children*, pp. 14-24.

Brown, R. T., Abramowitz, A. J., Dulcan, M., and Modan-Swain, A. (1989). "Attention Deficit Hyperactivity Disorder: Diagnosis, Management, Prognosis, and Current Research." *Emory University Journal of Medicine, 3(2)*, pp. 120-131.

Brown, R. T., and Sexson, S. B. (1989). "Effects of Methylphenidate on Cardiovascular Responses in Attention Deficit Hyperactivity Disordered Adolescents." *Journal of Adolescent Health Care, 10*, pp. 179-183.

Butler, K. G. (1988). "Preschool Language Processing Performance and Later Reading Achievement," in R. L. Masland and M. W. Masland, *Prevention of Reading Failure*. Parkton, MD: York Press.

Buzan, T. (1983). *Use Both Sides of Your Brain*. New York: E. P. Dutton.

Campbell, R. (1977). *How to Really Love Your Child*. Wheaton: SP Publications.

Cantwell, D. P. (1972). "Psychiatric Illnesses in the Families of Hyperactive Children." *Archives of General Psychiatry, 27*, pp. 414-417.

Cantwell, D. P. (1985). "Hyperactive Children Have Grown Up." *Archives of General Psychiatry, 42*, pp. 1026-1028.

Cetron, M. (1985). *Schools of the Future*. New York: McGraw Hill Book Company.

Clark, F., and Clark, C. (1989). *Hassle-free Homework*. New York: Doubleday.

Coles, G. (1987). *The Learning Mystique*. New York: Pantheon Books.

Collins, B. E., Whalen, C. K., & Henker, B. (1980). "Ecological and Pharmacological Influences on Behaviors in the Classroom: The Hyperkinetic Behavioral Syndrome." In S. Salzinger, J. Antrobus, & J. Glick (Eds.), *The Ecosystem of the "Sick" Child*.

New York, Academic Press, pp. 103-137.

Copeland, E. D. (1988). The Joy of a Job Well Done. Confident, Capable, Cooperative Children Series. Atlanta: 3 C's of Childhood, Inc.

Copeland, E. D. (1991). *Medications for Attention Disorders (ADHD/ADD) and Related Medical Problems*. Atlanta: SPI Press.

Copeland, E. D., and Love, V. L. (1990). *Attention Without Tension: A Teacher's Handbook on Attention Disorders*. Atlanta: 3 C's of Childhood, Inc.

Cowart, V. S. (1982). "Stimulant Therapy for Attention Disorders." *Journal of the American Medical Association, 248*, 286. Reporting on paper delivered by Dr. Robert J. Lerer at meeting of American Psychiatric Association, Chicago, Illinois.

Cowart, V. S. (1988). "The Ritalin Controversy: What's Made This Drug's Opponents Hyperactive?" *Journal of the American Medical Association, 259(17)*, pp. 2521-2524.

Cowen, E., Pederson, A., Babigan, H., Izzo, L., & Trost, M. (1973). "Long-term Follow-up of Early Detected Vulnerable Children." *Journal of Consulting and Clinical Psychology, 41*, pp. 438-446.

Crook, W. (1991). *Help for the Hyperactive Child*. Jackson, TN: Professional Books.

Crook, W. (1980). *Tracking Down Hidden Food Allergy*. Jackson: Professional Books.

Davis, M. K. (1989). "Preparing Teachers for Developmentally Appropriate Kindergarten Classrooms." *Dimensions, 17*, pp. 4-7.

DeMilio, L. (1989). "Psychiatric Syndromes in Adolescent Substance Abusers." *American Journal of Psychiatry, 146(9)*, pp. 1212-1213.

Dobson, J. (1978). *The Strong-willed Child*. Wheaton: Tyndale House Publishers, Inc.

Egger, J., Carter, C. M., Graham, P.J., Gumley, D., and Soothill, J. F. (1985). "Controlled Trial of Oligoantigenic Treatment in the Hyperkinetic Syndrome." *Lancet*, March 9, pp. 540-545.

Elia, J. (1989). In "Helping Children with Attention Disorders" by Dixie Farley, *FDA Consumer*, February, pp. 11-15.

Elkind, D. (1987). *Miseducation: Preschoolers at Risk*. New York: Alfred A. Knopf.

Feingold, B. F. (1975). *Why Your Child is Hyperactive.* New York: Random House.

Feldman, B. N. (1987). *Kids Who Succeed.* New York: Rawson Associates.

Feldman, R. D. (1987). "How to Earn an A+ in Helping With Homework." *Woman's Day,* November 24, pp. 24-29.

Fontenelle, D. (1983). *Understanding and Managing Overactive Children.* Englewood Cliffs: Prentice-Hall, Inc.

Forster, P., and Doyle, B. A. (1989). "Teaching Listening Skills to Students with Attention Deficit Disorders." *Teaching Exceptional Children,* (Winter), pp. 20-22.

Fulghum, R. (1986). *All I Ever Need to Know I Learned in Kindergarten.* New York: Villard Books.

Gardner, H. (1983). *Frames of Mind.* New York: Basic Books.

Gern, J. E., et al. (1991). "Allergic Reactions to Mild-Contaminated Non-Dairy Products." *New England Journal of Medicine, 324(14),* pp. 976-979.

Gittelman, R., Mannuzza, S., Shenker, R., and Bonagura, N., (1985). "Hyperactive Boys Almost Grown Up. I. Psychiatric Status." *Archives of General Psychiatry,* 42, pp. 937-946.

Golden, G. S. (1988). "The Relationship Between Stimulant Medication and Tics." *Pediatric Annals, 17(6),* pp. 405-408.

Goldstein, S., and Goldstein, M. (1990). *Managing Attention Disorders in Children.* New York: John Wiley & Sons.

Hagerman, R. J., and Falkenstein, A. R. (1987). "An Association Between Recurrent Otitis Media in Infancy and Later Hyperactivity." *Clinical Pediatrics,* 5, pp. 253-257.

Healy, J. M. (1987). *Your Child's Growing Mind.* Garden City: Doubleday.

Holdsworth, L., and Whitmore, K. (1974). "A Study of Children With Epilepsy Attending Ordinary Schools: 1. Their Seizure Patterns, Progress, and Behavior in School." *Developmental Medicine and Child Neurology, 16,* pp. 746-758.

Horn, J. C. (1989). "Drafted at the Age of Nine." *Psychology Today,* January/February, p. 22.

Hunt, R. D. (1988). "Clonidine and Treatment of ADHD." *The Psychiatric Times,* September, pp. 10-12.

Hunt, R. D., Capper, L., and O'Connell, P. (1990). "Clonidine in Child and Adolescent Psychiatry." *Journal of Child and Adolescent Psychopharmacology, 1,* pp. 87-102.

Ingersoll, B. (1988). *Your Hyperactive Child - A Parent's Guide to Coping with Attention Deficit Disorder.* New York: Doubleday.

Interagency Committee on Learning Disabilities (1987). "Learning Disabilities: A Report to the U. S. Congress." Washington, DC: Government Printing Office, pp. 194-217.

Jaffe, P. (1989). "The Other ADD." *The Chadder Box, 2,* November, p. 3.

Jaffe, P. (1991). "ADD and American Psychiatry." *Addendum, 5* (Summer) pp. 6-7.

Jagger, J., Prescott, B. A., Cohen, D. J., et al. (1982). "The Epidemiology of Tourette's Syndrome: A Pilot Study." *Schizophrenic Bulletin, 8,* pp. 267-277.

Joneja, J. V., and Bielory, L. (1990). *Understanding Allergy, Sensitivity and Immunity: A Comprehensive Guide.* New Brunswick, NJ: Rutgers University Press.

Kaplan, B. J., McNicol, J., Conte, R. A., and Moghadam, H. K. (1989). "Dietary Replacement in Preschool-aged Hyperactive Boys." *Pediatrics, 83,* pp. 7-17.

Kavanagh, J. F. and Truss, T. J. Jr. (Eds.). (1988). *Learning Disabilities: Proceedings of the National Conference.* Parkton, MD: York Press.

Kinsbourne, M., and Caplan, P. J. (1979). *Children's Learning and Attention Problems.* Boston: Little, Brown & Co.

Kirby, E. A., and Grimley, L. K. (1986). *Understanding and Treating Attention Deficit Disorder.* New York: Pergamon Press. In *Psychology Practitioner Guidebooks,* Arnold P. Goldstein, Leonard Krasner, Sol I. Garfield (Eds.).

Klein, R. G., and Mannuzza, S. (1988). "Hyperactive Boys Almost Grown Up." III. Methylphenidate Effects on Ultimate Height." *Archives of General Psychiatry, 45,* pp. 1131-1134.

Klein, R. Q. (1987). "Prognosis of Attention Deficit Disorder and Its Management in Adolescence." *Pediatrics in Review, 8(7),* pp. 216-222.

Klorman, R., Coons, H. W., and Borgstedt, A. D. (1987). "Effects of Methylphenidate on Adolescents with a Childhood History of Attention Deficit Disorder: I. Clinical Findings." *Journal of the American Academy of Child and Adolescent Psychiatry, 26(3),* pp. 363-367.

Kohn, A. (1989). "Suffer the Restless Children." *The Atlantic Monthly,* November, pp. 90-100.

Kumar, A. et al. (1991). "Sweeteners, Flavorings, and Dyes in Antibiotic Preparations." *Pediatrics,* March, pp. 352-360.

Kwasman, A. (1989). "Letter to the Editor." *Clinical Pediatrics, 28(7),* pp. 336.

Lou, H. C., Henriksen, L., Bruhn, P., Børner, H., and Nielsen, J. B. (1989). "Striatal Dysfunction in Attention Deficit and Hyperkinetic Disorder." *Archives of Neurology, 46,* pp. 48-52.

Matthews, W. S. (1988). "Attention Deficits and Learning Disabilities in Children with Tourette's Syndrome." *Pediatric Annals, 17(6), pp.* 410-416.

Menninger, W. C. (1964). The Meaning of Work in Western Society. In H. Borow (Ed.), *Man in a World at Work.* Boston: Houghton Mifflin Company.

Mesulam, M. M. (1986). "Frontal Cortex and Behavior." *Annals of Neurology, 19,* pp. 320-325.

Morrison, J., and Stewart, M. (1971). "A Family Study of Hyperactive Child Syndrome." *Biological Psychiatry, 3,* pp. 189-195.

National Institute of Mental Health (1981). "Workshop on Attention Deficit Disorders." U. S. Department of Health and Human Services. *Psychopharmacology Bulletin, p. 21.* Washington, D.C.: Government Printing Office, Monograph reprint, 1.

Okimoto, J. D., and Stegall, P. J. (1987). *Boomerang Kids.* New York: Pocket Books.

Oppenheim, J. (1989). "Kids, Parents and Homework." *Good Housekeeping,* September, 148, p. 165.

Ortlund, A. (1978). *Children are Wet Cement.* Old Tappan: Fleming H. Revell Company.

Ostrander, S., Schroeder, L., and Ostrander, N. (1989). *Super-Learning.* New York: Dell Publishing.

Parker, Harvey C. (1988). *The ADD Hyperactivity Workbook for Parents, Teachers and Kids.* Plantation: Impact Publications, Inc.

Peter, L. L. (1977). *Peter's Quotations, Ideas for Our Time.* New York: William Morrow & Company.

Peterson, E. H. (1987). *Growing Up With Your Teenager.* Old Tappan: Fleming H. Revell Company.

Physician's Desk Reference. (1990). Oradell, NJ: Medical Economics Company, Inc.

Prochnow, H. V. (1958). *The New Speaker's Treasury of Wit and Wisdom.* New York: Harper and Brothers.

Rapp, D. J. (1979). *Allergies and the Hyperactive Child.* New York: Simon & Schuster.

Riddle, M. A., Nelson, J. C., Kleinman, C. S., Rasmusson, A., Leckman, J. F., King, R. A., and Cohen, D. J. (1991). "Case Study. Sudden Death in Children Receiving Norpramin: A Review of Three Reported Cases and Commentary." *Journal of the American Academy of Child and Adolescent Psychiatry, 30,* p. 1.

Robin, A. L., and Foster, S. L. (1989). *Negotiating Parent-Adolescent Conflict: A Behavioral-Family Systems Approach.* New York: Guilford Press.

Rooney, K. J. (1989). "Independent Strategies for Efficient Study: A Core Approach." *Academic Therapy, 24(4),* pp. 383-389.

Safer, D. J., and Krager, J. M. (1988). "A Survey of Medication Treatment for Hyperactive/Inattentive Students." *Journal of the American Medical Association, 260(15),* pp. 2256-2258.

Sanger, S., and Kelly, J. (1988). *The Woman Who Works, The Parent Who Cares: A Revolutionary Program for Raising Your Child.* New York: Harper & Row.

Satterfield, J. H., Satterfield, B. T., Schell, A. M. (1987). "Therapeutic Interventions to Prevent Delinquency in Hyperactive Boys." *Journal of American Academy of Child and Adolescent Psychiatry, 26(1),* pp. 56-64.

Schrag, P., and Divoky, D. (1970). *The Myth of the Hyperactive Child.* New York: Pantheon Books.

Schwartz, S. (1964). "Effect of Neonatal Cortical Lesions and Early Environmental Factors on Adult Rat Behavior." *Journal of Comparative and Physiological Psychology, 57,* pp. 72-77.

Seabrook, C. (1990). "CDC: Lead Levels Still Poisoning Kids." *The Atlanta Constitution,* July 17, p. 1(A).

Shapiro, L., and Koehl, C. (1991). "Feeding Frenzy." *Newsweek,* May 27, pp. 46-53.

Shaywitz, S. E., and Shaywitz, B. A (1988). "Attention Deficit Disorder: Current Perspectives." In J. Kavanaugh and T. Truss, Jr. (Eds.), *Learning Disabilities. Proceedings of the National Conference.* Parkton: York Press.

Silver, L. B. (1984). *The Misunderstood Child.* New York: McGraw-Hill Book Company.

Sleator, E. K., and Pelham, W. E., Jr. (1986). *Dialogues in Pediatric Management.* Attention Deficit Disorder, p. 1(3). Norwalk: Appleton-Century-Crofts, 52.

Smith, L. (1979). *Feed Your Kids Right.* New York: McGraw-Hill.

Spock, B. (1990). "It's All Up to Us." *Newsweek* (Spring/Winter), pp. 106-107.

Stewart, J. (1989). "The Homework Dilemma." *Parents,* February, pp. 80-85.

Stewart, M. A., and Olds, S. W. (1973). *Raising a Hyperactive Child.* New York: Harper & Row Publishers.

Still, G. F. (1902). "The Coulstonian Lectures on Some Abnormal Physical Conditions in Children." *Lancet, 1,* pp. 1008-1012.

Stoop, D. (1987). *Living With a Perfectionist.* Nashville: Oliver-Nelson.

Swanson, J. M. (1988). Discussion in J. Kavanaugh and T. Truss, Jr. (Eds.), *"Learning Disabilities: Proceedings of the National Conference."* pp. 532-546. Parkton: York Press.

Taylor, J. F. (1980). *The Hyperactive Child and the Family.* New York: Dodd, Mead & Company.

Taylor, J. F. (1990). *Helping Your Hyperactive Child.* Rocklin: California, Prima Publishing and Communications.

Uphoff, J. K., and Gilmore J. (1986). "Pupil Age at School Entrance-How Many Are Ready For Success?" *Young Children,* January, pp. 11-16.

U. S. Office of Child Development (1971). *"Report of the 1971 Conference on the Use of Stimulant Drugs in the Treatment of Behaviorally Disturbed Young School Children."* Washington, DC: Government Printing Office, pp. 4-8.

Vaillant, G. E. (1977). *Adaptation to Life.* Boston: Little, Brown and Co.

Wallinga, C. R., and Sweaney, A. L. (1985). "A Sense of Real Accomplishment: Young Children As Productive Family Members." *Young Children,* November, pp. 3-7.

Weiss, G., Kurger, E., Danielson, U., and Elman, M. (1975). "Effect of Long-term Treatment of Hyperactive Children with Methylphenidate." *CMA Journal, 112,* pp. 159-163.

Weiss, G., and Hechtman, L. T. (1986). *Hyperactive Children Grown Up.* New York: The Guilford Press.

Wender, P. H. (1987). *The Hyperactive Child, Adolescent, and Adult.* New York: Oxford University Press.

Whalen, C. K. (1988). Discussion in J. Kavanaugh and T. Truss, Jr. (Eds.), *"Learning Disabilities: Proceedings of the National Conference."* Parkton: York Press, pp. 524-531.

Willerman, L. (1973). "Activity Level and Hyperactivity in Twins." *Child Development, 44,* pp. 288-293.

Williams, M. (1975). *The Velveteen Rabbit.* New York: Avon Books.

Wolkenberg, F. (1987). "Out of a Darkness." *New York Times Magazine,* October 11, p. 62.

Zametkin, A. J., and Borcherding, B. G. (1989). "The Neuropharmacology of Attention-Deficit Hyperactivity Disorder." *Annual Review of Medicine, 40,* pp. 447-451.

Zametkin, A. J., Nordahl, T. E., Gross, M., King, A. C., Semple, W. E., Rumsey, J., Hamburger, S., and Cohen, R. M. (1990). "Cerebral Glucose Metabolism in Adults with Hyperactivity of Childhood Onset." *New England Journal of Medicine, 323,* pp. 1361-1366.

Ziglar, Z. (1985). *Raising Positive Kids in a Negative World.* Nashville: Oliver-Nelson Books.

Index